MOTHERHOOD AND REPRESENTATION

From novels of the nineteenth century to films of the 1990s, American culture abounds with images of white, middle-class mothers. In *Motherhood and Representation*, E. Ann Kaplan considers how the mother appears in three related spheres: the historical, in which she charts changing representations of the mother from 1830 to the postmodernist present; the psychoanalytic, which discusses theories of the mother from Freud to Lacan and the French Feminists; and the mother as she is figured in literary and film texts such as *East Lynne*, *Uncle Tom's Cabin*, *Christopher Strong*, *Imitation of Life*, *Three Men and a Baby*, and *The Handmaid's Tale*.

Kaplan's analysis complicates two commonly noted dominant paradigms of the mother as "Witch" and as "Angel," evident in nineteenth-century women's writing and twentieth-century women's melodrama. She includes discussion of the appropriation of minority mother-discourse, and then charts the contesting and often contradictory discourses of the mother in present-day America through cultural perspectives, with emphasis on reproductive technologies, science and consumerism, as well as on new fathers.

E. Ann Kaplan is Professor of English and Comparative Studies and Director of the Humanities Institute at Stony Brook, the State University of New York. She is the author of *Women and Film* and *Rocking Around the Clock*, and editor of *Psychoanalysis and Cinema*.

MOTHERHOOD AND REPRESENTATION

The Mother in Popular Culture and Melodrama

E. Ann Kaplan

London and New York

First published 1992
by Routledge
11 New Fetter Lane, London EC4P 4EE

Simultaneously published in the USA and Canada
by Routledge
a division of Routledge, Chapman and Hall, Inc.
29 West 35th Street, New York, NY 10001

© 1992 E. Ann Kaplan

Typeset in 10/12pt Linotron Baskerville by
Falcon Typographic Art Ltd, Edinburgh
Printed and bound in Great Britain by
Butler & Tanner Ltd, Frome and London

British Library Cataloguing-in-Publication Data
A catalogue record for this book is
available from the British Library.

Library of Congress Cataloging-in-Publication Data
Kaplan, E. Ann.
Motherhood and representation : the mother in popular culture and
melodrama / E. Ann Kaplan.
p. cm.
Includes bibliographical references and index.
1. American literature – 20th century – History and criticism.
2. Mothers in literature. 3. American literature – 19th century –
History and criticism. 4. Motion pictures and literature – United
States. 5. Women and literature – United States. 6. United States –
Popular culture. 7. Motherhood – United States. 8. Mothers – United
States. I. Title.
PS228.M66K36   1992
810.9'3520431 – dc20   91–45539

ISBN 0–415–01126–X
ISBN 0–415–01127–2 pbk

*For my mother, Gertrude Mercer,
and my daughter, Brett Kaplan*

CONTENTS

CONTENTS

ILLUSTRATIONS

PREFACE

I have dedicated this book to both my mother, Trudie Mercer, and my daughter, Brett Kaplan. My complex and contradictory relationships with both people fuelled the desire to write the book: I wanted to find out how mothers are constructed in patriarchy on the assumption that such research not only would contribute to knowledge but also enlighten my own struggles, both as daughter and as mother. I aimed to place these struggles within a larger historical and intellectual context than I had at the time in the hopes that, like the best research, the book would combine intellectual contribution with personal exploration.

One of my aims was to untangle the specific daughter- and mother-subjects that I embodied from, in Lacan's terms, the unconscious Imaginary and Symbolic Mothers over which I had no control and yet which positioned me. This led to the book's primary focus on discourses and representations *discourses & representations* rather than on the immediate, subjective level of mothering, which many scholars in other disciplines have addressed.

But to comment briefly on that personal level, motherhood has been one – if not *the* – major emotional, inter-subjective experience of my adult life to date. It was only when I became a mother that I fully understood some of my mother's struggles with me. My new position as mother brought us closer, and enabled a new kind of intimacy that had not been possible before. My mother's intuitive grasp of what my daughter meant to me never ceased to move me: her fondness for my daughter – and her much-needed care taking of my daughter in England during the long, hot USA summers – seemed to me evidence of what I meant to my mother.

In my role as single mother, the unconscious pleasures and deep satisfactions of mothering from the start vied with the equally pressing and self-defining needs to be intensely involved with intellectual and political pursuits, and to be sexually active within a meaningful adult relationship. At the time my daughter was born in 1968, combining sex, work and motherhood was still rare and barely socially acceptable, so that support systems were minimal. The costs to both my daughter and myself, living as we were (after 1971) in a little dyad in New York, took years to overcome.

This book, begun just before my daughter left home for college, was motivated partly by the desire to help my daughter understand the pain she endured because, given reigning discourses and institutions, I could not happily combine sex, work and motherhood during all those years we lived together without any "third" to provide a cushion or to usefully intervene in the dyad. This is pain that can never be taken away, but in recent years we have worked it through, in Freud's sense of that kind of "work." As this book goes to press, our relationship is close and developing in ways that are new and satisfying for me. I will not speak for my daughter. My hope is that I will be enabled, partly through the writing of this book, to help my daughter better understand the special difficulties of her own mother-position if she ever becomes a mother.

The book is also an attempt to account to myself for my difficulties in being the kind of either daughter or mother I really wanted to be. My emphases on history, motherhood as an institution, on patriarchal constraints and unconscious male needs regarding the mother, on the mother-in-the-unconscious and, finally, on compelling motherhood images in the melodrama that dominated my mental landscape about what a mother should or should not be – these emphases helped me to grasp the long traditions of which my own experiences became a part. Indeed, these traditions constructed my experiences as daughter and mother, and produced the unconscious operations that burdened me in ways in which, at the time, I was unaware.

I had to come to terms with how deeply a woman can need a full professional or activist life to feel whole – with how incomplete a life as *only* a mother can be for certain women. Although, as I said above, having my daughter has been a/the major emotional/personal experience, I could not have been happy being *a mother and nothing else*. I would have felt empty, incomplete – just as women who never have children are sometimes said to feel. I wanted my daughter, but I also wanted to contribute to society and to intellectual life. And culture did not, at the time, reward that duality.

I sometimes envy friends who become mothers in 1991: in many senses, it all seems so much easier for them. Lovers or partners now often share in the labors and pleasures of child rearing; society accepts women who combine motherhood and careers, at least, if not open sex; free enterprise has made available all kinds of economical devices and toys that make life with the baby happier, easier, more pleasant all around.

Yet, as is clear in Chapter 9, old concerns about a child's achievements have now intensified and become more widespread. There is a new level of competition for the most advanced, indeed accomplished baby, and this feeds the sense that one's baby must have the latest, most stimulating toys. Advertising and media child "hype" have reached a new level, as images of babies managing computers and other electrical devices abound. Middle-class parents now must make many decisions about whether or not to buy the latest technical toys for their children, and the struggle over which children's television programs are desirable has increased with ever new offerings on more and more channels.

But even more ominous is that all kinds of dangers I never dreamed of in my relatively privileged position now cloud mothers' horizons, including child abuse in day care centers and with baby sitters, increasing child kidnapping, or the fear that one's child will be killed by a stray bullet. While such happenings have long been a reality for many groups in North America, their increasing frequency across class and race lines, together with heightened publicity, has added stress to all parenting.

In the twenty-first century, motherhood will be something else again. This book records how motherhood was shaped by the nineteenth century for the first half of the twentieth century for white, middle-class women living in North America. It is written at a moment of dramatic transition in concepts of the mother produced through changing economic, social and political relations and discourses, through new consciousness about ethnic difference as well as about how race and gender intersect, and through new scientific discoveries regarding reproduction, gestation and birth. As I argue in the final chapter, the foetus now begins to take center stage. When that happens, the mother is dramatically re-positioned: she is relegated to the margins and her needs now subordinated to those of the foetus, who becomes the new subject almost from the moment of conception. The increasing practice of mother-surrogacy in a wide variety of forms greatly complicates, not only mother–foetus and mother–infant relations, but also relations between husbands and wives. These kinds of dramatic social/emotional changes obviously will require careful research as we enter the twenty-first century. If this book alerts scholars to take up more research on the many kinds of mother-topics that need exploring, especially in relation to minority and gay/lesbian discourses, it will have achieved a main aim.

New York, 5 July 1991

ACKNOWLEDGEMENTS

I have many people to thank for making possible this book's final emergence after many years' research. My husband, Martin Hoffman, has been an unfailing source of information about psychological research as well as an indefatigable discussant about issues in the book. He has been the sounding board for many of the arguments made here.

My students – over the years since I began teaching courses on motherhood in literature and film at Rutgers University in 1982 through to similar courses at Stony Brook in 1987 and 1988 – have provided invaluable insights and telling responses to materials and theories that I first tried out on them. I thank them for their patience and their intelligence in sometimes trying sessions on topics emotionally and intellectually difficult.

I thank my colleagues in literature, film and psychoanalysis, for all their help and stimulation over the years of this project. Thanks to Christine Gledhill, who challenged many of my ideas as I prepared a paper for inclusion in her edited volume, *Home is Where the Heart is: Studies in Melodrama and the Woman's Film* (London: British Film Institute, 1987). I thank especially the faculty at Stony Brook who participated in a seminar on "Motherhood and Representation" in Spring 1988: I worked through some of my theories in that context, but faculty all made invaluable presentations from diverse disciplinary areas. I learned a great deal from them all, but let me mention especially Helen Cooper, Ruth Schwartz-Cowan, Lou Deutsch, Adrienne Munich and Susan Squier.

I want also to thank the organizers (Muriel Dimen, Jessica Benjamin, Adrienne Harris and Virginia Gouldner) and participants in a seminar at the New York Institute for the Humanities on "Psychoanalysis and Sexual Difference." In stimulating meetings I learned a great deal that was important for the book about diverse psychoanalytic mothering theories. I look forward to the series of essays, edited by Donna Bassin, Maureen Honey and Meryl Kaplan, about motherhood (including some of my post-MS thoughts on mothering) that will represent much of the work in that seminar. I want in particular to thank Meryl Kaplan and Donna Bassin in this regard, and also Jessica Benjamin for useful feedback on a chapter in the book.

ACKNOWLEDGEMENTS

Thanks go to Helen Cooper for her steady, careful final reading of the last version of the MS, just before it went to press. Helen provided just what I needed at the time – a careful reading within the framework of my discourse rather than a reading that began to query some of my positions: thanks go to earlier readers (whose names I do not know) who had questioned and probed assumptions at an appropriate stage of the project.

I want to thank both Don Ihde, Dean of Humanities and Fine Arts at SUNY at Stony Brook, for granting a vital research leave in Fall 1989, and the Humanities Research Center (HRC) at Australian National University for a Fellowship during that time. I revised the MS while at HRC, and delivered papers on Chapter 9 at several Australian universities. I thank the various audiences for their useful comments.

Thanks also to the Museum of Modern Art and the British Film Institute for permission to reproduce the film stills featured in the book.

Finally, I want to thank my (then) secretary at the Humanities Institute, Diane Godden, who retyped my MS for a new computer program in 1988; Joe Greco, a graduate student in English at Stony Brook, for his patient work on the book in Summer 1990; Pablo Nagel and Jan Hochman, also graduate students at Stony Brook, for invaluable help with research; and my daughter, Brett Kaplan, for the tiresome work of compiling the indices.

Parts of the book have been published in different versions than appear here in the following journals and volumes: "The Case of the Missing Mother: Patriarchy and the Maternal in Vidor's *Stella Dallas*," *Heresies* (1983) 4 (4): 81–5; "Theories of Melodrama: A Feminist Perspective," *Women and Performance* (1983) 1 (1): 40–8; "Mothering, Feminism and Representation: The Maternal in Melodrama and the Woman's Film from 1910–1940," in C. Gledhill (ed.), (1987) *Home is Where the Heart is: Studies in Melodrama and the Woman's Film*, London: British Film Institute; "Discourses of the Mother in Postmodern Film and Culture," *Westerly: A Quarterly Review* (Australia) (1989) 34 (9): 24–34; "Sex, Work and Motherhood: The Impossible Triangle (With Reference to Post 1960s USA Film and Fiction)," *Journal of Sex Research* (1990) 27 (3): 409–25; "Female Spectatorship," in *Camera Obscura* (special eds Janet Bergstom and Mary Ann Doane) (1990) 21–2: 194–8.

Part I

HISTORY AND THEORY
DISCOURSES

1

INTRODUCTION

Plan and assumptions of the book

When I first conceived of this book in 1982, it was still true to say that the Mother, as subject in her own right, had received relatively scant scholarly treatment (see E.A. Kaplan 1983c). The Mother was in sense everywhere – one could hardly discuss anything without falling over her – but always in the margins, always not the topic per se under consideration. The mother, that is, was generally spoken, not speaking; she was usually discussed as an integral part of a discourse (because she really is everywhere) that was spoken by an Other. She was a figure in the design, out-of-focus; or, if in focus, then the brunt of an attack, a criticism, a complaint, usually in the discourse of a child (male or female) or in that of an adult (male or female) concerned to attribute all ills to the mother.

An absent presence, then. Present but absent. Two scenes in two very different King Vidor movies demonstrate the point: in *The Crowd*, the scene of the hero's birth manages to refuse the birthing mother any reverse shot; the anxious father looks at the bed where his son is being born, and we have the reverse shot of the doctor bending over the bed where the mother is, but the spectator is not allowed to see her. Then, behind the father, we see in the mirror, the *doctor* hand the baby to the nurse (see Figure 1). The scene concludes with the son being handed to the *father*. In *Stella Dallas* (made ten years later), there is a breakfast scene in which the tired mother's labour goes as unrecognized as her actual presence; the image shows her bending over the sink in the rear, and she comes into the frame only to speak for the Father.[1]

It was not then so much that the mother had not received attention as that she had mainly been studied from an Other's point of view; or represented as an (unquestioned) patriarchally constructed social function. Few scholars had been interested in understanding her positioning or her social role from *inside* the mother's discourse, in whatever context, of whatever type. Few scholars studied the oppressive aspects of patriarchal maternal representation or the mother's unwitting acceptance of mythic ideals impossible to achieve on the level of the social formation; or looked at the maternal as figuring the archetypal patriarchal feminine inherited from nineteenth-century sentimentalism.[2] The lack of cultural discourses setting

3

Figure 1   King Vidor's *The Crowd* (1928)
John Smith's father waits nervously to learn he has a boy. The mother who has
given birth is excluded from the scene. Mirror image shows doctor and nurse with
the baby.

forth woman's *subjective* pleasures in mothering (apart from such pleasures
taking place under the auspices of the Father or the state) has still not been
adequately studied; nor has the possibility of a desire for the child for its own
sake been examined. No one has yet answered Kristeva's question, "What is it
about this representation (of the patriarchal or Christian Maternal) that fails
to take account of what a woman might say or want of the Maternal . . . ?"
(Kristeva 1985: 101), largely because the question is so difficult to answer.
How can any historical (i.e. "real life" mother) know whether what she thinks
she wants really reflects her subjective desire, or whether she wants it because
it serves patriarchy (that she has been constructed to want to please)? Since
patriarchy wants women to want children, in other words, how can a woman
distinguish her desire for the child from that imposed on her?
  While this question interests me greatly, my terrain here is representation,
not historical mother-subjects. The question about the desire for, and pleasure
in, the child (whether biological or adopted) informs my examination of

4

Figure 2   King Vidor's *Stella Dallas* (1937)
Stella's prematurely aged mother silently slaves away at the sink in rear of the
frame, while Stella and her brother discuss his lunch.

cultural products (i.e. I am looking for discourses setting forth a mother's
subjectivity), but, as will become clear, dominant materials (significantly)
are rarely interested in any such subjectivity – a telling fact in itself. I will
show that at the very moment when mother-subjects start to gain attention,
this subjectivity is displaced into concern with the foetus.

The 1980s have seen an unprecedented amount of attention paid to
the mother from a whole variety of perspectives, including feminist and
theoretical ones.[3] Much of the work has come out of the social sciences,
is of an empirical nature and involves contemporary mothers and children.
Since my work has to do with *representations* of the mother, and largely deals
with the past, I have not been able to use a great deal of this material.
Historians' work, on the other hand, has been invaluable, even if those
scholars and I sometimes disagree about the truth-value of the historical
account. Literary and psychoanalytic studies clearly overlap most with what I
am doing here, and the influences particularly of Julia Kristeva and Monique
Plaza from France, and of American theorists attempting to combine French

5

and American psychoanalytic perspectives, will be obvious (cf. Dinnerstein 1976; Friday 1981; Dally 1982; Margolis 1984; Chodorow 1978). I continue to believe that Lacan's theories are still central for work on *representations*, but I am interested in positioning psychoanalytic insights derived from Lacan within a broad framework that includes other theoretical views.

In its original conception, the book would have taken the rest of my life to accomplish – or, alternatively, a vast array of scholars from a variety of disciplines (as one publisher's reader pointed out). What I think needs doing (and over ambitiously had suggested I would attempt) is bringing together the history of social discourses about the mother, changes in the economic and technological spheres, literary and filmic images of the mother, and both psychoanalytic mother *discourses* and the psychoanalytic *processes* mothering involves. "Perhaps such a project," the reader noted, "would need a 'team' made up of scholars from a number of different disciplines."

I have thus drastically curtailed my aims in order to mitigate the problem of over-generalization and lack of sufficient focus that the original conception inevitably entailed. This book's contribution to the recent pro-liferation of work on the mother is first, its specific focus on *representations* rather than on what I will shortly call "the historical" or "real life" mother, who is usually the object of study; second, its theorizing the mother-representations as produced through tensions between the level of the "historical" (I use the word, for want of a better, to indicate the level of social institutions, political/economic discourses, scientific/tech-nological developments), and the level of the "psychoanalytic." (Again, this word is used for want of a better to indicate the psychodynamic level – the terrain of Freud's unconscious, of the individualist discourse, but also of the Lacanian Imaginary, and of how humans come to be subjects.)

Thus, while the weight of the book and its main focus is on mother-representations in literary and film texts (together with those in popu-lar magazines, journalism and writings by child-care experts), it was impossible to account for these representations without reference to the "historical" and "psychoanalytic" discursive levels. The book analyzes the mother within three distinct (but ultimately related) representational spheres, those of the historical, the psychoanalytic and the fictional. These roughly correspond to three main kinds of discursive mothers, namely, first, the mother in her socially constructed, institutional role (the mother that girls are socialized to become, and that historical or real mothers strive to embody); second, the mother in the unconscious – the mother through whom the subject is constituted – who is first fully articulated by Freud at the turn of the century as the split-mother: this mother is later theorized more fully by (largely female) analysts; and third, the mother in fictional representations who combines the institutionally positioned mother, and the unconscious mother. The fourth mother, who may be called the "real life" mother (the bodily mother) or the historical fig- ure who interacts daily with her child (and who can be studied by social scientists) lies outside my discursive scope, because I believe she is ultimately not-representable as such. She is, nevertheless, enormously important to me (as to many feminists), and it is hoped that the knowl- edge this study produces will have some impact on her often conflicted, difficult and marginalized life. To the extent that discourses construct mothers on the level of lived reality, work that helps to produce positive change on the discursive level (as I hope this book does) should be beneficial.

Since the level of the fictional lies at the intersection of the other two levels (i.e. the historical, the psychoanalytic), traces of those levels exist within the different kinds of discursive texts under study, and enter into the analysis. In some cases, the mother in the fictional is close to the institutionally constructed mother; but at other times she diverges widely. It is at those moments that the unconscious, Imaginary mother comes to dominate representations, often because some threat has emerged through social changes.

The book's opening sections, sketching in the historical and psychoanalytic spheres, are necessarily broad-ranging and generalizing, but hopefully this will be compensated for in the third, large section on mother-representations in literary, film and social texts. Where possible, I indicate relations among the three spheres, but I deliberately avoid constructing a theory that might explain ways in which the spheres are inevitably interconnected. If deconstruction has taught us anything, it is to suspect high-modernist, totalizing theories. In the context of ever-increasing "data" available to researchers, it is, in any case, virtually impossible to arrive at a "grand theory." The need is for phenomena broken down into manageable units within which coherence may be achieved. My contribution is to demonstrate how fictional mother-representations are produced through the tensions between historical and psychoanalytic spheres, and then to organize (and analyze) the contradictory mother-discourses and ideologies within spe- cific texts.

Other aspects of the book to be noted are, first, its broad historical span (it encompasses North American culture – including European influences – from 1830 to 1960, with a look at recent developments in the final chapter); second, its linking of nineteenth-century popular literary texts with twentieth-century film; third, its attempts to locate clearly the terrain on which it works, thereby situating social science research as different from, but orthogonal with, what I am doing; and finally its addressing filmic and literary mother-representations and discourses via a series of interlocking theoretical frameworks – those of nineteenth-century melo- drama and its twentieth-century film versions, mothering theory (past and present), and recent feminist research on female subjectivity, spectatorship and representation.

The first section on the "historical" (Chapter 2) outlines the broad historical context for the book; it charts changes in motherhood as a social institution, and in corresponding motherhood discourses, from Rousseau and the nineteenth century to postmodernism. I locate a pre-modern mother (who lies beyond my frame); an early modern mother (who emerges in Europe with Rousseau and the institutions needed by the first Industrial Revolution, but whose influence on North American discourses is clear); a high-modernist mother constructed through social changes in post-Romanticism (leading up to the First World War) and evident in full-blown modernism (between the two World Wars); finally, a postmodern mother. This latter figure is currently being constructed in response to social developments, particularly those arising from various 1960s movements (including feminisms), the rapid rise of multinational corporate capitalisms (the international financial elite) and the electronic technological revolution.

This "macro" historical sphere references the broad historical movement produced by economic conditions, political movements and scientific/technological developments. The macro sphere moves inexorably in tandem with these forces, which produce changes, not only within nations, but also in relations between nations: they also produce the discourses I indicate, which move from the construction of the "mother" as a new, self-conscious, patriarchal social *role* (with Rousseau); through the revolutionary modernist discovery of subjectivity (with Freud, and his theory of the unconscious, which, ironically, did not lead to discussion of the *mother's* subjectivity; rather it produced the mother as the one through whom "I," the child, *become* a subject); to recent mother-discourses in reaction to (but also reflecting) postmodern theories of the decentered subject, and of the end of totalizing narratives.

In the past century, changes in the macro-historical sphere have been dramatic and rapid, impacting directly on both the family as institution, and particularly on the mother. The impact of reproductive technologies, and the discourses they have spawned, is merely the most awesome recent example of what I have in mind.

The danger of invoking the broad historical span lies in the difficulty of amassing empirical evidence to support generalizations, and of taking into account specific historical contexts, cultural, racial and class differences, the changing nature of the reading/viewing public, the contexts of production and exhibition, and so on. In order to narrow the project and make possible a coherent tracing of select historical mother paradigms, I decided deliberately to limit this study to what I call the "Master" Motherhood Discourse as it worked to position white, middle-class women as subjects in very specific ways. The concept of a "Master Discourse" derives ultimately from

8

Nietzsche, who, in his *Genealogy of Morals*, comments on the difficulty of eradicating ourselves from the intellectual traditions of established authorities:

> The masters' right of giving names [he notes] goes so far that it is permissible to look upon language itself as the expression of the power of the masters: they say "this *is* that, and that," they seal finally every object and every event with a sound, and thereby at the same time take possession of it.
>
> (Nietzsche 1954)[4]

Nietzsche was uninterested in the specifically *male* domination of the moral traditions he warred against, but this is central to my purposes here. The discourse of motherhood that I am exploring is not accidentally a "master" discourse: its patriarchal aspects are precisely what I want to unravel.

But the method here mainly relies on Foucault's work, particularly his discourse theory as evident in the volumes on sexuality (see especially the Introduction in Foucault 1978). I explore the ramifications of what is a prevailing cultural discourse (in the period of study) of the Ideal "angel" Mother pitted against her evil "witch" opposite, as it was developed (and then embodied itself) in specifically nineteenth- and early-twentieth-century iconography, myths, images and representations. My study is, then, limited to tracing paradigms in white, North American, middle-class culture, as this culture consolidated itself in the early nineteenth century following Rousseau's lead.

Understanding this prevailing or "dominant" discourse is crucial even for groups that the dominant marginalizes (e.g. Black, Jewish, Hispanic and other American ethnic groups, the various working classes, the poor and the homeless, the non-traditional family, where the stepmother, the adoptive mother, or surrogate may be central; or where homosexual couples are raising children, and so on). A study could be made of mother images in the sub-culture of each of these groups (and hopefully this book will inspire such studies, if they are not already underway), but such a study could benefit from knowledge of how the dominant paradigm, oppressive for the minority group, came into being, how its very presence constructs (as part of its ideology) other groups as "marginalized." I do deal with the appropriation of minority discourse by the dominant in *Uncle Tom's Cabin* and *Imitation of Life*.

I do *not* argue that mothers in particular, or individual families (even those fitting into the white, heterosexual, biological norm) necessarily operated according to the dominant discourse. Some presumably did, others did not; as in any period, on the level of lived experience there is clearly a wide range of social practices. These, I believe (following here Tony Bennett and others who have developed the concept of "reading formations": see Bennett 1986; Laclau undated, cited by Bennett; Laclau 1980; Pêcheux 1982) depend on one's particular sub-cultural group, be that ideological (feminist, minority, class), ethnic, institutional or other. Feminist

9

historians have begun to discover the surprising resiliency of women to their oppressive positioning across the decades; they have found moments in every period when women took up rebellious stances against practices that created hardship and suffering. But this in no way negates the constant presence of myths on a totally different, unconscious level. It is this level that I deal with in the book's second section on the "psychoanalytic" sphere.

I argue here that women's activist capacities and resilience in the face of oppressive institutional positioning exist alongside the centrality to their lives of the intra-psychic and unconscious terrain, which often produces women's complicity with patriarchal norms. Changes naturally take place in this sphere of the psychoanalytic, but compared to that in the macro-historical sphere, change in the intra-psychic terrain is more slow; it can act as a kind of brake for the economic, technological and political forces which would otherwise proceed unimpeded. It is therefore an ideologically ambivalent terrain.

Nevertheless, there are dramatic changes in the early twentieth century in thinking about this terrain. High modernism's most central discovery, along with Marx's theories, was Freud's theory of the unconscious and his "discovery" of subjectivity. Freud's thinking revolutionized concepts of the human being from those that prevailed in the nineteenth century by positing an inner, psychic life not theorized before even if there to be glimpsed in the western literature (that is my concern here) from as far back as at least the Greek civilization. In the book's second section on the Psychoanalytic (Chapter 3), I examine the various kinds of psychoanalytic processes and discourses as they pertain to dominant motherhood images and as they have been revised by feminist scholars on both sides of the Atlantic and elsewhere (e.g. Australia) in developing recent Mothering Theory. The chapter looks at how far recent psychoanalytic theories may help us to understand what is happening on the unconscious, mythic level exposed in film representations, as it interacts with the historical sphere. I am here concerned both with psychoanalysis as describing an inevitable process of subject-formation (my "foundationalist" moment), and with psychoanalytic theory as a *discourse* itself producing certain powerful mother representations, particularly in the post-Freud period. Understanding the process of subject-formation from a psychoanalytic point of view is crucial for later arguments in two ways: first, the level of family subjectivity needs to be set alongside that of the historical/political and institutional sphere, whose theorists have often neglected the familial subject; second, later arguments about film reception rely on showing how psychoanalytic processes are activated in viewing films.

The main body of the text deals with the third sphere, that of mother-representations in select North American texts from 1830 to 1990. I have limited myself deliberately (for the most part) to the melodrama genre for two reasons: first, I was interested in popular materials addressing a "mass" audience; dominant myths/fantasies/ideologies emerge most clearly in popular commercial texts addressing a huge audience, and melodrama is precisely the form which contains the ingredients for mass appeal. Second, melodrama in the modern period is the form that has always most explicitly addressed a *female* audience.

In searching for the paradigms underlying twentieth-century mother-representations in films made (largely) by men (my main focus in the book), I found myself back in the nineteenth century and in *women's writing*, in particular. This at first surprised me, until I realized that in North America at least, the terrain of the domestic and the feminine was excluded from nineteenth-century male fiction, for reasons I allude to in Chapter 7. It was Hollywood's specifically *commercial* context that led male directors and producers to make (often scorned) melodramas: for there was a lucrative female audience for this material. The stories, meanwhile, were to be found in the plays (made from the original fiction) to which script-writers usually turned, as will be discussed in the case of *East Lynne* (Chapter 5). Melodrama theory is pertinent to both imaginary modes (i.e. nineteenth-century women's writing and twentieth-century film), although it has not been so applied hitherto. The continuing twentieth-century convention of women's melodramatic writing (as in the Harlequin Romances, for example), or of male-produced visual dramas (as in TV soaps), lies beyond my specific focus on film (although other materials are referred to in the final chapter).

Since the linking of literary and film texts provided difficulties for some early readers of the book proposal, let me note that while the two kinds of text (literature, film) were obviously produced in vastly different institutional and historical contexts, nineteenth-century popular fiction and twentieth-century popular (commercial) cinema are closely linked as narrative forms that have wide appeal (they are often literally linked in the mining of popular fiction by film studios eager for "safe," ready-made stories).

Scholars working on the popular woman's novel, as noted, have not been particularly interested in the theory of melodrama per se, or in locating the woman's novel within this aesthetic mode. Feminist film critics on the other hand have focused on melodrama precisely in an attempt to define and differentiate those films specifically addressed to women from those addressing a largely male audience. Looking back at the nineteenth century from the perspective of these recent feminist film debates enabled me to see that many nineteenth-century women's popular novels in fact take place in the terrain that Peter Brooks (1976) has called the "melodramatic imagination" – a terrain that (as Thomas Elsaesser (1972) showed some time ago) dominates certain twentieth-century films. Returning to nineteenth-century roots for twentieth-century film narratives about women's issues helps to illuminate what is going on in these mass narratives of our period. (I leave it to other scholars to analyze links between nineteenth-century literary melodramatic modes and contemporary forms – TV, popular fiction, comic books, etc. – other than film.) The first decades of film – from 1900 to 1920, say – are particularly bound to nineteenth-century literary and dramatic models, as film historians are now demonstrating (see e.g. Staiger 1980; 1985; Vardac 1977). Since I am concerned with larger narrative issues – rather than technical matters involving the particular form (i.e. novel, film) – I see little problem in talking about the same paradigms within different imaginative modes. I am interested in issues of textual address, spectatorship (and reader-response), the gendered audience, and different forms and meanings of identification. These kinds of issues pertain to, and thus link, both fiction and the fiction film.

Theories of melodrama central to analyzes in this section of the book will be developed fully in Part II introducing "Fictional Representation": here I will merely outline some textual concepts central to the choice of materials and to their organization.

First, the concept of the "Maternal Melodrama" versus "The Maternal Woman's Film:" (Or "Complicit" versus "Resisting" Melodramas). The theory of a "Master" mother-discourse, involving an "angel" versus a "witch" figure structures the choice of specific melodramas on one obvious level. But a theory of different *kinds* of female melodrama provides a second organizational and interpretative level. The distinction is between melodramas I call "complicit" (maternal melodramas) and those I call "resisting" (the maternal woman's film). As the terms suggest, the former comply passively with the dominant patriarchal mother-discourse (labelled above the "Master" Mother Discourse), while the latter question or expose this discourse.

Second, the concept of Psychoanalytic versus Conscious-Rational Texts. The "complicit"/"resisting" categories are meant to be deliberately *ideological*, but they are linked to a further concept of a psychoanalytic/conscious-rational distinction on the narrative level. The distinction refers to the way the narrative assumes the mother is either positioned by unconscious, mythic processes beyond her control, or sees her as positioned historically by social institutions (theoretically open to change). The term "conscious/rational" connotes conscious psychological processes of knowing and understanding the world, including how institutions function to constrain or define historical subjects; while the term "psychoanalytic" (fully developed in Chapter 3) connotes the unconscious level of the subject's relations and modes of functioning – the level of the Imaginary – that moves the subject without his/her conscious knowledge. The terms reflect ideal-types rarely achieved in practice: most actions, texts and representations include both cognitive/constructive and psychoanalytic elements, but one mode is usually primary. It is the *primacy* of one mode over the other that governs the *kind* of text that results, that is whether it is "complicit" or "resisting" melodrama.

Third, the Concept of the Reader and the Film Spectator. A final set of concepts requiring brief mention have to do with the vexed question of the film spectator. Because I am limiting myself to a study of *representations*, I am unable to discuss the *historical* reader/spectator (i.e. the individuals receiving any particular novel or film in their specific historical moment). I theorize two kinds of reader/spectator positions: *that which the novel/film offers*, whether or not the historical subject takes it up (I call this the "hypothetical" reader/spectator); and *that which the subject brings to novel/film reception*, which has to do with the reading formations of his or her historical moment. Potentially, the reading-subject and the subject in the cinema are constructed both by the novelistic strategies (or the cinematic strategies of the film being viewed), *and* by the social practices and institutions through which the subject lives out her or his historical moment. There is a delicate negotiation in any textual reception between the hypothetical spectator offered by the novel/film and the reading formations of the reader/viewer (E.A. Kaplan 1985a; 1985b). Depending on the social practices through which this reader/viewer is constructed, she or he will be more or less receptive to the hypothetical spectator-position of the novel/film. Given my disciplinary constraints, in this book I confine myself to theorizing the hypothetical reader/spectator that any one novel/film offers.

The complicit/resisting melodrama theory provides the central organizing structure for Part II on Fictional Representation. In this schema, both the maternal sacrifice melodrama, figuring the "angel" mother-figure, and those melodramas figuring the evil, "witch" mother, fall into the complicit type, and are dealt with first: Chapter 5 addresses the maternal sacrifice paradigm, taking the nineteenth-century woman's novel, *East Lynne* (1861), and some of its play and film versions, as a case study. Chapter 6 looks at the second dominant maternal paradigm, that of the evil "phallic" or witch mother who is the underside of the self-sacrificing ideal mother. This "monstrous" mother, evident in both Greek and Renaissance narratives (viz. *Medea*, *King Lear* as examples) is all but eclipsed by nineteenth-century sentimentalism. By and large, the paradigm of the fearsome, dominating mother becomes central only in the wake of the Second World War. After discussion of the paradigm in social materials (like Philip Wylie's *A Generation of Vipers*, 1942), I look at the monstrous figure in the 1940s prototype (*Now Voyager*), and in its 1960s version (*Marnie*). The revival of the dominating mother-type in some 1980s films, together with a rewriting of the Wylie text by Hans Sebald in the late 1970s, will be taken up in Chapter 9.

But, after these examples of the complicit maternal melodrama, I turn in the next chapters to examples of the resisting type, the "maternal woman's film." Chapters 7 and 8 analyze the "resisting" woman's form that is arguably in the tradition of nineteenth-century "domestic" feminism as embodied in Harriet Beecher Stowe's *Uncle Tom's Cabin* and as revolutionized by Charlotte Perkins Gilman in *Herland*, written at the turn of the century. I analyze select films from the 1920s to 1960, showing how more cognitive-constructive and transgressive textual elements are often fused with the specifically mythic, unconscious ones in ways that make disentanglement difficult. Mythic elements intrude particularly in the pathos-ridden endings of some of

13

the films that lift the narrative on to the level of the oppressive social imaginary. The films will be distinguished according to their relative degrees of complicity with, and resistance to, dominant mother paradigms. Chapter 7 explores silent films by Weber, Brennon, Mamoulian and Vidor, while in Chapter 8 I deal with four 1930s films in detail (Arzner's *Christopher Strong* and *Craig's Wife*, Stahl's *Imitation of Life* and Vidor's *Stella Dallas*), followed by brief mention of two related 1950s Sirk films, *All That Heaven Allows* and his *Imitation of Life*, that arguably look toward ideological and social changes that were to take place in the 1960s.

Chapter 9 explores the discourses that perhaps account for some of the recent motherhood representations. Obviously, things seem even more complex and multiply determined in the 1980s and 1990s, which have seen not only unprecedented technological and industrial change, but also the articulation of a plethora of often contradictory and oppositional motherhood and other discourses. These new discourses (the result of feminism and other 1960s liberation movements – gay and minority liberation, the sexual "revolution") and their accompanying reproductive technologies (test-tube babies, in-vitro sounding, gene manipulation, surrogate mothering) confront the continuing traditional discourses that I have discussed and shown in operation in earlier chapters.

The most dramatic alteration in mother-representations addressed in the final chapter involves the new focus on the foetus that has emerged in connection with the rapid advances in reproductive technologies. The foetal discourse increased rapidly in the late 1960s, following the 1965 publication of Lennart Nilsson's stunningly presented progressive photographs of the foetus during gestation. The increase in scientific knowledge about the foetus, together with developments in photographic technologies, have produced visual foetal images. The power of these images stimulated anti-abortion discourse and a concern for the foetus that once again marginalizes the mother: the foetus now takes her place at the center of things, while the mother's body and subjectivity recede.

Indeed, the foetus is seen not only as a being *in its own right*, but a being *with its own rights*, which are often in opposition to (and privileged over) those of the mother. It is discursively constructed as if it already were a *subject*, and one which once again supersedes the *mother's* subjectivity; "mother" is literally reduced to a holding vessel – the non-subject that makes possible the child's subjectivity – in a bitterly ironic exaggeration of the way patriarchal culture has *always* positioned the mother (whether or not she in fact took up, or resisted, this position).

It is not that the new discourses and their accompanying technologies sweep aside the old order of things, or found a totally new language: they enter into a culture already laden with older discourses, causing a general shake-up, disruption, dislocation – a scene of struggle of one discourse against another, with often bitter, hostile and violent results.

14

The deliberate limitation of this book to discussion of complicit maternal melodramas and resisting maternal women's films is part of a strategy to narrow my project to manageable proportions. I am thus far from claiming to have covered all the possible mother images in nineteenth-century fiction by and about women, or to have accounted historically for the continuance of these images in the twentieth-century film. I merely demonstrate the narrative parallels in the mother paradigms found in my selected examples. I validate arguments by focusing on *East Lynne*, which provides an example of one set of film texts that are remakes of a well-known popular nineteenth-century novel and play. I am interested in the persistence of certain kinds of melodramatic themes and myths, which is not to deny that quite other themes, myths and images also occurred. My selection comes from the repetition of certain paradigms over time, and from their extreme popularity (as measured by *Variety*'s figures). When a myth has such persistence, one can assume it touches something basic in the white, middle-class cultural unconscious. It is the analysis of this "something" through theories of history, psychoanalysis and representation, that this book attempts.

This is not to deny that the functions that melodrama serves and the paradigms it works with change as society changes. Such changes expose alterations in the way woman is thought in patriarchy. Alterations, however, all reflect adjustments within a basic positioning of woman as lack, absence in the cultural dominant; or, perhaps to put it more clearly, mythic changes embody patriarchy's adjustment to new threats that emerge from changes in the social formation.

It is clear that in any one historical mother-subject a number of conflicting representations jostle for dominance: my discussions aim to examine some of these. The representations exist on a different level than that of material bodily sensations and experiences in the daily physical contact with the child: not that the latter aren't also socially constructed. But the level of the material maternal body, and of how the mother-subject represents her body to herself, necessarily lie outside the purview at least of the main "body" of this text.

The mythic level, as Roland Barthes and Jacques Lacan have amply shown, is linked to the level of the unconscious. Althusser's concept of ideology takes this level into account, "ideology" for him being precisely that which, in social practices, is assumed to be natural, the truth, unquestioned, that is *unconscious*. Lacan showed that the structuring of the subject in the mirror-phase as in the lure of an Ideal-I makes it vulnerable to subject-ion to a Transcendental Subject. Lacan identifies this Transcendental Subject as the phallus, but Althusser's broader definition of it in relation to Ideology is useful in linking the psychoanalytic and the social terrains.

There is, however, always a lag between the level of Ideology or what I am calling "Master Discourses," and that of changes in the social formation. For instance, changes set in motion in the post-war period are only now beginning to alter the dominant motherhood discourse that has in fact been archaic since at least the 1960s and that is still part of current debates. A dominant discourse positions women in certain ways of which they are often not conscious; only when they band together to take up arms against some particular hardship, suffering or frustration may women begin to be aware of the codes that confine and limit them. At such a moment one might say that the unconscious is becoming conscious, and that a "female," as against a (patriarchal) "feminine" discourse is beginning to develop. That is, a "female" discourse manifests itself, not in any return to some "essential" femaleness, but in the very processes of struggle against dominant discourses that position women in oppressive ways; it emerges, that is, in the "gaps" of patriarchal hegemony discovered in moments of struggle, disruption, rebellion.

It is the unconscious level that I unravel in looking at motherhood from the perspective of *representation*. I am not a positivist historian making claims about lived realities in the sense of daily self-concepts, personal interactions, or women's historical struggles in the social formation for rights, and so on. It is on the level of what underlies the daily, conscious actions that representations exist and that we can uncover the mythic signifieds of a culture.

These mythic signifiers are most evident in the popular texts that I will explore here and offer as "evidence" of myths being at work in the culture at any given time. My premiss is that women, like everybody else, can function only within the linguistic, semiotic constraints of their historical moment – within that is the discourses available to them. We cannot, thus, expect in the mid-nineteenth century the kind of feminist consciousness that erupted in the 1970s: nineteenth-century women had their own form of feminism that (following women historians) I am here calling "domestic" feminism, while we are today confronting a mother-paradigm shift analogous to that with which this book starts: this shift has been brought about by a second-stage industrial revolution marked by the move from the machine to the electronic age that postmodernism signals. The entire semiotic field in which we live in postmodern America contains the dramatic alterations in technologies and the decentering effects of the multi-corporate capitalisms that have developed since the 1960s. The new postmodern mother-constructs, both positive and negative, that are emerging in this context will be explored in the book's conclusion by examining both popular and feminist materials. The book aims here to contribute to the crucial work of analyzing the ideological frameworks, representations and discourses that construct the new reproductive technologies and the new social and political institutions that position the postmodern mother.

Three historical epochs + mother-discourses
(1) Pre-modern (proceeding from Rousseau, dominating late 18th + the 19th centuries)
(2) Modern (ca. 1900 - 1953) — breakup of trad
industrialism
Darwin, Marx, Freud
(3) Post-modern (WWII → present ; war, electronic technology

2

THE HISTORICAL SPHERE

Motherhood as institution and social discourse

Theorizing satisfactorily the complex interrelationship between a cultural discourse and economic/social/technological change is beyond the scope of this book. The historical shifts in major institutions affecting the mother, like the family, are long, slow and arduous, moving more rapidly in some nations and regions of nations than in others, and happening usually first in the cities, and later in the country. There is no overnight, uniform change either in rela-tions of production or in cultural/ideological discourse. What we are talking about is a change in institution and, correspondingly, in discourse that can be seen only from some historical distance; the precise links between discursive and technological changes again may become visible from an historical perspective, but most often remain unclear. Does the change in discourse precede or follow the technological changes? Do the two kinds of change happen more or less in tandem? Do pressures from traditional paradigms and positionings impede implementation of technological discoveries?

For my purposes here, I will posit three major economic/political/tech-nological eruptions that affected the historical mother and produced cor-responding changes in mother-discourses. I do not attempt to show *how* such mutual changes happened; nor will I try to substantiate claims for institutional eruptions, which are in any case readily recognizable, generally accepted, and have been usefully summarized by the historians and sociologists I rely on (Cott 1977; Welter 1966; Degler 1980; Ehrenreich *et al.* 1978).[1] Positing a tentative link between changes in mother-institutions and mother-discourses seems reasonable enough, if one takes a broad perspective, although I will not try to *prove* such links: I am satisfied to show parallels.

The three historical eruptions are first, that of the Industrial Revolution, second, that of the First World War, and third, that of the recent, electronic revolution following the Second World War. The first eruption marked the economically necessary transition of the pre-modern mercantile-class wives and mothers out of their roles as producers in the old pre-industrial economy into that of consumers in the new middle-class home (Cott 1977; Degler 1980; Filene 1986; Chafe 1972; Bernard 1974).[2] This shift may be said to inaugurate the early modern mother in the modern nuclear family.

17

The second eruption marks the first, disturbing challenge to the nuclear-family institution, by 1914 in its fullest, most complete stage. Women's entry into the work-force in large numbers during the First World War, the women's suffrage movement, and the first waves of female liberation in the 1920s, all severely threatened the nuclear family, whose cornerstone was the modern mother. Historians have charted the (relatively) large numbers of women entering higher education in this period, the number of women remaining childless, the increase in lesbian relations, despite their having to be carefully hidden (see e.g. Filene 1986). Through all this, the nuclear family remained intact and the mother was still central, but defensively so. This shift may be said to mark the "high modernist" mother.

The third eruption is that of the Second World War, and its aftermath, coming to its head in the various 1960s liberation movements, with new challenges to all dominant institutions, but particularly the nuclear family. The development of multinational corporations, of the high-finance elite, and the rapid evolution of technologies in the wake of the electronic revolution has drastically altered our social relations; but these changes have had particular impact on the already altered and challenged nuclear family, caught between its outmoded, nineteenth-century forms and new ones. In the 1980s the increase in middle-class women engaged in full-time, professional work has had enormous ramifications for the old nuclear family, and produced significant alteration in traditional family gender roles. In the middle class at least, the father now takes on some of the nurturing in unprecedented ways, although research shows that the burden still rests mainly with women. With the development of sophisticated new reproductive technologies (such as in-vitro fertilization, artificial insemination, embryo freezing and experimentation, micro injection of sperm), and in a situation where mother-surrogacy is on the increase (if often outlawed), the old centrality of the mother, and especially her location in anything like the nineteenth-century family, has been challenged in a particularly dramatic manner. This final shift may be signalled by the concept of a "postmodern" mother-construct, which usefully signals the political and feminist ambiguities in relation to recent changes.

We have little evidence about the actual nature of mothering work in any historical period, or about the quality of mother–child relations, or how historical mothers "managed" their institutionally assigned roles. Historians continue to seek such evidence (Gillis 1985; Schwartz-Cowan 1983), but much more research is required in this area. Doubts remain as to whether such data can be recovered adequately, and historians further worry about the confusion between levels of discourse and of empirical data. A brief look at debates over Elisabeth Badinter's 1970s work on motherhood in eighteenth-century France will clarify issues at stake, particularly since these issues are relevant to the pre-modern, pre-Rousseauian mother who provides the backdrop against which Rousseau's innovations need to be set.

Badinter (1980) argued that before Rousseau, childhood in France had

18

not been particularly valued, as a stage. She shows that some experts, for example, continued to espouse Augustinian assumptions about the child as an imperfect being, weighed down by original sin; others followed Juan Luis Vives' denouncement of mothers who were affectionate or playful. Badinter implies that the discourses she discovered were evidence of *social* practice, and has thus aroused some historians' ire:[3] historians have shown that the specified theories by no means complete the existing discourses, and that we cannot infer much about *actual child-rearing practices* from such material. Some mothers may indeed have tried to follow one or another of the above mentioned authorities, but others surely disregarded them, or had never even heard of the theories. George D. Sussman (1977) reads the sending of children to wet-nurses so excoriated by Badinter not so much as a sign of motherly neglect (Badinter's argument) but rather as a necessity for urban, working, French mothers. From various historical records, Sussman shows how much of rural women's behaviour with children derived from superstition and folklore rather than from any articulated religious pronouncements. He infers that the mothers did not see the use of wet-nurses as desirable but as their only means of survival; this does not mean, as Badinter had argued, that the child him/herself was not valued.

Another example of excellent empirical historical work relating to motherhood is Valerie A. Fildes's (1986) thorough research into infant feeding practices in Britain (with important reference to other cultures). Her work provides suggestive material for theorizing mother–child relations on the social level, but such scholarship does not interpret its findings or pretend to tell us about the psychic terrain.

We should assume that, as now, mothering practices and relations varied enormously within specific historical moments, but that the details of these practices and relations are lost to us in their specificity on the level of the Real. An additional problem is that mother-representations in any one period are also always contradictory, multiple, many-sided; a variety of images exists at the same time, and depending on how researchers look (with what questions in mind) they may find something different. What one scholar views as the "dominant" representation may also vary according to the kinds of questions being asked, the interests and biases of the researcher.

For my purposes here, the value of experts' pronouncements lies precisely in their *discursive* properties that indicate dominant discourses that influence the level of representation. If the scholar studying the history of ideas is to develop any argument at all, hypotheses have to be formulated and patterns traced. In this book, I am using the word "dominant" to refer to representations that appear to have been given a wide circulation in North American culture by a variety of means – child-care manuals, women's magazines, popular women's writing, popular Hollywood film. From this perspective, it seems reasonable to distinguish three broad "Master" mother discourses or narratives corresponding to the above three historical eruptions producing the early modern, high-modernist and postmodern mothers. These mother-related discourses may be described as first, Rousseauian discourses (produced along with the early modern mother institution); second, Darwinian/Marxist/Freudian discourses (produced along with First World War and high-modernist challenges to the family); and finally, recent, postmodern mother discourses (produced along with even more drastic challenges to the family through the electronic revolution and its impact on corporate capitalisms).

In the pre-modern era, mother paradigms have a long and complex history, and could presumably be charted in analogous ways (see e.g. Gould 1980). But to situate what I am doing in that kind of historical context would take me beyond the scope of this book. It was western culture's turn, at the time of Rousseau, to a new focus on the *child*, that produced the modern mother (in her role as there specially to care *for the child*) who is the object of this study. There were obviously contradictory discourses about childhood in pre-Rousseauian France, as we saw, but Rousseau's ideas of child-rearing, first articulated in his well-known *Émile* (1762), were revolutionary. It is their revolutionary implications, together with their deep implications for future mother discourses within the period of my study, that warrants the detailed treatment here given to the ideas originating in eighteenth-century France but developed in nineteenth-century North America. The relatively detailed treatment is further warranted by the degree of attention given to nineteenth- and early-twentieth-century materials still governed by nineteenth-century ideas in this book. The early-modern-mother paradigm, indeed, turns out to be the one most difficult to dislodge, largely because of its close links to nineteenth-century religious ideologies and authorities. Its traces *still* influence struggles on the discursive level today.

Rousseau's contribution to the new motherhood-discourse is his description of a regime of total attention to the child from an early age (Rousseau 1974: 325–8, 348–9). His disapproval of wet-nursing was merely one of many ways in which he set up a new organization of child-rearing. In general, his book established a conception of child-rearing as a long preparation for adulthood, carefully overseen by the parents.

In the process of doing this, Rousseau introduces a new mother discourse, almost, indeed, as an aside. By this I mean that it is only because the early education of man (*sic*) is necessarily in woman's hands (because of her large biological role) that the mother comes into things at all. Most of Emile's education is in either the Father's or the male Tutor's hands, but because the woman must have a part, Rousseau has to attend to her preparation for mothering. For Rousseau, the girl's biological processes shape her to be a mother, and thus require an attention that has no parallel for the boy. The very survival of the human race depends, for Rousseau, on the woman's function in cementing the family through her skills in emotions and relationships. "Naturally" the complement, the pleasure and the mother of

20

man, woman should learn only what is "suitable" for her given role. (It is significant, however, that this did involve a certain level of education for the purpose of training the child intellectually in the early years.)

Taking on an imaginary proponent of sexual equality (he was later to have a real one in Mary Wollstonecraft),[4] Rousseau concludes that

> Although here and there a woman may have few children, what difference does it make? Is it any the less a woman's business to be a mother? And do not the general laws of nature and morality make provision for this state of things?
>
> (Rousseau 1974: 328)

In France, the emergence of a new social class, the bourgeoisie, arguably created the need to articulate appropriate male/female sex-roles for the changed situation. The child assumes a new importance for Rousseau possibly because what happens to him (*sic*) will determine the kind of man/citizen he will make. Rousseau thus re-inscribes in cultural discourse a division of labour that, while to some degree pre-existing, is now shaped for the development of modern capitalism. He theorizes the public/male, private/female split that will structure a conception of separate spheres in the nineteenth and twentieth centuries, regardless of whether women in fact worked or not. Rousseau's articulation is "classic" in ascribing to nature what is in fact cultural, and in assuming the white, western and middle-class ethic to be the norm.

Rousseau, then, inaugurates the first phase of modern motherhood discourse, which filtered through to North America in the early nineteenth century, replacing an earlier "pre-modern" mother (who lies beyond my frame here). Various historians, feminist and otherwise, have suggested a link between the solidifying of certain motherhood discourses in the mid-nineteenth century and the economically necessary transition of wives and mothers (referred to above) out of their roles as producers in the old pre-industrial economy into the new middle-class home, designed to promote consumption.

Motherhood discourses quickly arose in North America to "educate" the new mother. An array of so-called authorities – priests and clergymen, doctors, philosophers, professors, writers, journalists, and others, all largely male – were constantly proclaiming about mothering in the nineteenth century; they took it upon themselves to define for mothers what their role should be, perhaps just because in a transition period there is confusion and doubt. The voice of authority emerges as a way of making people secure. As industrialism got underway, so the voices multiplied, and diversified, bringing together, often indiscriminately, pieces of so-called "wisdom" from the long past of such pronouncements intermixed with the latest theories. Once child-care experts got into the act, it was a free-for-all that feminist historians have delighted in exposing (Ehrenreich *et al.* 1978).

In the case of North America, a further problem arises from the reliance upon, and ready importation of, European ideas. America still looked to Europe in the nineteenth century for guidance in ideas as well as fashions. What Europeans did was still regarded as superior to what Americans did; there was a snobbishness about the European, and Anglophiles seem to have been in their heyday. This climate meant that whatever was articulated in Europe became holy gospel overnight, particularly (obviously) on the East Coast.

The danger of this hasty importation was the disparity between the intel-lectual/historical/social/political context of a certain theory's production in a European nation, and the North American context into which it was taken. Ideas clearly took on quite other casts in the different context. On the other hand, sometimes a European theory fitted precisely practices and ideologies that had already evolved in North America in the course of the immigrant process, and that merely awaited a certain articulation and formalization to be thoroughly integrated into cultural discourse.

If Rousseau's ideas quickly became popular in America (Cott 1977: 166–7), it was because they found an unexpected resonance despite the vastly different intellectual and cultural contexts. As David Leverenz (1980: esp. ch. 3) has shown, Puritan discourses about the mother already valued tenderness, and wet-nursing was not a regular custom in North America. In other words, Rousseau's ideas were not nearly as radical in the USA as they had been in France, and were easily assimilated because they evidently did not involve major changes in either practice or discourse.

Nevertheless, the impact of the Industrial Revolution, happening in North America about a hundred years later than in Europe, stimulated a more elaborate and institutionalized articulation of the mother's duties than had been evident in Puritan times. As Linda Kerber (1980: 231) points out, "the domestic function of the pre-industrial mother had not needed ideological justification; it was implicit in the biological and political economy of her world." Kerber notes that the nursing mother was the obvious candidate for keeping the spinning wheel turning and tending the open-hearth fire in pre-industrial days. Before the American Revolution, thus, there was no sharp disjunction between ideology and practice, Kerber argues, but she sees the Revolution as the watershed:

> It created a public ideology of individual responsibility and virtue just before the industrial machinery began to free middle-class women from some of their unremitting toil and to propel lower-class women more fully into the public economy. The terms of domesticity were changed, and the pundits could not bring back the past.
>
> (Kerber 1980: 231)

It is at the very point of this technological change that ideology begins to take on a life of its own, to become, in Althusser's words, "images, myths, representations," a distinct sphere no longer necessarily in accord with social practices, the means of production or the division of labour. "Ideology" becomes what is precisely taken as "natural," what is assumed: it becomes, in fact, *unconscious*.

Kerber isolates a moment in the development of one particular ideological construct that is our concern here, namely that of the "Republican Mother." Revolutionary rhetoric in general necessarily entailed woman's entrance into the political sphere. And yet, ideologically (and perhaps institutionally) culture was no more ready for woman's complete equality and autonomy than it was in the mid-nineteenth or even the mid-twentieth centuries. Cultural discourses then as later found a way to at once pay lip service to woman's increased share in government, and severely to restrict her activities – in this case through the concept of the Republican Mother. "Motherhood," says Kerber (1980: 200) "was discussed almost as if it were a fourth branch of government, a device that ensured social control in the gentlest possible way." Woman's political function was neatly confined completely within the home.

Kerber's analysis is important because it shows how cultural discourses emerge to take care of threatening social changes. (The knowledge that such discourses are produced to reduce threatening changes is naturally repressed.) Kerber's analysis is also important in anticipating a similar manoeuver that took place about a hundred years later at the time of women's entry into the political sphere around the anti-slavery issue. At that point the new concept also centered on the Mother as the position that could *safely* be granted a certain power as long as it remained intact – that is, as long as women were not demanding the freedom totally to leave the home and the family.

One female American voice taking up the kind of discourse suggested by Kerber is Lydia Sigourney, in 1839. Sigourney discusses the issues of the mother's power at length, picking up as she does so the earlier notion of the "Republican" mother outlined by Kerber. For Sigourney (1839) Motherhood is precisely a branch of government, with responsibilities and powers analogous to those of the Statesmen. As historians have shown, mid-nineteenth-century women strategically used their assigned power to serve their own political ends.

Only a few women, however, could actually contrive to engage in political work; for some, a discourse like Sigourney's would presumably provide feelings of empowerment through the elevation of mothering to an important task serving the state, analogous to tasks men engaged in, in the more specifically designated public sphere. For others, needs for empowerment had to come through vicarious identification with fictional figures in the more resisting literary forms, such as those analyzed in Chapter 7. Meanwhile, representations and discourses speaking to male fears and fantasies about women – to the ongoing patriarchal discourses about the mother –

23

continued alongside ones arguably addressing women readers oppressed by the governing ideologies.

In order to understand the commitment to woman's presence in the home at mid-century, one has to realize how strongly entrenched "The Cult of True Womanhood" was by that time. Rousseau's representation of Sophie in *Emile* was but one of the many forces participating in the construction of the True Womanhood image. Nancy Cott shows how the identification of woman with the "heart" in the late eighteenth century signalled the inequality of the sexes in making woman inextricably dependent on men:

> If women are considered dependent on others (men) for their protection and support, self-preservation itself demanded skill in personal relationships. Rousseau's portrayal in *Emile* was the most unequivocal and influential formulation for this reasoning in the 18th century. . . . [His] central meaning resonated through the decades as a description of women's social options and a prescription for their behaviour.
>
> (Cott 1977: 167)

In a well-known early article, Barbara Welter (1966) outlined the four basic qualities of what was, by the mid-century, an entrenched ideology of womanhood – namely, piety, purity, domesticity and submissiveness (see also Ulrich 1982). The similarity of these qualities to those advocated by Rousseau for the ideal mother is obvious. And these were the qualities impressed on mothers by self-chosen child-care "experts" such as ministers, in mid- and late-century, as will be explored in more detail in later chapters. Indeed, it is precisely the intervention of religious authorities in matters of child-rearing that kept alive the self-sacrificing "angel" mother, and traces of Rousseau's discourse long after other discourses, and social/technological changes, had prepared the ground-work for her disappearance (see e.g. Gardiner 1974).[5] eruption of the First World War first challenged the codes that had seemed revolutionary in 1762, and the norm in the following century and a half. If high modernism began at the turn of the century with the various artists' movements (the "*blaue reiter*" and competing "*brücke*" groups in Germany – Berlin being considered the European center for radical activity in this period) its wide-spread institutional impact, particularly in relation to the family, was fully felt with the onset of the First World War and the sudden entry of large numbers of women into the work-force for the war effort. The aftermath of the war was to be seen in the intense struggles women were to mount for the vote, and, in the 1920s, in the freedoms particularly middle- and upper-class women managed to win (education, primarily, but, secondarily and also important, sexual and social freedoms).

The theoretical discourses significant for thinking about the mother and the family in this high modernist period are, of course, those of Darwin, Marx and Freud. Significantly, the male narratives divide themselves into those dealing with larger, abstract biological and social forces (Darwin,

24

Marx), and those dealing with the "inner" (or private) sphere (Freud). Darwin's theories about the origin of the species and the descent of man had been prepared for by others since the late eighteenth century, but had an enormous, revolutionary (and contradictory) impact on nineteenth-century thinking. To begin with, his theories partly inspired Marx and Engels to develop their dialectical materialist analysis of human/social forces (they saw their ideas about society as similar to those of Darwin on natural selection (McLellan 1971: 124; Huxley and Kettlewell 1965: 80–1)). Lewis Henry Morgan's research on *Ancient Society* made use of Darwin's interpretation of biological evolution (see Leacock's Introduction, Engels 1972). But while Darwin's theories, as reworked by Marx and Engels, questioned the sanctity of the family in challenging its God-given eternity and seeing it as a social and class construct (the result of evolution), they also, ironically, gave rise to conservative biological theories for keeping the mother in the home. For the discourse of biological survival focuses on the need of the human species in the earliest communities, and on the mother, required for their protection to be devoted to the young. (Recently, the possibility of hormonal programming in women for nurturing has been researched.) Such theories bolster already dominant ideas about the mother's importance within the constraints of the middle-class family. Darwin's theories about the animal world and about the survival of the fittest produced later eugenic theories, as I discuss in Chapter 8.

Meanwhile, Marx's theories advocating the end of the "bourgeois family" (there *was* only this family, according to Marx),[6] and showing the bourgeois family's negative links to private property, capital and oppression, provided a negative analysis of the family not theorized fully before. As Shulamith Firestone (1970: 12) has noted, Marx "was on to something more profound than he knew when he observed that the family contained within itself in miniature all the antagonisms that later develop on a wide scale within the society and the state." Firestone goes on to extrapolate from Marx the need for something to disturb the biological family, namely, in her terms, the "sexual revolution," something Marx precisely omitted, as she shows.

Freud's theorizing about unconscious childhood sexuality and the Oedipus Complex revolutionized Rousseauian ideas by positing an unconscious, inner sphere; in so doing, Freud prepared the way for the "sexual revolution" Firestone locates. As will be clear in Chapter 3, which deals exclusively with the psychoanalytic sphere charted by Freud and his followers, Freud's ideas, like those of Marx and Darwin, can be seen as themselves phallocentric: even where women are implicated, there is rarely treatment of the specificity of their situations, least of all specific attention to the mother, who is simply (so significantly) absent, per se, from all these narratives.

Nevertheless, these powerful modernist narratives have provided the tools for feminist subversion of both dominant discourses and of the male-biases of the theories themselves.[7] These theories have also provided feminists with the tools to look at what the male theorists (even Freud) found so hard; namely, at the daily, lived, pleasures and pains of women within the intimate, personal, psychic/unconscious familial sphere they have so long inhabited and known so well. (It is because this terrain is foregrounded in domestic melodrama modes that I have made melodrama the focus for this study; feminists can find traces of this sphere in the melodrama genre and in little else.)

But a third, major historical eruption, signalled by the Second World War and its aftermath, problematizes both the high modernist narratives themselves and some feminist revisionings of them. Particularly in the ten years from 1978 to 1988, dramatic alterations in motherhood discourses have taken place. These are, briefly, the result of a complex combination of new scientific/technological developments, the 1960s–1970s feminist movements, and political and social changes. Alterations amount to a paradigm-shift analogous to that which took place in the 1830s in the context of the first industrial revolution, and which a large section of this book charts in the sphere of representation. While women's biological and reproductive roles were not only unquestioned at the time of that paradigm-shift – on the contrary, those roles were being privileged by it – now it is precisely around women's biological/reproductive capacities that new discourses are developing. The "given" (that woman's main purpose is to reproduce) has been irrevocably challenged by the residues of the great modernist narratives. Anxiety emerges just because there is a "question" as to whether or not woman should mother, and if so, *how* to reproduce (a question occasioned by the choice of new reproductive technologies and alternative contexts for child-bearing and rearing). The whole previously conceived "natural" terrain is adamantly self-reflexive and problematized in the 1990s, giving rise to a plethora of contradictory, heterogeneous motherhood ideologies and unconscious fantasies. It is these discourses and contradictory developments, particularly as they impact on 1970s feminist theories and practices in relation to the mother, that I will briefly explore in this book's concluding chapter. In the 1980s, we find a plethora of discourses in which the mother now figures as *subject*. But, as we will see, her subjectivity causes dislocations, problems, that cultural productions and articulations now address. Unlike the Father, who was always viewed as a subject, it is the mother's very coming into *subjectivity* that produces a new set of issues in culture around day care, the combining of work and mothering, the impact of the mother's work on the child, on the father, and so on, which will be explored. As already noted, it is also in the context of mother-as-(new) subject that cultural discourses begin to display interest in the foetus-as-subject, vying with, if not already displacing, mother-as-subject.

26

3

THE PSYCHOANALYTIC SPHERE
AND MOTHERHOOD DISCOURSE

This chapter looks at the mother in the intra-psychic and unconscious terrain, which, as noted earlier, must be separated out from the historical/political. This is not to deny that there is a social dimension to the psychoanalytic level – a dimension that Freud himself failed to pursue. As Eli Zaretsky has pointed out,

> Freud's thought opens the way for an understanding of the role that instinctual sexuality plays in social life. It makes it possible to talk about transforming our sexual lives as we now talk about transforming our economic and political systems.
>
> (Zaretsky 1976: 131–2)

Zaretsky also notes that psychoanalysis nevertheless considers sexuality only as it takes shape within the family, seen as a relatively unchanging form.

I assume that the family *is* a changing form, but most of this book is concerned with the particular bourgeois form of family that evolved from the first Industrial Revolution. That family's high modernist form (the family now small, nuclear, isolated, with husbands often distanced from the work-place) provided the need for, and subsequent findings of, psychoanalytic theory. For it was the forced close, daily contact between the mother (situated in the home, without a career) and her child – a contact now divorced from the labor within the pre-Industrial home in which children also engaged – that elicited the Oedipal neuroses Freud theorized. I use psychoanalytic theory here to explore the particular form the sexual drive takes within this family, whose demise we are perhaps already witnessing: twenty-first century, postmodern family modes may well produce a different form of the sexual drive because very different social, biological and psychological conditions may well prevail, as my final chapter suggests. I focus in this chapter on the special form of psychic relation between mother and child that the bourgeois family produced between 1830 and, say, 1970 (to choose a cut-off point) in North America. Given the limitation of my study to complicit maternal melodramas and resisting maternal women's films between 1830 and 1970, I will confine my discussion of psychological processes to those that are particularly

27

relevant to illuminating these melodramas: in relation to *complicit* maternal melodramas, unconscious pre-Oedipal, fusional or symbiotic processes are relevant, and take precedence over conscious/rational functioning; in relation to *resisting* melodramas, conscious/rational processes take precedence over the unconscious ones, which are nevertheless still operating.

The chapter has two parts to it: in the first, I explore select psychoanalytic processes as they have been theorized to take place within the bourgeois family defined above; in the second I explore psychoanalysis *as an historically constituted ideology*. I look at ways in which psychoanalytic theory, particularly in the post-Freud period, becomes itself a *discourse* producing powerful mother-representations in culture.

Both parts of the chapter prepare for analyses in Part II on "Fictional Representations." The first part is relevant because, having explored certain psychoanalytic theories of mother–child symbiosis, I show how maternal melodramas of both types represent desire for fusion with the mother. I distinguish between humanist/sociological Freudian theories which illuminate some nineteenth-century women's texts (and select twentieth-century films), and post-structuralist Lacanian theories, which can be used to explore how the symbolic order structures the mother. The former analyze relations between mothers and others (whether in texts or in lived experience), using Freudian Oedipal theories, while the latter analyze discursive organizations of language in texts and in culture. While both kinds of psychoanalytic theory inform my work in different ways, I privilege the post-structuralist ones in this book. Since these theories isolate discursive gender assumptions evident in symbolic processes crucial to subject-formation (in which the mother is central), they refer to the level of things also found in fictional materials.

I am interested in links between psychoanalytic theory showing unconscious need for closeness with the mother's body, and the basic cinematic institution. I will argue that the cinema is the closest analog in the realm of the Symbolic to access to the maternal body: it allows subjects to re-experience the pleasures of fusion with the maternal body in fact impossible after the pre-Oedipal period.

The second part of the chapter prepares the way for exploring psychoanalytic mother-discourses, as these are picked up and deployed in various ways within specific film texts. Psychoanalysis is here presented as a discourse that engenders cultural representations and explanations of a specific kind. This discourse serves an ideological function in the sense of supporting woman's position as centrally that of mother within the bourgeois home. It is a discourse that the maternal melodrama in turn adopts as part of furthering capitalism's needs in the first half of the twentieth century.

It is the tension between concepts like the unconscious, central to psychoanalytic theory and privileged by me as "true" given specific historical and social contexts, and psychoanalysis as a discourse that culture picks up

28

and uses for its own ends (particularly for positioning women in certain ideological ways: Kofman 1985) that is central to this book.

Since there remains a debate in feminist circles about the value of psychoanalysis as a tool (Birns 1988; see Appendix A, pp. 52ff), let me say something about my reasons for making the method central in my text: first, psychoanalytic theory enables me to understand fictional phenomena that other methods cannot account for. I began thinking about this project by noticing certain repeated fictional mother-representations, which I wanted to explain. Psychoanalysis offered itself as a system that may account for what I noticed. In the absence of research to the contrary, I assume that these representations fulfill important psychic functions if they are so prominent, over so much time, in popular materials.

Feminists are not the first to attack analytic theories and practices, which have been criticized by psychologists and others since Freud's own time. Attacks usually take the form of outright rejection of the existence (or importance) of unconscious processes. But adequate alternative explanations for the phenomena that psychoanalysis tries to explain are still lacking. Academic psychologists disagree as to whether or not unconscious motivation has been scientifically demonstrated. However, most psychologists accept the concept of an unconscious, albeit not necessarily of a Freudian kind. Psychoanalysis is in the odd place of being an unproven theory. Some of the issues in psychoanalytic theory are amenable to empirical testing, and a number of researchers are engaged in such work (Shevrin and Dickman 1980). As long as psychoanalysis has not been disproved, it seems reasonable to adopt it as a method where it appears to account for what is otherwise hard to explain.

Even though Freud does not directly address the mother,[1] nor say much about female sexuality per se, his theories revolutionized nineteenth-century motherhood discourses as Rousseau's theories had revolutionized pre-modern motherhood discourses. Freud's theory of how the baby comes to know itself as an entity separate from its mother ushers in the concept of subjectivity, although this was Lacan's, not Freud's, term for the phenomena Freud analyzed particularly in the fort-da game. Freud alluded to the difference between the level of *fusion* with the mother in the pre-Oedipal stage, and the post-Oedipal level of self-hood (achieved through the Oedipus Complex, where the female child accepts castration, and the male child *fears* castration), but did not develop this theory. He hypothesized that both male and female children learn to use language as the means for replacing loss of the mother, who recedes into the unconscious at latency. As Parveen Adams (1983) puts it, "Freud's concept of psychical reality requires the repression of the desire for the mother, an instinctual renunciation which is the price of civilization."

According to Freud, this repression takes place at the time of the Oedipus Complex, which Freud then primarily focused on in his work to the neglect of the pre-Oedipal period. Although he did finally acknowledge what he called the "Primal" mother (the pre-Oedipal mother), Freud had difficulty in "defining her other than as object of hatred or place of pathology" (Plaza 1981). Since for Freud, the phallus mediates the symbolic level, there is, from the child's point of view, only the pre-Oedipal phallic mother, or the post-Oedipal (and powerless) castrated one.

Lacan's reworking of Freudian theories is useful in stressing the parts of Freud that dealt (if only implicitly) with the level of representation/the symbolic. Lacan's movement from concern with biology to concern with language resulted in more attention to the pre-Oedipal stage, and to its heady pleasures, even if for Lacan, female desire remains impossible. Lacan stresses how we come to be *sexed* subjects, how sexual difference operates on the unconscious level, namely that of the "Imaginary," as set in opposition to the level of culture, the Law, and language that he calls the "Symbolic." Lacan's mirror phase represents the transition between the pre-Oedipal and the phallic phases. It represents early realization of subjectivity (which is really a *split* subjectivity) as the child at once clings to illusory oneness with the mother in the world of the Imaginary, and begins to be aware of the mother as an object distinct from itself. For Lacan, the incipient awareness of the mother-as-object is linked to the child's awareness of its "mirror" self (its Ideal Imago) as an entity also distinct from itself. The Imaginary unitary self (whether a mother-self Self or a mirror-self Self) is now split into two objects: mother and self; mirror-image and self.

In the Lacanian system, the child/adult, however, never forgets the world of the Imaginary, and he/she continues to desire, unconsciously, the illusory oneness with the mother he/she experienced. But there are differences in the male and female fantasies and in the ways in which unsatisfied pre-Oedipal longings can be channelled.

The boy's longing for, and identification with, the mother suffers a severe blow with the entry of the Father and the need for individuation. The shadow of the phallus indeed falls over the boy as he finds his place in a symbolic order organized around the phallus as signifier. Fear of castration at the Father's hands if he continues his erotic desire for the mother and the identification that this involves (carried over from the pre-Oedipal stage) plummets the boy into identification with his Father and with the phallus. He looks forward both to one day having symbolic power like his father, and to recuperating his mother through marriage to someone like her. But note that the original feminine identification still remains a problem, something that troubles him, that is disturbing and needs to be defended against, as in negative/derogatory representations of the mother.

The girl's dilemma is more complicated, as Juliet Mitchell has noted, in that the shadow of the phallus also falls over her, but now because the phallus is what the mother desires rather than because there is any identification of her own. Her masculine identification is thus at one remove, but meanwhile

Useful review of Freud/Lacan/cinematic theory

it has overwhelmed the original feminine identification. It is in this sense that any specifically *female* desire becomes impossible – at least within the symbolic order, which is the order of discourse.

Nevertheless, Lacanian theory does provide a certain space for a special, pre-Oedipal, fusional, pleasure (which Lacan calls *jouissance*). This *jouissance* is a specifically feminine, bodily, kind of ecstasy which Lacan says lies beyond the phallus, and is for that reason not able to be spoken within discourse. The concept of *jouissance*, as well as that of the mirror-phase, is important for the texts I call "complicit," and for understanding the phenomenon of the self-sacrificing maternal figure so common in melodramas. Lacan's theories are also useful in analyzing the way readers/viewers attach themselves to texts, as if seeking to replicate the mirror-phase and its fusion/separation duality. It is precisely the politics of the fusional phenomenon, taken up as a discourse within certain melodrama texts (like *East Lynne* and *Stella Dallas*) that I will explore in Part II of the book on "Motherhood and Fictional Representation."

Female theorists have struggled to clarify the implications for feminism of both Freudian theories and the Lacanian revisions of Freud. Positions range from outright rejection of Freud and psychoanalytic theory (Baym 1984),[2] to interest in Freudian-based theories (object-relations or ego-psychology) (Gardiner 1986; Chodorow 1978: 133–4; Benjamin 1988), to exploring questions and concepts raised in Lacanian theories.[3] While both of the latter groups are interested in psychoanalysis, their focuses differ greatly: the first, Freudian-based group leans in the humanist/sociological direction, while the latter Lacanian group stresses the construction of the female subject through language and signifying systems generally.[4] Lacanian theorists aim to discover how femininity and masculinity are constructed as the child enters the order of language and culture; often, theorists hope this knowledge will enable them to learn how to change things.

Some essays in the so-called "L'Ane Dossier" in *m/f* usefully summarize the basic differences between the Lacanian and the Freudian/sociological theories, while themselves favoring a more orthodox Lacanian position than I want to present here: Nancy Wood usefully notes the different mothers that psychoanalytic and feminist research claim to have resuscitated. She says that

> While feminism has primarily sought to expose and reclaim the "social" mother by illuminating all her material tasks and functions, psychoanalysis conjures a maternal "imago" whose relationship to any bodily counterpart is greatly attenuated. In the case of Lacanian psychoanalysis, we might say that it is not even an unconscious image which is encountered in the analytic situation, but the subject's desire for the mother, the desire to be the mother, and the desire of the mother. In short, the profile of the mother which Lacanian psychoanalysis offers

to view is primarily a "figure" of the subject's desire. The question of interest to a feminist analytics of mothering, then, is whether or not the social and psychical mother ever coincide.

(Wood 1983)

But in this volume that "interest" in "whether or not the social and psychical mothers ever coincide" is not followed up: authors are far more interested in the psychical mother, per se. I differ from them in being concerned about the social mother, and in wanting to take note of *both* mothers. I am interested in the layering of the social mother ontop of the psychical one.

Marie-Christine Hamon (1983), in the same *m/f* issue, insists on the necessary and permanent dissatisfaction of the human child (an insatiable demand for love) first noted by Freud and having nothing to do with the real (historical) mother's deficiencies. For in the Lacanian system, it is the mother who introduces the child to lack, castration, representation; and whichever historical person were taking care of the child (literal father, nurse or other surrogate), the same *figure* of loss (a figure under the sign "mother,") would remain. The figure is the price of separation and individuation essential to human growth and autonomy. Hamon usefully points to the gender differences involved in this process: the boy has to overcome the incestuous representation and to recognize that the mother can be both virgin and whore. He has to learn that the mother also has a sexual life – a life which must exclude the son, while the girl refinds the mother in the father or husband or child. For the girl, it is a matter of *being* the mother rather than *having* the mother.

The humanist/sociological feminist Freudian position is best represented by Nancy Chodorow, who has been taken up extensively by feminist literary and film scholars. Other psychoanalytic feminists, like Jessica Benjamin or Maud Mannoni, have been important for my research, but, for the sake of retaining a certain coherence, I leave them till later. (See Appendix A, pp. 52–55, for summary of psychoanalytic feminists not explored here.)

Working within the American Freudian object-relations tradition, Chodorow modifies standard theory in stressing not only the girl's strong pre-Oedipal feminine identification, but also the long continuation of such attachments well into the Oedipal period, and even into adult life:

Because mothers are the primary love object and object of identification for both genders . . . the oedipus complex in girls is characterized by the continuation of pre-oedipal attachments and preoccupations, sexual oscillation in an oedipal triangle, and the lack of either absolute change of love object or absolute oedipal resolution.

(Chodorow 1978)

Chodorow is not concerned with the role of language/ representation/the

Symbolic in the constitution of the subject, thinking rather in terms of the self as an essence that is shaped through unconscious relation to other "object" selves. In this model then, the girl remains attached to the mother since she gets her feminine identity in this way (as against the boy who gets his masculine identity through precisely negating his earlier "feminine" identification with the mother), and merely adds on her relationship to the father.

Chodorow points out that at puberty all the girl's early pre-Oedipal bonding with, and ambivalence towards, her mother re-emerges. Here Chodorow recognizes the unconscious desire at work in explicitly differentiating her analysis from that of Helene Deutsch (1926) who focuses on the girl's object relationships, as against the primary (unconscious) identification that Chodorow shows is really at work. "That is," Chodorow says, "a daughter acts as if she is and feels herself unconsciously one with her mother" (1978: 136). A little further on, she says that girls "In relation to their mother (and similarly, the mother in relation to her daughters) . . . experience themselves as overly attached, unindividuated and without boundaries" (1978: 137). This often leads to overt criticism and/or rejection of the mother, but in fact, the daughter "has fled to intense identification-idealization-object loves, trying to merge herself with anyone other than her mother, all the while expressing her feelings of dependence on and primary identification with this mother" (1978: 137). Chodorow concludes that while girls "usually make a sexual resolution in favor of men and their father, [they] retain an internal emotional triangle" (1978: 140).

What is important about Chodorow's work is its challenge to Freud's phallocentrism, its attention to the *girl's* pre-Oedipal and Oedipal struggles, its positing of a specificity in itself to the feminine (however encumbered that notion might be by essentialism, it has a rhetorical force that is important and provoking); its suggestion that female identity is less rigid than men's because of the girl's *double* identification (pre-Oedipally with the mother – an identification that continues – post-Oedipally with the Father); and finally its hopeful suggestion that the exclusivity of the reproduction of mothering to the female child is not inevitable or unchangeable. Chodorow believes that different psychic patterns would result from men taking primary responsibility for child-rearing and from releasing the mother from the position of sole nurturer and care-taker.

The solution is problematic because Chodorow confuses the social and psychic mothers. Parveen Adams (1983) points out that Chodorow's work privileges the social over concepts of desire and the unconscious in relation to the construction of sexual difference. That is, she replaces "desire" and "drive" with "needs" and "instinct." While Adams perhaps overstates the case (I've shown that Chodorow does, at times, make use of some theories of the unconscious), Adams is correct in noting that Chodorow's image of good mothering ends up close to that of Winnicott: that is, it ends up putting the

33

emphasis, again, on the capacity of the mother (now helped by the father, however) to be the kind of secure presence arguably needed for the child's development. The theory assumes that the infant's self can be a unified, coherent one, but that its "continuity of being" is dependent on parents' providing the secure base.

Particularly important is Adams's point that the relational potential Chodorow discusses might itself be the effect of practices that have constructed the modern mother and bound her to her set of tasks (as outlined in Chapter 2). Adams argues convincingly, following Lacan, that the subject is always a "split" subject, "that which does *not* have the continuity of being that Winnicott deems so essential for the ego" (Adams 1983: 47).

Interestingly enough, Adams agrees with Chodorow that we need new norms that would free the socially constructed mother from that construction. But she is not satisfied with Chodorow's treatment of the social, or with her solution to the mother's dilemma, namely an increased role for the father. Adams argues that Chodorow conflates the psychic and the social here, and misses the point that "the role of the parent is itself a social construction which needs to be understood in historical terms" (1983: 51). Adams questions that Chodorow's "principle of equity is in itself a critical alteration of social relations" (Adams 1983: 51). This is something that I will return to in the final chapter.

I am interested in Chodorow because her a-historic, a-specific theories for me function as part of the modernist period I am working with. That is, her theories usefully describe the reproduction of white, bourgeois, mothering in the period from 1860 to 1960. What Chodorow has to say about the adolescent girl's struggle to separate from her mother illuminates some mother–child representations in "resisting" maternal women's films to be discussed later on. Chodorow's theories helpfully illuminate the project of some nineteenth-century female writers who also aimed to "recover" the mother through identification with the nurturing role. Women's popular narratives deploy an internal emotional triangle similar to the one Chodorow describes, and the theory partially explains the slippage I am interested in between mother–child "romantic" (merged) love and such male/female love. Even though they were writing before Freud articulated his theories (and even longer before Chodorow, of course), nineteenth-century women (like Harriet Beecher Stowe and Charlotte Perkins Gilman, discussed in Chapter 8) saw the mother role as potentially a socially progressive and beneficial one. The theories, that is, are useful as tools to unlock some fictional aims in certain historical texts by and about women, even if I might want to question the strategies women employed from my own, post-structuralist historical moment.

Some French feminists also working in the theoretical context of post-structuralism (in the wake, that is, of such writers as Barthes, Derrida, Althusser, Lacan and Foucault), objected to Freudian psychoanalysis per se, as a *discourse*, and raised issues in the context of language/representation/the Lacanian Imaginary and Symbolic. These authors were particularly interested in Lacan's positing of a specifically feminine *jouissance*, of a bodily feminine ecstasy "beyond the phallus," and proceeded to develop theories from this premiss. Some understanding of these theorists of the female *body* is important, not so much for readings I will myself undertake here as, first, for situating my readings in relation to others, and second, for illuminating aspects of mother–daughter merging/symbiosis which provides some of the pleasures of "complicit" melodramas. Such theories may be helpful in understanding the utopian appeal to female spectators of the mother-child (especially *boy*-child) "romance" that often has the fusional quality some French feminists see as subversive.

Luce Irigaray perhaps best represents this alternate approach. Writing in response to the specifically Lacanian formulations of Freudian theory, her work naturally takes on a cast different from that of Chodorow:

> The issue is not one of elaborating a new theory of which woman would be the *subject* or the *object*, but of jamming the theoretical machinery itself, of suspending its pretension to the production of a truth and of a meaning that are excessively univocal.
>
> (Irigaray 1985a: 78)

She notes that women should not focus on Freud's question "what is woman?", but rather

> repeating/interpreting the way in which, within discourse, the feminine finds itself defined as lack, deficiency, or as imitation and negative image of the subject, they should signify that with respect to this logic a disruptive excess is possible on the feminine side.
>
> (Irigaray 1985a: 78)

It is precisely this "excess" that Irigaray believes leaves open the possibility of another (female) language.

Irigaray believes that this excess has its source in woman's body that manifests, in its very structure, "nearness" – "those rubbings between two infinitely near neighbors that create a dynamics" (1985a: 79). This implies "a mode of exchange irreducible to any *centering*, any *centrism* . . . a proximity that confounds any adequation, any appropriation" (Irigaray 1985a: 79).

We see that while Chodorow was at pains to illuminate the girl's psychic processes within the Freudian system (something that Freud himself overlooked), and to show how psychoanalytic processes reproduce mothering and the status quo, Irigaray not only critiques the system itself, revealing it as a particular kind of discourse, but also tries to find ways for women to transcend that system, to move beyond its constraints. The focus on language/the Symbolic/representation allows Irigaray to expose the cultural construction of the discourse that confines women, thus opening up at least the theoretical possibility for change, however difficult such a change might be precisely because of the centrality of the Symbolic. Irigaray is, however, willing to suggest that women can discover a different "language," other modalities of being, through the *body*.

Two closely linked essays ("And the One Doesn't Stir Without the Other;" "When Our Lips Speak Together" reveal Irigaray's understanding of the psychoanalytic discourses (and corresponding family structures) that position mothers and daughters negatively. Her analysis here is similar to Chodorow's when the latter deals with the unconscious and primary process. The essays also attempt to suggest ways for women to create a new modality, to re-construct themselves. Both essays are important to my concerns in discussing the maternal sacrifice narrative in their focus on the mother–daughter (or, more generally, woman-woman) merging/symbiosis, although my stance toward symbiosis (and its "subversiveness") will differ.

Irigaray explores in a poignant, poetic, beautifully evocative manner the impact on the daughter of "fusional" mothering, and also (assuming that the daughter has managed to free herself from the negative effects) celebrates what is seen as a healthy kind of coming-together-as-one of two women, not literally mother and daughter.

Interestingly enough, Irigaray's analysis of the first step of working one's way through the mother (to be found in "And The One Doesn't Stir Without the Other": Irigaray 1981) was articulated after celebrating a (perhaps utopian) concept of female–female relating in "When Our Lips Speak Together" (Irigaray 1985b). As Hélène Wenzel points out, the first essay imagines the pre-Oedipal daughter "speaking" her experience that "maternity fills in the gaps in a repressed female sexuality" (Wenzel 1981: 27), and makes concrete what Monique Plaza (1981) has to say about why mothers engage in "fusional" relating: the child compensates for the woman's general frustrations rather than opening up any new possibility of its own. Indeed, later in the essay, Irigaray seems afraid that, given leeway, the female imaginary might privilege the maternal over the feminine, and in so doing simply repeat the male system of "jealous possession of its valued product." In accepting a certain social power in the maternal, woman reduces herself, for Irigaray, to sexual impotence; if she were to try to reverse the order of things, the inevitable phallic maternal involved would mean reversion to sameness, to phallocratism (Wenzel 1981: 33).

The essay goes on to describe the daughter's turning to the father, not because of her sense of lack but, as Wenzel again notes, paradoxically because of being "overstuffed" with the mother's nurturing. The father leaves her empty inside but does at least give her space. We see the girl now taking on the attributes of the patriarchal feminine, becoming socialized into the prescribed cultural role, and finally leaving the mother, but not without pain.

The next section shows the daughter trying to explain the mother to herself – to explain the emptiness (the result of her patriarchal positioning) that led the mother to mirror herself in the daughter: "I received from you only your obliviousness of self, while my presence allowed you to forget this oblivion. So that with my tangible appearance I redoubled the lack of your presence" (Irigaray 1981: 65). The final section of "And the One" suggests how it is that the mother and daughter have been locked in such negativity, "captives of our confinement" (Irigaray 1981: 67). The daughter implores the mother to "remain alive" in giving her birth.

Irigaray posits the possibility for simultaneous autonomy and oneness between women in "When Our Lips Speak Together." She repeats the notion already mentioned of bodies nourished by mutual pleasure:

> Our abundance is inexhaustible: it knows neither want nor plenty. Since we give each other (our) all, with nothing held back, nothing hoarded, our exchanges are without terms, without end. How can I say it? The language we know is so limited.
>
> (Irigaray 1985b: 213–14)

The women here do not need children (woman does not need to become "mother"), since Irigaray sees the child as the way for men and women to "embody their closeness, their distance" (1985b: 209). Two women together do not need such strategies, since they are able to be directly close, not needing to go via the child as *symbol*.

Obviously, Irigaray realizes that children are necessary in the larger scheme of things (for the continuation of the human race). Her theories are important in freeing women from the oppression of desire for the symbolic child: but she does not account for the "deliberately chosen" desire for the child that is, at least theoretically, possible once women have worked their way to consciousness of patriarchal socialization.

Cixous's theories, in many ways similar to Irigaray's, nevertheless differ in terms of which elements of the female body are seen as presenting a challenge to the Lacanian patriarchal symbolic (Cixous and Clément 1986). While Irigaray focuses on *touch*, Cixous focuses on the *voice*, which is transformed into *writing* (écriture feminine). If Irigaray's grounding signifier is the material (ultimately maternal) female body (albeit a body multiple, dispersed, with fluid boundaries), Cixous's is the female voice. She foregrounds her own speaking voice in her writing which follows the rules of speech rather than the conventions established for writing. Her prose is then riotous, full of stops and starts, repetitions, reversals, punctuated with expletives, rhetorical questions, exclamations, as impassioned speech would be. Seizing this Voice posited as being *different*, a denunciating voice, Cixous proceeds to analyze woman's oppression. The energy in her prose belies the negated, absent female position that she describes; it is as if she is willing her female readers to follow her in seizing a lost voice, intent on inspiring her readers, waking them up from their "Sleeping Beauty" sleep.

Significantly, Cixous believes that women can find this Voice because it was given to them by their mother: "The Voice sings from a time before law, before the Symbolic took one's breath away and reappropriated it into language under its authority of separation" (Cixous and Clément 1986). Cixous here is describing something similar to Kristeva's "semiotic," except that the situating of the Voice concretely within the mother's body gives it a different emphasis. In an extraordinary passage, Cixous strives as far as is possible in words to express the complex rhythms and flowing boundaries between mother and child that results in passing the Voice on to the female child:

> In women there is always, more or less, something of the "mother" repairing and feeding, resisting separation, a force that does not let itself be cut off but that runs codes ragged. The relationship to childhood (the child she was, she is, she acts and makes and starts anew, and unties at the place where, as a same, she even others herself), is no more cut off than is the relationship to the "mother," as it consists of delights and violences.
>
> (Cixous and Clément 1986: 93)

While it is unclear why Cixous puts the quotation marks around "the mother" (she is not here referring to the Christian/patriarchal construct – quite the opposite), the passage conveys the fluid boundaries between mother and child – the subject's retaining of both positions at the same time. The second half of the passage is more difficult in that here Cixous's use of pronouns is such as to deliberately prevent the coherent "I" and "You" positions of the patriarchal symbolic:

> Text, my body: traversed by lilting flows; listen to me, it is not a captivation, clinging "mother"; it is the equivoice that, touching you, affects you, pushes you away from your breast to come to language, that summons your strength; it is the rhyth-me that laughs you ... the part of you that puts the space between your self and pushes you to inscribe your woman's style in language. Voice: milk that could go on forever. Found again. The lost mother/bitter lost. Eternity: is voice mixed with milk.
>
> (Cixous and Clément 1986: 78)

Poetic, evocative prose, this passage posits the mother, not so much as a solid, physical presence, but as a voice-off (the voice that Laura Mulvey (1977–8) argued was that of the Sphinx, calling from the long past of history). The "mother" means the pre-Symbolic world of song, rhythms, as against the symbiotic/merged mother of Irigaray. Indeed, this mother pushes the child away from the breast, liberating the child into *her* language, not his-story. For Cixous, then, the mother is the daughter's source of speaking, not a forbidden place that prevents the voice or against which the subject must struggle to emerge as a subject (as in Kristeva).

Because they ultimately have to rely on the biological structuring of the female body to arrive at a new female "language," a new female way of relating to the world, to other women, Irigaray and Cixous have, like Chodorow, been accused of essentialism. The biological determinism apparently underlying Irigaray's theories is a problem, although one can argue that in Irigaray the body is a discursive entity, not a literal, biological one. I am not convinced by this argument, and I also think it is hard to escape essentialist traps. Nevertheless, it is important to develop theories that clearly operate on the discursive rather than the biological level, since only discursive theories prevent women and men from being locked into specific positions.

My concern with both Cixous and Irigaray has also to do first with the problem of *desire*, particularly with the notion that this desire can ever find expression and/or be satisfied; and second (following from this) with the utopian level on which theories function. By this, I mean that Cixous and Irigaray attempt to open out the Lacanian paradigm, which cannot account for how the girl ever retrieves her lost "feminine," and which assumes that the girl is forever situated in the position of lack. I have taken this space to explore their theories, along with some of Chodorow's, because, as is already clear, my analyses of nineteenth-century texts by women will seek to show the underlying search for a similar, early feminine identification through fantasies/images/representations of romantic love or of mother–child bonding. But I will also be asking what exactly investment in this search *means*: I want to question *celebrating unproblematically* female fusional orientations, to ask whose interests these orientations ultimately serve? I differ from Irigaray and Cixous in relation to evaluating this psychoanalytic phenomenon of "merging." Irigaray and Cixous are often used to construct theories of feminine subversion via the female body per se, just because the female body is said to be "beyond the phallus." I rather see the female body (and in particular mother/child bodies) as constructed by/through the patriarchal Imaginary to fulfill specific patriarchal or capitalist needs. In this case how can any politics of the body be liberating other than on the most basic individualist level?

Constructing a feminine pre-Oedipal mother might enable us to see Motherhood as one way for the girl to re-establish her lost feminine identification through means other than via the phallus. The woman would, in this scenario, recover the lost part of herself as Mother, or with her own Mother through identifying with herself as Mother, or with her own Mother through adopting the mother-position. But the danger is in theories being mere wish-fulfillments, mere rhetorical strategies for structuring the possibility of non-castration. (Chodorow does acknowledge that merging may produce an obstacle for the girl's proper individuation, autonomy, independence: indeed, she accounts for the girl's turn toward the father as a means for her to escape the mother). Nevertheless, Chodorow (1978) clearly values the orientation toward relatedness that comes from closeness to the mother, without asking how this has been ideologically required). Thus, the difficult question remains: is such mother-identification only to identify with a patriarchal construct? Does it mean continuing to be in an oppressed position, the woman marginalized like her own mother? To put it another way: can there ever be anything subversive or progressive in our identification with our mothers in the Symbolic? How can motherhood ever be non-patriarchal, non-complicit? Honoring the mother's subjectivity, the mother's voice, may be important in a culture where that subjectivity and voice have been silenced; but the question is: what precisely is it possible for the mother to *speak as* in a patriarchal culture? If the mother's position is patriarchally constructed, can she only speak within the confines of that construction? How could she speak *otherwise*?

Kristeva was one of the first to address these difficult questions and to theorize possible answers. Many theorists of motherhood, including those briefly discussed above, end up looking from the child position. That slippage from talking about the mother to talking from the child's perspective seems endemic to research in this area, and in itself revealing of the instability in the mother construct. In her essay, "Stabat Mater," Kristeva (1985) claims that we cannot simply turn to motherhood as something that definitely attributes existence to woman: for "motherhood" turns out "to be an adult (male and female) fantasy of a lost continent." Things are further complicated by the fact that when we try to think motherhood, what we end up thinking is rather the idealized relationship between her and us. This relationship is unlocalizable, according to Kristeva, and ends up being "an idealization of primary narcissism" (1985: 99). On the cultural level, traditional representations (largely deriving from Christianity) are broadly accepted. Feminists have rejected these as oppressive and confining, but in so doing have then denied the entire "real experience" (Kristeva's words) of maternity that Kristeva wants to address.

By the words, "real experience," Kristeva does not intend any naive essentialism, although in this area the Symbolic, the unconscious and the "real" (here meaning lived, daily experience) are always collapsing into each other. Kristeva's writings about motherhood follow on her work in linguistics and semiotics, and are intricately bound up in those theories. In "Stabat Mater" and "Motherhood According to Bellini," (1980) we see Kristeva bringing together her concepts of the "semiotic" and "the chora" (developed in relation to male avant-garde artists) with theories about motherhood. In one sense, Kristeva is saying that women have privileged access to the semiotic, the Imaginary and the pre-linguistic "chora" through their biological experience of giving birth. It is not that this level of things is limited to women – she has shown the male avant-garde's participation in it already – but that motherhood provides another access. But Kristeva implies that language is man's access to *jouissance*, biology woman's. And this is a problem.

① "the mother was standing"
Latin hymn @ sorrows of the Virgin
at the Crucifixion

cp??
29'

Accordingly, in the essay on Bellini, Kristeva (1980) is at pains to show how through his artistic creativity, Bellini, a male Renaissance painter, can reach back to the *jouissance* of the pre-linguistic that is most evident in the display of color in the works – particularly the rhythms and pulsations the color produces. Kristeva evidently believes that the male artist can identify with the mother's *jouissance* and in some sense achieve it in his art. But I question whether it is the *mother's* experience that Bellini reproduces or that of the child in the dyad that is always so inseparable from the maternal being. That is, isn't the maternal indeed a relationship, as Kristeva says, and as such not inhering in either party alone? I am only a mother in relating to my child, not outside of that relation. It is precisely patriarchal culture that has essentialized and fixed the concept "Mother" to my being-in-the-world, instead of permitting it to be a mobile part of my being that comes and goes depending on whether I am in relation or not to the child. I will return to this discussion in Chapter 9.

Kristeva's theories about mothering appear in two contrasting sets of the work: the essays mentioned above and written about the time of the birth of her child and her entry into psychoanalysis; and her *Powers of Horror*, written in 1980 (translated in 1982). The first body of work analyzes the split between the hypostatized Christian cultural representation of the mother, and the lived, non-symbolic aspect of giving birth and mothering. Kristeva here comes close to feminist concerns in her discussion of motherhood as "reunion of a woman-mother with the body of *her* mother" (Kristeva 1980). Arguing that no one can actually occupy the position of "Mother," because it represents merely a patriarchal function, Kristeva nevertheless opposes to the "symbolic paternal facet" of motherhood, a "nonsymbolic, nonpaternal causality," that consists of unrepresentable (because outside of culture) biological movement: "Cells fuse, split, and proliferate; volumes grow, tissues stretch, and body fluids change rhythm . . . . And no one is present . . . to signify what is going on" (Kristeva 1980: 237). This cannot be appropriated by patriarchy. In giving birth, Kristeva argues, "the woman enters into contact with her mother; she becomes, she is her own mother; they are the same continuity differentiating itself" (1980: 239). In this process, then, woman "actualizes the homosexual facet of motherhood, through which a woman is simultaneously closer to her instinctual memory, more negatory of the social, symbolic bond" (1980: 239). (This should be the case for the mother whatever the child's gender, but I suspect it would be a doubly strong identification when the baby is a girl.)

In this model, motherhood does not imply a reaffirmation of the phallus but rather a subversive moment, the "nodule of a biosocial program" whose *jouissance* is mute, and whose archaic basis Kristeva argues must be censured for women so that the "symbolic destiny of the speaking animal" can take place (1980: 241).

41

Here Kristeva seems for a moment to imply a specificity to the level of the semiotic for woman not dominant in her thought. We can honor Kristeva's attempt to include all humans in the level of the Imaginary and of *jouissance*, but nevertheless it would seem that we need to think about the different later implications of this pre-linguistic moment for males and females in the patriarchal Symbolic. Once we know and live out our positions as "male" or "female," the meanings of the pre-linguistic terrain are different for each gender. As a feminist, knowing about this theorized terrain, I am interested in exploring what of that terrain might be of use to my situation in the patriarchal Symbolic. I might conclude that nothing is useful; or I might find that what Toril Moi has identified as Kristeva's real concern, that is "marginality, subversion, dissidence" (Toril Moi 1986: 117), is of use in developing strategies for change and even more locally for survival. And that through being female, through knowing motherhood differently from males, I might have privileged access to that knowledge. Also, because I am a female in the Symbolic, I may find a way to relate differently from males to the patriarchal/Christian construct of the cultural mother by which historical mothers are overwhelmed.

I turn now to Kristeva's later work that involves theorizing the mother, namely her *Powers of Horror* (Kristeva 1982). What is fascinating here is how Kristeva's two reworkings of concepts of the mother might be seen as repeating, yet once again, that old duality of the idealized and monstrous mothers. No matter how hard we try, our language order would seem to insist on these polarities. Perhaps what Melanie Klein first fully theorized simply is the fact, namely, the primal mother is both idealized primary narcissism (total merging, total pleasure/bliss, total plenitude – which is the same thing), and the primal experience of abjection. The two kinds of mother would be related to the child's development: the mother as the abject would result from the necessary separation from the mother. All later objects "are based on the inaugural loss that laid the foundations of (the subject's) being" (Kristeva 1982). For Kristeva, "all abjection is in fact recognition of the *want* in which any being, meaning, language or desire is founded" (1982: 5). Perhaps most graphic for what Kristeva is talking about is the following:

> Out of the daze that has petrified him before the untouchable, impossible, absent body of the mother, a daze that has cut off his (*sic*) impulses from their object, that is, from their representations, out of such daze, he causes, along with loathing, one word to crop up – fear.

(Kristeva 1982: 6)

It seems that for Kristeva there are two choices: one either lives searching for a return to the primary narcissism of the first phase of relation to the mother, in which case one lives in desire for objects; or one lives with non-objects. Since this latter case is less usual, a brief clarification is in order. Kristeva calls the one who lives a life based on exclusion the "deject":

the deject has fluid boundaries, and is preoccupied therefore always with demarking territories. The deject lives with non-objects because he/she lacks the clear boundaries which constitute the object-world for normal subjects. His/her solidity is thus constantly in jeopardy, and he/she is constantly starting afresh, as Kristeva notes.

Kristeva goes on to link the abject with a particular form of *jouissance*, since like *jouissance*, the abject has to do with elimination of boundaries. But whereas for most people *jouissance* is a brief, ecstatic moment (the orgasm, joy in nature, spiritual ecstasy, and so on), for the deject it is the norm – often though in a terrifying sense. For the deject lives in the sphere of the Other (he/she has, as noted, no boundaries), and it is only by the fear and repugnance of being *possessed* – abjection, then – that the deject exists.

Kristeva here seems to be doing two things: first, trying to get inside the very being of the pre-linguistic baby – to imagine what it felt like to be that baby – to speak for that baby's feelings; and second, to be talking as the adult still experiencing such loss of boundary, which we clinically call "schizophrenia."

I am interested in how this all relates to the mother: Kristeva seems to be talking about the mother from the child perspective, whereas in the earlier work she tried to speak from the (impossible) mother position. She is thus able to articulate the two sides of the mother–child dyad, and to explore the poignant problem the child has in releasing hold of the maternal entity. Given the structure of the child as possessed by the mother (as not knowing her as an object, of having no boundary), the mother can be released only by the child's making her the abject – the reviled, the repugnant, all that is horrifying and disgusting. It is because of the prohibition placed on the maternal body (a defense against autoeroticism and the incest taboo) that abjection becomes necessary.

For Kristeva, then, woman is particularly implicated in abjection by virtue of being the one against whom the child has to develop subjectivity. If woman culturally is defined as the one at the margin between culture and chaos, order and anarchy, reason and the abyss, then she typifies abjection. She is the deject on the brink always of losing herself; but for culture she represents that dangerous zone against which culture must struggle to retain itself. Hence, women are sometimes reviled as too close to chaos, as outside of culture; but may then be idealized and elevated as supreme defenders against the wilderness that would envelop man.

Kristeva usefully reworks the tradition of the mother-virgin/mother-whore split (basically a *Christian* formulation) in psychoanalytic terms. Her theories are useful for specific film analyses of texts in Part II, particularly in relation to *East Lynne*, and later to *Marnie*. (If *East Lynne* is a text dramatizing the Kristevan "semiotic," *Marnie* represents Kristevan "abjection.") Unlike Chodorow, Irigaray and Cixous, Kristeva keeps on insisting on the limits/constraints of the Symbolic order, and on the centrality of the Law of the Father in defining female subjectivity. These are difficult issues for feminists because they pose problems for theories of a female subjectivity independent of male culture, but I believe they are essential to address. I also believe Kristeva's theories illuminate the impossible contradictions under which the mother (as subject *and* as sign) labors, and are thus particularly useful for Part II on *Fictional Representation*.

It is precisely in re-examining theories of the pre-Oedipal mother–child relation that we may begin to see whether it is possible for the mother to offer resistances against those imaginary positionings (Mannoni 1970). I will be arguing that it is precisely a fantasy of pre-Oedipal female and male desire, doomed never to be satiated but always searching for an object, that causes the "trouble" in maternal sacrifice narratives. We need to examine representations of the pre-Oedipal mother–child relation in regard to both genders if we are to understand the phenomenon of romantic love for both sexes. The pre-Oedipal haunts men as much as it haunts women, if differently, so that we are dealing with a phenomenon broader than some simple sexist one. Indeed, John Donne's haunting poem "The Compass" expresses almost the same emotions and identical structure of interpersonal relations for the male and female lovers as does Irigaray's essay about two women; the comparison, however, illuminates that within dominant, adult heterosexuality, males approximate satisfaction of pre-Oedipal desire more closely than women, since culture supports their finding the mother in heterosexual marriage.

Freudian theory has too categorically accepted the boy's clear renunciation of the feminine in his taking on of masculine identity. Janine Chasseguet-Smirgel's work, building on Karen Horney's initiatives, is important in seeing Freud's sexual monism and his attribution of a "natural scorn" for women on man's part, as a defense against the primal omnipotent mother with "her faculties, her organs and her specifically feminine features" (Chasseguet-Smirgel 1970b: 23–6).[5] The girl's penis envy, according to Chasseguet-Smirgel, is not linked primarily to castration but to "her need to beat back the maternal power" (1970b: 26). Chasseguet-Smirgel, thus, recognizes the powerful maternal image in the child's mind in a way foreign to Freud.

But we have, precisely here, to ask why patriarchy constructs the mother-images we have in dominant, popular texts: this brings me to the second aim of this chapter, in relation now to psychoanalysis as a *discourse* that can be used for specific ideological ends. Psychoanalysis used as a *discourse* has to be distinguished from psychoanalysis used to explain how we come to be *subjects* (which is the level with which this chapter has hitherto been concerned). I hope that this and previous chapters have together shown that within the modernist historical period, the mother is the one through whom we come to be subjects. This is the consequence first, of the formation of the nuclear family with the onset of Industrialism, and second, of the psychic processes taking place in the mother-centered/father-dominated family. The mother is the one through whom we come to be subjects in this formation, in our similarity and difference from her: she is therefore deeply lodged in the unconscious. This subjectivity is, moreover, prior to other subject-identities (such as class, race, or nationality). For all these reasons, an analysis of psychic processes underlying subjectivity has been undertaken. I assume that these processes are involved in representations produced in Hollywood and in the reception of commercial films.

But having looked at the implications for the viewing/reading subject of the mother's specific psychic centrality, and at the contribution that feminist theory has made to understanding the female child's subjectivity, it is now important to see what *uses* of its own North American culture has made of Freudian (and other) psychoanalytic discourses. As we've seen, Freud's theory of the Oedipus Complex provides an explanation, on a level other than the economic, for the mother's first being installed as symbolic Mother, then relegated to the margins of patriarchal culture. In addition, the Oedipus theory suggests psychic origins for the polarized paradigms of the "virgin" and "whore" mothers that have a long representational history. When read on the level of representations, it is perhaps not surprising that Freud's discourse duplicates dominant literary paradigms: since signifying practices in general are phallocentric, the semiotic field in the nineteenth century produced similar literary and psychoanalytic discourses about the mother. Psychoanalytic theory, as a representation of a representation, was bound to construct itself according to, as well as to account for, the binary opposites of the good and bad mothers that the child creates at an early age. In addition, Freud parallels earlier theories in looking from the *child* position, and then mainly from that of the *boy* child; Freud did not discuss the mother's representations of the mother–child interaction, nor analyze the psychic consequences of mothering for the woman. As will be clear in the following film analyses, North American culture has been able cleverly to use the theory of the child's "good" and "bad" mothers developed by analysts following Freud, to construct representations whose purpose is to manipulate women in, or out of, the work-force, in accordance with capitalism's needs. The powerful ideology of the masochistic, angelic, all-sacrificing mother, produced through psychoanalytic theories as representing the healthy "feminine" woman, has functioned (and is *still* functioning, although in ways strikingly altered via new technologies) to construct women in ways that serve forces that have nothing per se to do with women.

Given my focus on the maternal melodrama and particularly on the pre-Oedipal fusional figure, what is capitalism's *ideological* investment in unconscious fantasies of this symbiotic mother–child relationship in the period under study? Are fusional mothers validated or excoriated? Why?

First, it is important to note that, having once "discovered" the pre-Oedipal mother, psychoanalytic theory proceeds to belittle her and to represent her only through phallic constructs. Freud, and many object-relations theorists, could think of the child's meaning to the mother only in terms of the phallus, just as they could think of the mother's meaning to the child only in such terms; that is, theories of the meaning of the child to the mother are derived from Freud's prior theories of how the *child* thinks the mother. Analysts proceeded to construct two ways that mothers could relate to the child-phallus, the one "good," the other "bad." In the first, the child represents the longed-for penis and signifies the end of women's envy. She now enters into her "natural" masochistic feminine, subordinate to the Father, whose authority is accepted because partly possessed through the child. The mother is happily passive, receptive to her child's needs, and without her own desire (see e.g. Deutsch 1944).

Clearly, such images served economic needs at the turn of the century, when the institution of the family, with its unpaid (and underpaid) female labor, was essential in capitalist economies. But, on the psychoanalytic level, this discourse, when taken up in the "complicit" maternal melodrama, also satisfied *male* longings for the loss of the idealized mother.

In the second construct, the child still represents the phallus, but instead of placing herself in abjection towards it, the mother tries to take it into herself. Now construed as the "bad" phallic mother, she is, in Irigaray's words, "Closed in upon the jealous possession of (her) valued product. Rivaling man in his esteem for productive excess" (Irigaray 1985c: 30). In the strictest sense, the mother is always "phallic" in the Freudian and Lacanian systems, since the feminine can be defined only via the phallus. But the term is usually reserved for the second phenomenon of a jealous/possessive stance toward the child, just because it represents the much-longed-for phallus that is now aggressively seized upon. This second, negative kind of fusional mother image serves to punish women who fall away from the angelic mode, and who then do not serve patriarchal unconscious needs. (These polarized cultural discourses of the mother will be discussed more fully in chapters dealing with each paradigm as it emerges in film representations.)

Having now looked, first, at Freudian and Lacanian theories of how subjects are constituted in modernist culture, second, at feminist revisions of male psychoanalytic theories, and having finally suggested ideological uses of psychoanalytic theories in mainstream USA culture to be explored in film analyses, I want to conclude this chapter with a brief look at the psychic consequences for women of their subject construction in modernism. The recognition of ideological uses of psychoanalytic theory is useful in helping us to understand often conflicting responses on the part of young adult women (usually not yet mothers) toward their mothers. We are familiar with the oft-expressed hostility of young women (including feminists) towards their mothers. In fact, most of the early feminist literature ignored the mother, when not blaming her for women's ills. This perhaps represented a deep-seated anger, a wish to run from the painful memories of the mother. The hatred of the mother here is similar to that found in psychoanalytic theory, and was perhaps produced by the fusional mothers that psychoanalysis addresses – mothers themselves produced, like psychoanalytic theory, by patriarchy.

Monique Plaza (1981) has usefully theorized how the fusional mother processes that Freud and others have analyzed, and that have produced the familiar bi-polar dominant mother-representations, result from psychoanalysts (from object-relations theorists to Lacan) blaming the mother for the child's madness. In Lacanian terminology, the mother keeps her child down with her in the Imaginary – not allowing the child to become a subject, not yielding the child up to the Symbolic and allowing the Paternal Signifier to happen for the child (Plaza 1981: 77). In Plaza's words, this is the mother, who "negative and normative . . . is inscribed in the ideological problematic based on patriarchal dominance." While psychoanalysts have decried this tendency as evidence of the Mother's self-indulgence, Plaza rather sees it not only as an understandable urge on the part of mothers to gain some satisfaction for themselves in return for the sacrifices they have undergone, but also as the natural result of the abnormal cloistering of the mother–child dyad in patriarchal society. Situated as subject to the Father's Law, why should mothers not attempt to get some benefit from their maternal function by possessing the child and getting internal satisfaction, unavailable to them otherwise, from living through it? In attacking this tendency, Plaza notes, society is able to regulate family interactions and to "save" the child for the Father. Hence, perhaps, one reason for the ambivalent coding accorded fusional mothers in many of the maternal melodramas to be discussed here. That is, the ambivalence results from, on the one hand, the male spectator's pleasure in images of idealized, beautiful mothers totally devoted to the *boy* child; and on the other, his fear that such devotion will turn out not to be so selfless as it is supposed to be – that it will suddenly turn dangerous, and suffocating.

Building on Plaza's work, I want to argue that the two kinds of mother so criticized by establishment patriarchal discourses – child-care experts, doctors, clergy, psychoanalysts and psychologists i.e., the over-indulgent mother and the phallic Mother – both in fact represent strategies whereby the mother-as-constructed-in-patriarchy attempts to get something for herself in a situation where that is not supposed to happen. Plaza's "fusional" mothers, the one identifying with the child to the extent of vicariously mothering herself, the second getting gratification through exercising control over the child, can be found in many film melodramas. The indulgent mother takes something for herself by satisfying needs for love, nurturance and merging through the child; while the phallic mother satisfies needs for power that her ideal function prohibits. She may also project on to the child her resentments, disappointments and failures for which the child is also to suffer. Like the master–slave psychic phenomenon analyzed by Hegel and then Franz Fanon, in which those who are (or were) slaves identify with the master position once freed, mothers take out their subjection to their husbands on their children. They identify with the Law of the Father when interacting with the child, who is now given their own "slave" position. As with real masters and slaves, mothers are linked symbiotically to the child in this process. Both of these fusional mothers thus resist, in the only ways they can, the impossible masochistic, ideal, selfless maternal function that patriarchy demands, and therefore bring down on themselves the weight of critical discourses.

The phallocentric logic of the classical Freudian scheme brilliantly occludes any possibility for a pre-Oedipal feminine identification with the mother; the mother is always viewed by the child as having the phallus, until the disillusionment that instigates the Oedipal crisis and ushers in the castrated, powerless mother of the Symbolic order that I have already mentioned. A different set of meanings for motherhood emerges, however, if we rethink the model – as have some American and French feminists discussed earlier – from the positions of both child and mother so as to allow for an early identification with the mother's femaleness. Yet this female identification is mainly explored in women's texts that rarely become commercially successful. Or, when popular texts represent female–female bonding, such bonding is usually subordinated to patriarchal demands by the text's end.

It is significant that popular culture represents all three types of mother in its main mother paradigms, namely the all-sacrificing "angel in the house," the over-indulgent mother, satisfying her own needs, and finally the evil, possessive and destructive all-devouring one. Part of my project is to explore how phallocentric Freudian images prevail in popular culture, but also the degree to which some resistance to these myths is evident. I will in addition be showing how a close reading of mother representations reveals the inadequacy of the classical Freudian model, particularly in texts by female authors. I want to theorize a different kind of pre-Oedipal mother along the lines mentioned above in the work of some feminist Freudian revisionists, while not claiming that this pre-Oedipal mother is *beyond* patriarchy. It is a matter of acknowledging that more than one process can be going on simultaneously. While the Lacanians are correct in noting that the primal "cruel" mother, the one who introduces the child to lack, representation and language, is unavoidable, it is also true that other kinds of unconscious mothers come into being later on, built on traces of the pre-Oedipal feminine identification.

It is this negative mother who predominates in much Hollywood imagery – so much so that the image of the hated mother in psychoanalysis immediately evokes for Plaza the mother in the Hollywood melodrama: it is Mrs Danforth in *Rebecca*, Mrs Vale in *Now Voyager*, Carrie's obsessive mother in the film of that name, and so on – the mother that I'll discuss in Chapter 6.

This evil mother is, as will shortly be demonstrated by materials in Chapter

5, balanced by her bi-polar opposite, the saintly, self-sacrificing stereotype. But theories are being developed to deal with mother modalities that do not fit into either of these dominating mythic figures. Alternate theories are necessary to account for some of the so-called "resisting" mother-figures I will discuss in Chapters 7 and 8. To this end, I will conclude with mention of research that might prove useful to those, as well to future work on images.

Some recent research on early mother–infant interaction, initiated by Daniel N. Stern (1976), opens up a paradigm more hopeful for the future than the Lacanian one that has dominated certain feminist positions. The contributions of Lacan, which came to fruition in the 1960s and 1970s, included his attention to the level of language, structure, the Symbolic in psychoanalytic processes. As is well known, he developed Freud's glimpses into these levels into a complex theory in which he distinguished three separate realms, those of the Imaginary, the Symbolic and the Real. Lacan is excellent at showing how the realm of the Imaginary is the sphere that preoccupies us much of the time, and in which we invest a lot of Imaginary affect: for fantasies (such as those of an erotic relationship with a friend's wife or husband, with one's boss or colleague, with one's analyst) carry a great deal of affect even if nothing is acted out, one's body *does* nothing. Lacan shows how such Imaginary couplings and desires have to do with inevitable lack inscribed in Oedipal processes. His attention to this dream-like sphere in which we live was important, as was also his clarity about the level of the Symbolic – that is Laws, institutional, familial, religious and other codes that hem us in, that define what is, and is not, possible, define our place in culture. Both spheres are differentiated from the third realm of what he calls the Real, that is violent irruptions or events like death or revolution or natural disasters.

But the difficulty with the Lacanian paradigm has always been its disinterest in the level of affect or emotions, through its insistence that everything we know and feel arrives through signifying systems. This resulted in neglect of the pre-verbal, pre-Oedipal terrain in any sense other than an hypothesized insatiable desire remaining from a posited mother–child symbiosis. This symbiosis precedes the attainment of a cultural/linguistic subjectivity with the acquisition of language. Lacan's important work on subjective positions, then, takes place in the realm of the Symbolic, while the specific processes of the Imaginary sphere (such as the mirror phase, imagos, the Ideal-I, etc.) are left rather vague.

The value of Daniel N. Stern's work, going back to his important studies of the gaze in mother–child interactions (1976), is his combining of psychoanalysis and perspectives from academic child-development psychology. In the study of infant–mother "gaze" behaviour, Stern noted the extensive, silent and apparently pleasurable *mutual* gazing that was an automatic part of mother–baby interaction. This mutual gazing interested me because it was so different from the predominant, voyeuristic and fetishistic gazing that feminist film theorists, including myself, had been discovering in the classical Hollywood film, and that we found also in sexual behaviour outside the cinema.

The early mother–baby gaze seemed to have intersubjective possibilities that the objectifying, often degrading, so-called "male" gaze totally erased in the popular film, and it suggested a number of questions: why do humans in our culture reject this gaze? Is this gaze continued in other cultures? What is actually going on, on the level of affect, during this gaze behavior? Is the mutual, as against the objectifying, gaze something that fosters an intersubjectivity many of us find threatening? How does this idea bear on the unconscious threat that the mother apparently represents? What are the theoretical implications for the Lacanian psychoanalytic paradigm of attributing to the baby sufficient agency for it to participate in a mutual gaze in the first place? How does the idea of a mutual gaze also affect theories about the mother's symbiotic relation to the baby, such that she believes the baby to be part of herself, making an *intersubjectivity* impossible?

In his most recent book, Daniel H. Stern (1985) has explored many of these questions, and argued strongly for the baby's capacities for intersubjective emotional relating from at least nine months on. He studies and theorizes about the mother–baby interaction from a whole variety of viewpoints too complex to summarize here, and is sophisticated about the role of representation (for both mother and baby) in such intersubjective affectivity. The emotional domain is then central to his theories, and usefully complements Lacanian work. Stern attempts to understand the infant's subjective affective states, to theorize about how such states are learned, how they develop, and what connections they have to the mother's "feeling states." His study stresses the mother in-relation-to the child that I mentioned in Chapter 1, and that I believe is important in understanding how the mother is thought in cultures. The mother, we see, is not a fixed, monolithic construct; "mother" does not signify in fact any particular attributes. What we rather have is what Stern calls a "partnership" that is unique to the individuals comprising it and that is determined by their interactions from the beginning. For the baby, according to Stern, "an evoked companion or internal representation or working model or fantasised union with the mother is not more or less than the history of specific kinds of relationships . . . or the prototypic memory of specific ways of being with the mother" (Stern 1988: 118). For the mother (and here the relationship is obviously not symmetrical because the mother brings her entire personal history to the encounter), she has

> not only a working model of her infant, but a working model of her own mother, . . . a working model of her husband (who the baby may frequently remind her of), and various other working models, all of which will come into play.
>
> (Stern 1985: 119)

Stern's model still places enormous burdens on the mother, since her

50

affective states are seen as so determining of those in her infant; but its virtue is the focus on agency in the child, and on the importance of non-verbal affect in the constitution of the subject. Non-verbal affective states are often impossible to express within the constraints of a language-system simply not flexible enough for them. Affect is often in excess of linguistic possibilities, but this does not mean that we cannot know a lot about it or that we cannot deal with it. (Note, for instance, the importance of non-verbal affect in any therapy relationship: intense and emotionally charged affective states will occur, and reveal themselves in body language, in alterations in voice, in facial expressions, etc. Like the mother, the therapist is attuned to these feeling states, and will respond empathically, again usually non-verbally.) Concepts of the mutual gaze, of people as always affectively "in-relation-to" others, are useful in correcting a linguistic and specular stress on structurally determined "positions" and on an objectifying, distancing gaze.

Building on theories of Stern and others, Jessica Benjamin (1988), as noted in Appendix A (pp. 53–54), approaches things from a specifically gender-oriented perspective. Benjamin notes the lack of attention to the need for *mutual* recognition, "the necessity of recognizing as well as being recognized by the other," in many theories of the self. "This means," Benjamin notes, "that the child has a need to see the mother, too, as an independent subject, not simply as the 'external world' or an adjunct of his ego" (1988: 23) Importantly, Benjamin notes that

> If we are going to discover woman's independent desire – a desire that does not have to be represented by the phallus – we should consider the intersubjective mode where the two subjects meet, where not only the man, but also the woman can be subject.
>
> (Benjamin 1988: 126)

We might say that Winnicott's, Stern's and Benjamin's arguments take place on an entirely different level than those of Lacan. I take Lacan's Imaginary, Symbolic and Real as givens, but these work in an unconscious register other than the dimensions of the here-and-now-interpersonal connecting (or what Benjamin (1988) calls "recognition"). The here-and-now affective bonding or attaching is one important mode of early infancy which prepares for possible later adult mutuality. This is a different level of interpersonal relationship than that described by Lacan (and noted above) as typical of our lives in the Imaginary. Instead of the level of unconscious erotic fantasy, or of an unconscious whose movements always remain obscure, in excess of our understanding, one is engaged in a mutual task with a student, in empathic sharing of inner states with an analyst, or mutual understanding with a loved one. This level of here-and-now sharing is not as important in theorizing the mother as the other levels that are the focus of this book because the latter predominate in the level of *fictional representation* that mainly preoccupies me here.

51

Having now looked at various kinds of psychoanalytic mothering theories, whose concerns in part motivated this project, let me move to Part II, on *Fictional Representation*. Case studies will deal first with the two dominant nineteenth-century and early-twentieth-century mother-paradigms, namely those of maternal sacrifice and of maternal aggression/possession discussed here. In subsequent chapters, I will look at resistances to these pervasive mother-figures, before exploring how such cultural mother legacies can illuminate what is going on today in relation to motherhood.

Appendix A: *Discussion of American Psychoanalytic Feminist Theorists and Freudian Revisionists*

Please note that details of texts mentioned here may be found in the bibliography. Discussion has been divided into three groups: feminists who condemn all psychoanalytic theories for feminist analysis, those who reject theories of pre-Oedipality, but are interested in Oedipal Freudian revisionists (like Kohut) and those those who revise further Freudian/Lacanian paradigms.

In the first group, **Beverly Birns** reads Freudian theory as claiming that "the infant's relation to the mother was 'unique, without parallel, laid down unilaterally for a whole lifetime'" (Birns 1988). She objects to neo-Freudian attachment theory because it assumes that "the nature of the child's tie to the mother in the earliest years will predict later behaviour and development" (1988: 3); and finally, she rejects Dorothy Dinnerstein's and Nancy Chodorow's theories because they attribute "to infantile experience a power that is not demonstrated to exist!" (Birns 1988: 4). The problem here is that Birns confuses theories about the unconscious with developmental studies of observable mother–infant relations. No Freudian would argue that the child's unconscious, imaginary mother had any direct relationship to the child's daily dealings with her *historical* mother; nor that a child observably "happy" was necessarily *psychically* satisfied; nor, finally, that the mother was the *only* significant factor in a child's life!

Nina Baym, meanwhile, condemns mothering theories as denigrating women and overstating the influence of the pre-Oedipal mother (Baym 1984). Baym resents the theory of pre-Oedipal bonding of mother and child because "it limits maternity to a global, non-verbal or pre-verbal, endlessly supportive, passively nurturing presence." For Baym, the concept of the pre-Oedipal is "an interested fantasy of the maternal. Its purpose – to contain and confine mothers and hence women within the field of the irrational." Baym here fails to differentiate between a given psychoanalytic structure and the way culture can *use* psychoanalytic discourse for its own ends. The fact that theories of the pre-Oedipal mother–child bond could be used to rationalize a social and economic need to keep women in the home in no way reflects on the psychic determinants of certain mother–child relations within historically constituted patriarchal institutions. In blaming feminists for their theories, and in seeing the pre-Oedipal as necessarily degrading to women, Baym is taking over standard (male) psychoanalytic discourse.

In the second group, some feminists, like **Judith Kegan Gardiner**, have rightly criticized Baym's over-hasty condemnation of mothering theory, but are still interested in some psychoanalytic theories. Gardiner is still convinced that the Freudian pre-Oedipal is derogatory, and is sufficiently in sympathy with Baym's general characterization of the pre-Oedipal in mother–child relations (and fearful of being complicit in consigning women to silence if she accepts that pre-Oedipal) that she seeks out alternate theories of child development, relying mainly on Kohut's neo-Freudian self-theory. This theory, she argues, although not gender-specific is "more congruent with feminist values" than orthodox psychoanalysis (Gardiner 1986: 10). It does not theorize any special mother–child bonding in the pre-Oedipal period, rather believing that any adults "can empathically mirror the child" in this stage. According to Gardiner, self-psychology "rejects a separation/individuation model of maturity. Instead, it sees all people embedded for life in a network of human relations, and it posits mature interdependence and altruism as adult developmental goals" (1986: 10).

I welcome Kegan Gardiner's attempt to move us beyond an apparent impasse, but I am unsure that self-psychology theory solves the problems. This is mainly because the theory does not account for the manifestations of psychic states or experiences displayed in the popular literary and film genres that I am exploring. I find no evidence that Kohut's theories are "truer" than Freud's; and Freudian-based theories at least relate to structures and psychic states in popular genres. Self-theory is attractive in offering a model for healthy female development, but in pre-empting exploration of pre-Oedipal symbiosis and the separation/individuation struggle, it may repeat Freud's error. Too many daughters have spoken graphically of individuation problems, too many mothers of over-identification with the child to rule out Freudian-based theories.

In a third group, **Jessica Benjamin** questions the classical Freudian scenario, asking why it is that psychoanalysis repeats "long-standing oppositions within Western tradition – between rationalism and romanticism, Apollo and Dionysus" (1988: 147). Benjamin questions in particular the way that the mother is never permitted the place of a reality principle or a principle of separation and individuation; she is always seen as the point of danger, the point of fusion, while the father is the place for understanding difference and reality, the place of rescue, the place of separation and rationality. Benjamin objects to the way the psychoanalytic conception of the Oedipus Complex returns us to ancient myths about the overthrow of matriarchy by patriarchy: why is it, she asks, that one civilization always has to overthrow the other? Why can't they coexist? By analogy with Bachofen's theories of such (overturnings), the Oedipus Complex also insists on the mother being "thrown over" in favor of the father: couldn't we see the child as wanting separation and individuation, as "wanting to be his own person, even as he resents having to be it," without, that is, insisting on "throwing over" the mother?

In other work, Benjamin extends Chodorow's and Irigaray's tentative gestures toward some kind of mother–child relationship as mutually loving but autonomous (separated) beings into a full blown theory. She offers some clinical support for a pre-Oedipal mother–child relationship different from the phallic one dominating classical psychoanalytic theory. Building on Winnicott and contemporary infancy research, Benjamin insists that there are "aspects of the self that each individual infant has from the beginning – agency and receptivity toward the world. While this self needs the other's response to develop, it exists a priori, before the response." Benjamin posits a "presymbolic sense of self as having resources, a sense of self that evolves through relationships that validate what we can do for ourselves" (1980: 16–17). The pre-disposition toward differentiation and reality occurs in the mother–child dyad, according to Benjamin.

There is obviously a problem with asserting (developmental psychologists and Daniel Stern in particular have made powerful cases for this) that a child is born with certain basic (presumably biological) tendencies for individuation and agency that are outside the reach of culture; but on the other hand, the theory does provide a tentative way of opening up the impasse that the Lacanian model has produced. Unlike Kegan Gardiner, Benjamin does not assert that the intersubjective mode is ever the only one: she sees the possibilities for intersubjectivity existing side by side with the modality of a "self" structured through a Symbolic order premised on the phallus as signifier. As she puts it, "the self that develops and accumulates through such experiences of recognition is a different modality that sometimes works with, but sometimes is at cross purposes to, the symbolized ego of phallic structuring" (1980: 17).

While I find Benjamin's theories attractive for rethinking female development on the level of historical subjects, they are not only useful for illuminating some of the maternal melodramas that are the focus of Chapter 7. This is perhaps in itself significant: that is, the absence of much attempt precisely to represent the mother as the place of centrality, something other than the point of danger, of fusion, indicates the *ideological* necessity within capitalism in its modernist phases for underscoring the *fusional* mother paradigm. There may be ideological reasons for the child never being shown as wanting to be his own person, outside of help from patriarchal authorities (as in *Now Voyager* or *Marnie*, for instance).

54

Maud Mannoni has perhaps phrased better than anyone the lure of the Imaginary that must be taken into account in mother–child relations, and that represents yet one more modality than those that Benjamin theorizes. Mannoni makes clear that one has to deal with the often conflicting imaginary representations that operate in the complex of mother–child relations:

> When parent and child [she says] are brought to face the problem of desire in the relationship of each of them with the other from the very outset of the psychoanalytic treatment, the parents will be lead to reappraise themselves in the context of their past history; and from the child, now addressed as the subject, the analyst will get words that are sometimes astonishingly articulate. This poses the question of language in a certain mode of relationship to the Other and to oneself. To abrogate words – which may be described as alienated in that they are the words of others and of general opinion – is a painful adventure for the subject. The analyst's job is to help him undertake it.
>
> (Mannoni 1970: 73)

It should be noted that there is tremendous variety in terms of mother–child experiences – a variety reflected in the (presumably symptomatic) theories mentioned above. Theorists' differing preoccupations undoubtedly manifest their own diverse memories of being mothered and, in some cases, mothering.

Appendix B: *Freud and the Mother*

Freud rarely discussed the mother herself and evidently few of his patients were mothers. However, in 1893, he did describe a mother with a psychogenic disability to breast feed (Freud 1951a). But the essay is strangely detached and more technical than usual; one senses little empathy or identification with the patient: for example, take the following passage:

> I found her lying in bed with flushed cheeks and furious at her inability to feed the baby – an inability which increased at every attempt but against which she struggled with all her strength. . . . Her epigastrium was distended and sensitive to pressure; manual palpation showed morbid peristalsis of the stomach.
>
> (Freud 1951a: 118)

Freud manages successfully to overcome the mother's feeding problems through suggestion under hypnosis, but seems most concerned about not being recognized for having "saved" the situation: "Far from being welcomed as a saviour in the hour of need, it was obvious that I was being received with a bad grace and that I could not count on the patient having much confidence in me" (1951a: 119). Later on, he expresses annoyance that "no reference was ever made to my remarkable achievement" (1951a: 120). Freud finally is told that it was the woman's shame about needing recourse to hypnotism (as against being able to use her will to achieve her aims) that had governed her behavior, and is somewhat mollified.

One wonders if it was simply egotism that governed these particularly sensitive reactions to curing the mother. Could there have been counter-transference in the sense of being positioned as the child to the parental couple (the husband is mentioned several times as also not liking hypnosis)? One cannot help but recall the way Dora's mother is dealt with in the famous Case History, where she is relegated to silence and marginality; Freud sees her as of no importance to the case and dismisses her as a neurotic mother who has failed in her "duties" to both husband and daughter. Could Freud's much discussed closeness with his own mother have stood in the way of his treatment of mothers? Could he have needed to always occupy the "stern Father" position toward any mother, defending himself thus against any wishes to regress to the little boy?

Be that as it may, in this case, Freud significantly turns his attention away from the mothering situation per se in the "lessons" he draws from the case, talking rather about the difference between intentions and expectations as these relate to neurasthenics and to hysterics like his patient. Freud's main contribution in relation to the mother is not to be found in case histories like this one but rather in his discovery of the mother in the unconscious.

Part II

MOTHERHOOD AND FICTIONAL REPRESENTATION

4

WOMEN'S WRITING,
MELODRAMA AND FILM

This chapter seeks to explore the terrain at the intersection of what I have called the "historical" and the "psychoanalytic" discourses, namely "representation." The level of representation (whether fiction or film) always bears traces of both the historical and the psychoanalytic, and it is this realization that makes it logical to link nineteenth-century novels and twentieth-century films. But there are other reasons why the novels to be discussed are relevant to film theory and film analysis.

The literal (historical) relationship between nineteenth-century fiction and twentieth-century film has long been known (Vardac 1977; Elsaesser 1972; Staiger 1980). The relationship was usually mediated by theatrical versions of novels – versions which script-writers relied on (for obvious reasons) rather than go back to the novels. But scholars have not explored the relationship between novels and films with specific reference to how precedents set in women's writing (in relation to female representations) may illuminate gender aspects of women-oriented films made by men.

My reading of nineteenth-century women's novels alerted me to certain articulations of women's interactions in films made within a similar North American patriarchal paradigm. As I suggested in the Introduction (pp. 3–12), twentieth-century culture and its related films stand on the shoulders of nineteenth-century culture and *its* related fiction. The links are particularly true in relation to women, whose mythic constructs and social roles remained uncannily the same from the mid-nineteenth to the mid-twentieth century. The links I am making must be seen on the broad level of the modernist framework, outlined in the Introduction, which provides the backdrop for most of my analyzes. That is, similarities function on the level of social discourses which themselves contain individual texts. It is a level beyond the local, aesthetic specificities of individual novels or films. However, my analyses of individual texts will show how it is often only through the specific level that one can get access to the broader discursive level.

The different kinds of text (novels, films) each illuminate the other by being juxtaposed: novels, like Harriet Beecher Stowe's *Uncle Tom's Cabin* (1861) (discussed in Chapter 7), were subsequently seen by scholars as part of an early "domestic" feminism (Tompkins 1981). These address the female reader explicitly and speak from the mother-position as made possible within patriarchy. I looked for, and discovered in, film a parallel type to this domestic feminist literature useful in interpreting gender in film developments.

Further, I found it useful to apply theories developed in relation to one aesthetic mode to the other. Feminist film theory has focused on the issue of the "gaze," which, when applied to nineteenth-century literature, opened up new perspectives. Theories of film melodrama, such as those developed by Thomas Elsaesser (1972), also illuminate nineteenth-century women's writing.

Similarly, literary critics' focus on narrative identification in turn opened up new readings when applied to film. The pre-Oedipal paradigm so evident in a novel like Ellen Wood's *East Lynne* (1861), for example, alerted me to the less obvious operation of similar processes in certain films. Further, the apparently "strong" women in films like Brennon's *Dancing Mothers* (1926), which seemed hard to explain in terms of 1920s mother-images, made sense if viewed in relation to traditions in nineteenth-century women's writings, like those of Margaret Fuller (1848) or Gilman Perkins (1915).

I moreover began to see correlations between certain types of mother-images and social/political/economic disruptions. While within a certain historical period (say 1860 to 1960) psychoanalytic processes seem similar, social/political/economic conditions change. When the social situation permits, women make demands for subjectivity. Cultural productions, like novels and films, in periods when such demands are made bear traces of women's challenge to dominant culture.

Once I had seen a certain representational continuity operating, despite the novels being written by women and the later films produced by males, it made sense to link texts through the concept of melodrama, as a genre. This is the genre within representation relevant for my purposes, although I deal with the sub-category traditionally labelled, pejoratively, in fiction the sentimental novel, and in film the "woman's weepie." I further subdivide this category into two types, namely the "maternal melodrama" and "the maternal woman's text," depending on a novel's or film's degree of "complicit" and "resisting" elements: I will briefly define my use of the term "melodrama" and look at the politics of its historical emergence. This should further clarify the juxtaposition of nineteenth-century popular women's writing and twentieth-century film. I will then deal at greater length with the maternal melodrama subdivisions, and with feminist debates about representation in both film and literary theory.

The fact that melodrama is the genre which, in its recent form, arises with modernization – that is at the intersection of absolutist (or pre-modern) social forms and later specifically capitalist forms – makes it pertinent to my study of maternal images in the modern period. Geoffrey Nowell-Smith has argued that the contemporary melodrama arises in the late eighteenth century as a form that specifically addresses the new bourgeoisie. As Nowell-Smith (1977) puts it, "Author, audience and subject matter are put on a place of equality," as against the hierarchical relations implied in the earlier epic and tragic forms. "Mystified though it may be," Nowell-Smith (1977) notes, "the address is from one bourgeois to another bourgeois," and the subject matter is the life of the bourgeoisie. The Greek melodrama, while anticipating some of the modes of hysteria and excess of late eighteenth-century melodrama, is situated in a very different relation to its audience. The characters are far from mimicking the lives and status of those watching, retaining their mythic and ritualistic dimensions.

In the first half of the twentieth century, the Hollywood film is the dominant popular form through which both the maternal sacrifice theme and the more resisting discourse – analogous to that which critics inspired by the ideas of domestic feminism (Welter 1966; Cott 1977) found in the nineteenth-century novel – continues to find expression. The invention of film at the turn of the century is part of a crucial change taking place already in the late nineteenth century with the advent of modern consumer culture and advertising. As Allon White (1983) noted, this change "involved the displacement of pleasure into the realm of the signifier (form, style, association) and its disassociation from the 'real' world of work and dreary production." White notes that this "disassociation was a necessary correlative to the unfettering of commodity-centred, consumer capitalism," and that "the creaming off of the signifier from the signified marked a new phase in the production of Western subjectivity in its long march from Feudalism to a bureaucratic society of controlled consumption" (White 1983).

What happens is that a new self-consciousness is built into the subject's constitution. If the mirror phase had always been a necessary part of the subject's entry into the Symbolic, it now becomes an inherent part of cultural experience. Consumer culture hooks on to the subject's inevitable desiring mode, reinforcing and exploiting it by constant stimulation. Beginning with the department store and the stage melodrama, the culture of the spectacle is fully inscribed in society with the development of the cinema as an apparatus. Film becomes the form that replaces the popular novel in the way it addresses desires invoked by the new consumer culture: its mode as spectacle dovetails with modes of consumer culture in a vicious circle. In other words, film emerges at a certain stage of consumer culture; its modes increase consumerism and encourage upward class-striving through accumulation of consumer goods. Film, that is, produces new desires for goods signifying status. And while the popular novel continues, it is also affected by the culture of the spectacle, using description in a self-consciously "cinematic" style. The other self (in Lacanian terms) offered by the mirror becomes part of society's cultural mechanisms, transforming the subject's ways of perceiving and desiring.

Consumer culture and the bourgeois family are intricately linked to melodrama's re-emergence in the eighteenth century; its increasing importance in the late nineteenth and early twentieth centuries is evident in Hollywood's melodramatic film replacing stage melodrama. If one accepts Peter Brooks's general definition of the melodramatic (see pp. 63–4), then all the main Hollywood genres are melodrama in attempting an ethical recentering, a "search for a new plenitude in reaction to the decentering of modern consciousness" (Brooks 1976: x). This would be particularly true of the two genres traditionally viewed as the greatest in American cinema, namely, the Western and Gangster forms. These two undisputedly male genres are concerned with ethical values in the public sphere, a realm that patriarchy defines as largely excluding women. The Western and the Gangster film show a social order that needs to be purged and that contains blatant signs of good and evil. The film's work is to restore the community to health through the triumph of good over evil. Since traditionally women cannot be the arbiters of good and evil in the public sphere, they are assigned to the periphery of the narrative in these films, which are essentially constructed for the male spectator (E.A.Kaplan 1983d).

The juxtaposition of nineteenth-century women's writing (the so-called "sentimental" novel), and twentieth-century film melodramas makes sense in this context, and illuminates both aesthetic modes. Nineteenth-century popular women's writing and the classical Hollywood Woman's Film have at least two characteristics in common that arise from their shared reason for being, namely (as noted) culture's need at the time of industrialism/modernization for a new kind of drama. The fictional forms share first, a similar status as popular texts addressing a (newly developed) mass audience, and second, a common use of the melodramatic imagination. (These two aspects are themselves linked in that the melodrama is precisely that which contains the ingredients for mass appeal.)

Melodrama has been the object of much discussion in recent film theory, largely because of the new attention given to film and television melodrama forms explicitly seen as addressing female spectators, and as dealing with issues pertinent to women (Modleski 1983; Brunsdon 1983). Earlier (largely male) historians and literary theorists had been concerned to chart the history of melodrama as a critical category, as well as its history (and definition) as a specific theatre and film genre. As a critical category, melodrama was originally used in theatre criticism to describe a particular dramatic genre differing in essential ways from both tragedy and comedy. Scorned as an aesthetically inferior genre, theatrical melodrama gained significant critical attention only as late as the 1960s (Booth 1965; Grimstead 1986; Heilman 1968; Smith 1973).[1]

Scholars are concerned mainly to explain the genre's derivation from the Greek "melos" (music plus drama), to trace its modern evolution (dating most agree from Rousseau's *Pygmalion* 1774) and to describe what would become its archetypal form in Pixerecourt's plays. Scholars taking this approach examine melodrama on the pre-and post-Revolutionary French stage, and trace its degeneration into the "tawdry splendours of the Victorian melodrama" (Smith 1973: 5). Maurice Disher (1954) details the various kinds of British nineteenth-century melodramas, while David Grimstead (1986) studies the social conditions of American melodrama in roughly the same period. Authors often describe, in a literal way, the main characteristics of the stage melodrama, citing the stock characters and the (equally stock) plot structures. Frequently condescending toward the material being studied (although the degree varies), scholars reveal a discomfort in giving so much attention to what they perceive as "trash" (geared to an often uneducated mass of people) that should not, perhaps, be the object of scholarly study.

Eric Bentley's (1967) important essay, together with Robert Heilman's (1968) sensitive study of the differences between tragedy and melodrama, developed by Smith (1973), prepared the ground for a new consideration of melodrama that took place on an altogether different level. Writing at about the same time in the early 1970s, both Peter Brooks (1976) and Thomas Elsaesser (1972) expand the concept of melodrama beyond the confines of a specific theatrical genre to focus on a generalized type of aesthetic experience that produces specific emotional effects in the spectator. I use the term "melodrama" here in this generalized sense.

Brooks's main thesis is that melodrama is a response to the "loss of tragic vision" exacerbated by the Industrial Revolution and the creation of a society deprived of an organic and hierarchical order. The ensuing solidification of the bourgeois class, with its specific form of nuclear family, was accompanied by an ethical vacuum in the public sphere. Melodrama, then, is a type of sense-making characterized by "indulgence of strong emotionalism; moral polarization and schematization; extreme states of being, situations, actions; overt villainy, persecution of the good and final reward of virtue; inflated and extravagant expression; dark plottings, suspense, breathtaking peripety" (Brooks 1976: 4). According to Brooks, these qualities can be found in Balzac and Henry James.

As Brooks further notes, these ethical imperatives are often played out in the psychic as well as in the social sphere, particularly in genres like the novel that often adopt the melodramatic mode. For example, Brooks shows how the melodrama in its Gothic form foregrounds what the social order forbids and represses about familial relations. Hence its obsession with the themes of incest, adultery, sadism and masochism. In melodrama, Brooks says, "we are led back to the sources of the 'uncanny' in the processes of

63

desire and repression analyzed by Freud" (1976: 19). The Gothic castle, for instance,

> realizes an architectural approximation of the Freudian model of the mind, particularly the trap laid for the conscious by the unconscious and the repressed. The Gothic novel seeks an epistemology of the depths; it is fascinated by what lies hidden in the dungeon and the sepulcher. It sounds the depths bringing to violent light and enactment the force hidden and entrapped there.
>
> (Brooks 1976: 19)

For Brooks, characters in melodrama "assume primary psychic roles, Father, Mother, Child, and express basic psychic conditions" (1976: 4). At the end of his book, he summarizes the links between melodrama and psychoanalysis, showing that psychoanalysis is close to melodrama first in its "conception of the nature of conflict, which is stark and unremitting, possibly disabling, menacing to the ego, which must find ways to reduce or discharge it" (1976: 201); second, in the way in which characters in melodrama symbolize the superego, ego and id, figuring forth the unconscious always ready to betray figures standing for other parts of the mind. Finally, Brooks shows that both melodrama and psychoanalysis involve processes of articulating what has been repressed. "Cure and resolution in both cases," Brooks notes, "come as the result of articulation which is clarification" (1976: 201–2).

But Freud's explicit discussion of creativity and the "family romance" fantasies are useful in a general way for analysis (on the psychic level) of different types of melodrama texts to be discussed shortly: the analysis by both Freud (1909/1951) originally, and then by the female author, Marthe Robert (1980) following him, are phallocentric: both authors write as though the child-subject involved were inevitably male, and also as if all authors were male. I will, by contrast, focus on sexual difference, discuss the needs the mother-sacrifice pattern satisfies for both genders (but with emphasis on women), look at texts by female authors, and suggest differences in narratives that deal with mother–daughter as against mother–son relations. But the very fact of Freud's and Robert's automatic male-centredness reveals the dominance for both genders of patriarchal constructs – a dominance that, significantly, functions in (and helps define) one of my sub-categories, namely the "maternal melodrama."

A brief review of their theories is important not only for this reason, but also so as to clarify feminist revisions of the theories. Freud's well-known theories about story-telling are to be found in two rather slight essays, "Creative Writing and Day-Dreaming" and "The Family Romance" (Freud 1909/51). For Freud, story-telling is the means by which children deal with their anxiety about sex differences, sibling rivalry and beings upon whom they are dependent, especially the mother. While Freud is mainly concerned in the first essay to establish the relationship between children's play fantasies on the one hand, day- and night-dreams of adults on the other, in "The Family Romance" he distinguishes two different predominant fantasies, which Marthe Robert calls those of the Bastard and of the Foundling (Robert 1980: 28). Both have to do with the child's Oedipal relationship to the mother, and with concerns about origins; and both reflect the child's needs at the moment of disillusionment with the originally narcissistically idealized parents. Robert points out that both stories rely on the dual image of the good/bad mother; but in the earlier Foundling story (which Robert considers pre-Oedipal) the child does not differentiate his parents, rejecting them both as too lowly and flawed to be his real parents; he imagines that he is born of Royal parents who will one day come to claim him.

The Bastard fantasy, on the other hand, arises in the Oedipal period and is designed to deal with erotic feelings toward the mother. In this story, the child is illegitimate, having been born of the "real" lowly mother, but sired by a royal father, about whom he now fantasizes. The story breaks asunder the parental unit, and permits displacement of the child's erotic desire into fantasies of the mother having illicit sex with other men; it also enables the child to feel that he and his mother constitute the real family unit, since the father is excluded. In both cases, the fantasy frees the child from fear of castration by the father who would normally possess the mother, because in the fantasy she is not possessed.

Robert points out the way in which this fantasy necessarily demeans the mother. "His mother's lowly status," Robert notes, "is the price he (*sic*) [the child] has to pay for her intimacy – his love demeans her, while the loathed father inhabits the ideal regions befitting his rank" (1980: 28). But in addition, Robert says, the mother is also "branded with immorality, since the fantasy of his illegitimacy necessarily presupposes her adultery. . . . She is reduced to the status of servant, fallen woman or even prostitute" (1980: 28).

As we will see, the "complicit" maternal sacrifice theme appears very much to embody these Freudian "family romance" fantasies, and demonstrates the same male perspective. For instance, we find precisely this scenario in the main plot of *East Lynne*, discussed in Chapter 5. The close psychic links between heterosexual passion and the mother–boy-child bond (the displacements of the one type of bonding on to the other) will be clear in this and other popular narratives to be analyzed later on.

Freud's comments are very general, and he does not differentiate among kinds of literature: not only does Freud ignore the whole high/low culture division, but also he fails to differentiate various literary genres. This has the beneficial result of avoiding pejorative labelling, and possibly outright rejection, of much popular material. While it is obvious from reading their work that Freud and the first generation of psychoanalysts in their personal lives identified with the high-culture stance and scorned popular culture, their daily interactions with patients involved details of "narratives" very like those offered in melodrama. (For example, what could be more typically melodramatic than Dora's case history?)

A similar melodramatic imagination is very much in evidence in nineteenth-century women's writing, which should not, perhaps, surprise us: both Freud and women writers shared the same late-nineteenth-century semiotic field, which produced similar gender constructs. Most of my case studies are taken from films made between 1920 and 1970, but central to this project, as already noted, is juxtaposing nineteenth-century fictional forms and twentieth-century films that rely not only on "the melodramatic imagination" (as defined on pp. 63–4) but also on feminist revisions and emendations to the male theories.

Feminist critics have exposed precisely what is lacking in the theories about melodrama as male critics have developed them. Insufficient attention has been paid, first, to questions of the gendered spectator that the form addresses, and second, to the political dimensions of the social function that melodrama serves. If melodrama is indeed like psychoanalysis a "sense-making system which man has elaborated to recuperate meanings in the world," we need to assess the *kinds* of meanings it recuperates. Peter Schofer (1982) has analyzed Marcel Pagnol's films to show how their melodramatic function ultimately perpetuates a lie. The audience, Schofer says, "leaves the theatre with the satisfaction that the family and the economics of exchange are secure." But he notes that the film closes off discussion of the lie that is necessary to "perpetuate the family's honor and to guarantee the rebirth of the full family of Mother, father and children." This lie, Schofer concludes, is necessary to "guarantee survival of the family, and by extension, the survival of a stable society."

The "lie", namely that woman must of necessity be subordinated to the Law of the Father, is also concealed in the dominant Hollywood genres. The insistent assertion of the necessary subordination of woman within a film system centred on organization by *genre* (Staiger 1980) produced a subordinated set of films functioning as a counter-balance to the dominant male genres, which were often labelled "the woman's weepie." Interest in these films intensified in the second wave of film research in connection with attention to the subversive potential in Sirk's 1950s melodramas. These were seen to open space prohibited by the so-called Classical Realist Film text, restricted to oppressive patriarchal norms (Willemen 1972).

The largely male critics engaged in this work focused more on broadly defined bourgeois ideology about the family in general than on the films' specifically *female* address (MacCabe 1974). This is more of a problem than the fact that, as Tania Modleski has noted, the theory privileged melodramas that seemed critical of the status quo over those that were clearly not (Modleski 1988a: 41). If traces of the Frankfurt School, elitist, modernist, cultural position remain here, there is a parallel danger: uncritical acceptance of any materials that women enjoy because to do otherwise entails abhorring the "feminine." The debate highlights problems endemic to this sort of study: how to describe *differences* among kinds of text without getting caught up in the linguistic polarities inherent in western culture and its language-systems – polarities that always denigrate emotion/the irrational/kinesthetic, and the domestic in contrast to intellect/reason/culture, and the public sphere. I do not want to eliminate the ideological importance of Brechtian "distanciation" theories, but suggest that such theories can be applied without denigrating "femininity," or, indeed, locking any "feminine" into the binary opposite (i.e. emotion/the irrational) of "intellect" and "the rational."

In remedying the failure to deal with female address, feminist critics brought renewed interest in melodrama, and asked new questions of the form. In a first wave of work, critics like Laura Mulvey (1977–8) and Mary Ann Doane (1982; 1984) (to take two important examples), began to explore the important difference between films addressed to a male and to a female spectator. Mulvey defines the family melodrama as explicitly a form with female address, one that deliberately functions as a counter-balance to the dominant male genres. For her, "a dramatic rendering of women's frustrations, publicly acting out an adjustment of balance in the male ego is socially and ideologically beneficial" (1977–8: 54). But she goes on to assume that the melodrama involves "reaffirmation of the Oedipus complex" (1977–8: 54). That is, although in the family melodrama "The phallocentric, castration-based, more misogynist fantasies of patriarchal culture" are "sacrificed in the interest of civilization," Mulvey reads "civilization" in terms of how man comes to be man, that is as necessarily involving the male rejection of the mother, and the mother's position as a patriarchal function (1977–8: 56).

Nevertheless, Mulvey finds something important for women in these films about female victims: for her,

> in the absence of any coherent culture of oppression, the simple fact of recognition has aesthetic importance: there is a dizzy satisfaction in witnessing the way that sexual difference under patriarchy is fraught, explosive, and erupts dramatically into violence within its own stomping ground, the family. (Mulvey 1977–8: 54)

Building on this work, Mary Ann Doane has shown that most women's films construct a heroine who is a victim, entailing a masochistic identification for the female viewer. Doane (1984) goes to Irigaray to show how woman cannot assume the fetishistic position because

> the lack of distance between seeing and understanding, the mode of judging "in a flash" [a reference to Freud's theory of the girl's sudden reaction to seeing the penis for the first time] is conducive to what might be termed an "overidentification" with the image. (Doane 1984: 69)

Doane views this over-identification with the image as necessarily entailing a passive/masochistic position because of the position woman is assigned in cinematic narrative. On the other hand, woman may also identify with the active hero, in which case, as Mulvey had already argued, woman took up a masculine spectator position.

Doane (1987) developed aspects of this research in her study of the medical discourse in a certain type of woman's film. In addressing a specifically *female* spectator, the woman's melodrama must avoid the usual (male) mechanisms of voyeurism and fetishism because the female look is not permitted desire in the same way as the male look. Woman must be despecularized, and scopophilic energy directed away from the female body. According to Doane, the medical gaze is inserted in place of the erotic one to overcome the fear, anxiety and horror of the object-less, free-floating gaze. The result of this de-eroticization of the female gaze is that the female spectator is effectively disembodied. While the cinema generally denies woman that imaginary identification with discursive mastery available to the male spectator, Doane argues that the woman's film makes impossible even woman's narcissistic identification with woman as spectacle, producing, in Doane's words, "masochistic fantasy *instead* of sexuality" (Doane 1987: 67–8).

One of the problems with Doane's essay is her generalization of the mechanisms she explores to the entire woman's film genre. I will attempt to differentiate those films addressing women that involve such de-specularization of the female spectator from others which function to allow the female spectator certain kinds of pleasure in the struggle to resist patriarchal definitions and positionings.[2]

In a second wave of work on the family melodrama, critics like Linda Williams (1984) and Tania Modleski (1983; 1988a) have used spectatorship theory to argue that women are not merely offered identification with victims in these films. Often, they argue, victims are situated in relation to other female figures with whom the female spectator also identifies: out of the resulting multiple and shifting series of identifications, the spectator learns about victimization, about woman's deprivations, and glimpses other female ways of being. According to Modleski (1988a) woman's bisexual nature, "rooted in preoedipality, and her consequent alleged tendency to overidentify with other women and with texts, is less a problem for *women*, as Doane would have it, than it is for patriarchy" (1988a: 8). In addition, following Susan Lurie (1981), Modleski suggests that patriarchy has constructed a theory of female castration so as to deny a difference that would mean there could be non-castrated beings: discussing *Rear Window*, Modleski notes that Jeff's fear of Liz's perfection

is related to man's fear of women's difference and his suspicion that they may not, after all, be mutilated (imperfect) men, may not be what, as

Susan Lurie puts it, *men* would be if they lacked penises – "bereft of sexuality, helpless, incapable."

(Modleski 1988a: 33)

Finally, Teresa de Lauretis (1987) has asked that feminist theory refrain any more from disrupting man-centered vision by representing its blind spots, but move on to creating another – feminine or feminist – vision.

These theories fall, broadly speaking, into two groups: the first (represented above by Mulvey and Doane) assumes that the "feminine" is always reached via the masculine, making any specifically (and separately) *female* desire impossible. The second (represented above by Modleski and Williams) asserts that there is such a thing as an independent "feminine." In the first set of theories, women are seen to be castrated, and in that sense lacking their own desire; in the second set, women are viewed as being complete as they are, and capable of their own desire. These theorists argue that female castration is a patriarchal construct serving to prevent men from having to deal with *difference*, and enabling them to maintain a position of superiority.

On the level of representation, where these arguments are being played out, one finds texts structured according to both theories: the two kinds of maternal melodrama that I have distinguished, namely the complicit and resistant, each embody one of the polarized positions: the dominant complicit maternal melodrama represents the mother as a paternal function, and addresses a *male* spectator (it usually features an intense mother–son relationship – Griffith's *The Mothering Heart* (1913) and Wood's *East Lynne* (1931) provide the archetype); the second category, that I call the "Maternal Woman's Film" (the "resisting" type), speaks *from* the mother position and about its pleasures and oppressions (Stahl's *Imitation of Life* provides one archetype). The first paradigm, then, is a male fantasy about the boy-child's loss of the idealized mother, while in the second, although the basic Oedipal melodrama structure remains, the enunciative position is altered so that the story is fully positioned within the mother's perspective and subjectivity. Narratives in the first, complicit, type may appear to be spoken from the woman's position, but this is soon revealed to be that of an uncritical patriarchal function. In the second type of text, the position is still articulated within patriarchy (this type does not found a new order of language or of the "feminine"), but it assumes a feminine desire, even if its expression is constantly repressed or thwarted.

It is the specific type of *fantasy* that is addressed that makes the difference: in some historical moments, space is opened up for female fantasies within patriarchy. But most of the time dominant commercial forms, even those about the domestic sphere, proliferate *male* fantasies, which stress female castration. It may be, as Mulvey (1977–8) has argued, that these fantasies arise from male guilt at repression of the feminine, or to balance the "phallocentric, castration-based, more misogynist fantasies of patriarchal culture ... in contradiction with the ideology of the family" (1977–8: 56), but such fantasies nevertheless do not benefit women.

Some texts, then, themselves postulate female castration, while others postulate a definite female "wholeness." It is the politics of the two positions that I will be concerned with. Feminist critics, like Doane, interested in texts postulating (and acting "as if" women were castrated) do not necessarily themselves *agree* that women *are* castrated; their work aims to elucidate how *patriarchy* (through its dominant institutions, like Hollywood) represents women as castrated. Other critics have an investment in proving female "wholeness," and may set up a false polarity between feminist theoretical positions (Case 1989).

I argue that the differing feminist theories emerged from the differing types of text that scholars worked on. Complicit texts invite theories positing female castration, and theories of woman's over-identification with textuality. Those texts with resisting elements open up space for theories of the female subject complete in herself, with her own desire; or at least with contradictory desires (for the Law/Father and for the non-castrated mother).

My own position resists universalizing either female castration *or* female "wholeness." I see each of these positions as socially constructed within specific historical, national, intellectual/cultural contexts. At times, a culture may construct woman as castrated (and this will reveal itself in representations); at other times, it may construct woman as "one," and as generating her own desire. Often, which construct operates (or dominates) depends on gender address, as I am ultimately arguing here.

To summarize: centered on the female protagonist and on ostensibly female concerns (love, seduction, motherhood, marriage, children, abandonment, jealousy, role-conflicts, etc.) maternal melodramas of both kinds address the female spectator in ways other genres rarely do. But some melodramas (especially the complicit ones) realize male fantasies surrounding mother/son development, and in this also address the male spectator. They may be designed to allay unconscious male fears. After all, most of these films are produced within the patriarchal institution of Classical Hollywood. The fantasy of plenitude, of a return to illusory oneness with the Mother, governs the socially constructed desire of both male and female protagonists. The maternal melodrama comes closest to explicit representation of the etiology in showing the longing of the mother for the (lost) child object. The mythic pattern renders the romantic quality of this longing "safe," by displacing the desire from the (usually male) child and figuring it in the body of the *mother*. The cultural codes for mother love already contain an element of dedicated devotion, whereas the adult male is supposed to have freed himself from the "weakness," even "unnaturalness," that excessive mother love signifies. Through these complicit texts, culture perpetuates the "romance" of the biological, mother–child relation. Meanwhile, other films addressed specifically to women construct females as subjects capable of pursuing their own desire (at least, for part of the narrative), or mark out an enunciative position *critical* of dominant gender constructs, which exposes their oppressive nature.

Feminist critics of nineteenth-century women's writing have not situated the material in the context of the melodramatic imagination, but feminist debates have some parallels to those in film studies. Ann Douglas (1977) comes closest to dealing with the melodramatic terrain, but her thesis stands oddly opposed to mine; for while she reads nineteenth-century women's writing somewhat similarly, she takes a very different stance toward it. Far from valorizing women's attempts at finding their own spaces or empathizing with the oppression that the sentimental novel embodies, Douglas rather derides what she sees as a negative "feminization" of North American culture in this period. Douglas sees that "Nineteenth century American women were oppressed, and damaged," but goes on to blame them for the negative influence that they exerted just because they were "damaged" (1977: 11). Women, she argues, became oppressive in their turn, doing "the dirty work of society in several senses." She is particularly disturbed by a feminization viewed as morally weak, irrational, lacking in toughness that prepared for a mass culture that Douglas deplores: "Sentimentalism," she notes, "with its tendency to obfuscate the visible dynamics of development, heralded the cultural sprawl that has increasingly characterized post-Victorian life" (1977: 13).

In her treatment of women's writing, Douglas thus focuses on the stories as "courses in the shopping mentality, exercises in euphemism essential to the system of flattery which served as the rationale for the American woman's economic position" (1977: 62). At occasional, more empathic moments, Douglas does note the way some novels focus on "a confrontation between feminine sanctions and man-made dictates," allowing women some vicarious satisfaction in winning at least some battles; and the way that others turn passivity into heroism by having a protagonist too pure or naive to clear herself of a sin she has been accused of, bringing tears, presumably, to female readers.

But for Douglas, the literature mainly offers evidence of "the enormous need of its authors and readers for uncritical confirmation of themselves and instantaneous satisfaction of their appetites" (1977: 63). Douglas sees the cult of motherhood only negatively, as "an essential precondition to the flattery American women were trained to demand in place of justice and equality . . . a sanction for subjectivity and self-love" (1977: 75). Both ministers and women, for Douglas, substituted knowledge for sensibility, literature for life.

As Jane Tompkins (1981) has noted, Douglas here identifies with a classically patriarchal stance toward the feminine, much like the male film critics discussed above. The same binary opposition is in play. That is, Douglas first links high culture with order, rationality and discipline, and

71

then identifies all these with the masculine; meanwhile, popular culture, emotional excess and indulgence are identified with the feminine. In this way, she supports the established patriarchal view that popular culture is a derided terrain partly because it is the province of women and the domestic.[3] While Douglas implicitly positions women's culture in the melodramatic terrain, her conventional (and male-identified) scorn for this level of things leads in a direction away from feminist film critics. The latter, as we have seen, approach the melodramatic in the hopes of understanding the importance of the psychic and social processes at work. Douglas's work suffers from an overdose of rationalism and the dearth of any psychoanalytic insights that might permit a more empathic view of nineteenth-century women.

An updated version of Douglas's theory may be found in Alfred Habegger's (1982) discussion of differences between female and male nineteenth-century novels. He implicitly locates women's fiction in an again derided melodramatic terrain in the course of attempting to understand the origins of the rise of the realist male American novel. He perhaps correctly sees the male realist novel as produced through reaction against the fantasy-laden and heavily escapist qualities of women's novels. But the problem, as with Douglas, lies in the hierarchy that is implicit in the differences outlined between the fictional modes. The discussion usefully emphasizes that one tradition in the woman's novel (which finds its analogue in one type of woman's film – the maternal melodrama) is based on emotionalism, and encourages identification of the reader with a single heroine (the description would fit my example here, namely *East Lynne*): woman's fiction, Habegger notes,

> was characterized by an idealized heroine, a strong appeal to the reader's fantasies or day-dreams, a great deal of "domestic" social and psychological detail, and a plot based on love interest that lead up to a decisive speech – "I love you."
>
> (Habegger 1982: 106)

But the problem is the derogatory stance implied in Habegger's language. He refers to "the ideal gender types, daydreams and lies poisoning the novel and society," claiming that male novels attempted to "tell the truth about, to test and to get at." Habegger finds in the male realist novel what he misses in woman's writing, namely "balance between passionate identification with protagonists and a more detached judgement, a degree of rationality" together with "detailed verisimilitude, close social notation, analysis of motives, and unhappy endings."

While Habegger's distinction between fictional types is close to that which I am myself making here, his argument takes on quite another cast because of the pejorative, and essentialized, polarizing of the male and female novel. The types themselves echo those that Robert extracts from Freud, but the blanket gender attribution is Habegger's own. Distinctions among fictional modes in both literature and film along the melodrama/realism dimension are important to my argument, but it is crucial first, to avoid pejorative labelling of the melodrama mode; second, to avoid labelling the melodrama mode typically "feminine;" and third, to understand that nineteenth-century female writers (like the ones I explore in Chapter 7) also write novels that "tell the truth about, test, and get at idealized gender types, daydreams."

Drawing particularly on work by Richard Dyer (1981) and Fredric Jameson (1979), Tania Modleski (1986) and Janice Radway (1984) offer a corrective to both Douglas's and Habegger's positions. Unlike both latter critics, Modleski speculates about women's needs and fantasies that the popular narratives address. Using a psychological (and sometimes psychoanalytic) perspective, Modleski divides the recent popular woman's novel into the "hysterical" Harlequin Romance and "paranoid" Gothics, depending on the sorts of desires that the narrative patterns address. While Modleski sees these fictions as both reflecting and inducing the psychological states they embody, she is careful not to "blame the victim," asserting that "Even though the novels can be said to intensify female tensions and conflicts, on balance the contradictions in women's lives are more responsible for the existence of Harlequins than Harlequins are responsible for the contradictions" (Modleski 1983: 57).

Modleski, however, does not use recent feminist theories of melodrama in her analysis, turning rather to male clinicians for theoretical support; and when she occasionally makes links back to eighteenth- and nineteenth-century women writers, she draws on English rather than American writers.

Janice Radway's (1984) study also deals with the contemporary rather than the nineteenth-century woman's romance, but from a very different, empirical perspective. The study is based on extensive interviews Radway did with fans of the Harlequin Romances. Obviously, the interview is a mode of research no longer possible for any period other than our own, and, for that very reason, a valuable contribution, particularly for later critics. But the interview method necessarily elicits women readers' cognitive processes, as against the unconscious ones that Modleski had theorized. Radway's questions explore the constraints on women's daily lives that produce needs for certain kinds of fantasy. For example, the representation of men who dominate women, says Radway, in no way suggests that women approve of domination but rather gives satisfaction through "examining an all too common state of affairs in order to display possible strategies for coping with it" (Radway 1984: 75). Women both want images of people better and happier than they are in lived reality – they want a fantasy world where rewards come to the virtuous and where there is no ambiguity – but they also want accuracy on the physical level of the fictive world – accuracy about places, facts and history, which Radway found was stored as information to be used later on and even checked out through visiting novelistic locations.

While we learn interesting things from hearing about women's secondary processes in reading, we also need theories about the primary processes involved if we are fully to understand the nature of the desires that keep women reading Harlequins. Reading Radway in the context of Freud, Brooks and the others, one sees how closely allied her findings are to theirs, despite her not referring explicitly to the level of the unconscious. For example, the tension she notes between the realistic surface and the underlying fantasy realm is similar to that already discussed by Robert, Elsaesser and Brooks as characteristic of the melodramatic imagination.

Radway briefly refers to the mother by noting, rather than pursuing, the idea that the masculinized representation of heroines in Harlequins has to do with the reader's ambivalent needs at once to reject the mother – and therefore that kind of dependent feminine – and also to regain her. However, none of these writers discusses the maternal in woman's writing in any depth, perhaps because the romance, the sentimental and the Gothic novels do not usually have motherhood as an explicit theme: narratives focus on the woman's search for the ideal male lover and husband-to-be. The reasons for this surface omission are interesting, but I will be arguing that in fact the psychic pattern of such fiction about romantic love is based on repressed desires from the early mother–child relationship.

Female critics of women's fiction referred to are important for their explicit interest in popular culture and in women writers and readers. But none deal with differences among types of woman's novels in terms of the melodrama/realism/modernism/postmodernism distinctions that inter- est me, some of which Habegger addressed, however unsatisfactorily. The distinctions are crucial for understanding the way that popular culture functions – its similarities with, and differences from, high culture, and its psychological importance. Distinguishing the various aesthetic modes enables us to understand the importance of popular culture historically, and will provide the bases for analyses in subsequent chapters. In addition, discussion of these modes will make more clear exactly how the conflating of all three hitherto distinct modes (melodrama, realism, modernism) is part of what constitutes the postmodern that characterizes our own era.

Briefly, to recapitulate: texts whose melodramatic elements are uppermost (the "complicit") permit full expression to the patriarchal unconscious in which we are immersed and which we need to know about, but also allow issues around female desire to be addressed. The type of text whose realistic elements predominate (i.e. "resisting") are important in permitting address to the oppressive social institutions that confine women and in allowing expression of alternative social structures, albeit often in a merely utopian fashion. The last type of deconstructive text ("postmodern"), made possible through theories arising in the recent women's movement, offers the most possibility for constructing new textual subjects, which, in turn, may provide the historical female reader/spectator with the possibility for experiencing herself *otherwise*.

Given my interests here, the body of the book focuses on commercial texts that deal with the mother, although in the final chapter I give attention to some recent alternative modes. Chapter 5 on *East Lynne* looks at one powerful example of the complicit maternal melodrama (the mother-sacrifice model) as the paradigm is worked out in literature, drama and film. Subsequent chapters take up the second complicit phallic/evil mother paradigm, and then I analyze a series of texts with resisting (conscious/rational) elements. The final chapter explores the complex, contradictory and ambiguous mother-representations in a variety of popular and of less commercial texts, and attempts to situate these in relation to rapidly changing political, economic and social discourses.

THE MATERNAL MELODRAMA: THE SACRIFICE PARADIGM

Ellen Wood's *East Lynne* and its play and film versions

In this chapter, I focus on the maternal sacrifice paradigm whose representational heyday was the nineteenth century, for reasons suggested in Chapter 2. Taking a representative woman's popular novel, *East Lynne*, and some later stage and film versions, I situate the texts in the interlocking theoretical frameworks outlined in the previous chapters. Although the novel is British, it was quickly disseminated in the USA, showing that it satisfied imaginary desires in North America as well as in Britain.

In this, as in other case studies, representations are multidetermined, emerging from the complex interaction of authorial gender; historical gender codes at the time of the writing (including the broader familial discourse); codes of class and race produced by a culture's particular industrial/technological stage; the psychoanalytic discourse (that can be inferred in texts before psychoanalytic thought became explicit and public); and, finally, inter-textual processes concerned with aesthetic and formal conventions as well as specific influences.

In this case, melodrama, as a generalized aesthetic mode embodying a particular type of imagination, will provide one governing framework. As we saw earlier, the terrain of the melodramatic imagination is concerned to make sense of aspects of experience not normally imaged. Melodrama is geared toward representation of unconscious processes. Psychoanalysis, then, will be a second governing framework, while the political aspects of the narrative will also be explored. Indeed, it is the specifically political uses of the melodrama that interest me as much as the way nineteenth-century gender ideology is seen to shape representations of the relationship to the mother. The interaction of psychoanalytic and political discourses shows that some representations construct an erotic fantasy for the lost mother object, which, displaced into the terrain of passionate heterosexual romance, threatens the new bourgeois social order and must be curtailed.

After a full discussion of Ellen Wood's 1861 novel, I will briefly look at one of the play versions produced soon after publication of *East Lynne*. Focus will be on the codes that structured the Victorian stage in North America. These codes mandated that a text fit a specific genre and embody fixed rhetorical and spectacular features. The formal structures and codes peculiar to the theatre inevitably construct spectator-positions quite other than the novel's reading positions.

Finally, I will turn to two of the various film versions of *East Lynne*, made at differing moments in Hollywood's institutional, technological and aesthetic development. I will focus not only on the contrast between the two films, especially in relation to the construction of subjectivity, but also on the constraints of Hollywood codes. Ideological demands together with the specificity of the cinematic apparatus, produce new sets of meanings from the original novel.

A main concern is the meanings given to pre-Symbolic representations of mother–child bondings.[1] This relationship takes different forms and is differently valued in the various *East Lynne* examples, depending on whether or not there is identification with the mother-figure. When such identification is present, the mother-sacrifice paradigm may expose the oppressive aspects of the patriarchal positioning of the mother; the text may reveal how the mother strives to gain unmet gratifications by establishing a fusional relationship with her child. This may take the form of the over-invested mother or the powerful "phallic" one, as we saw in Chapter 4 (cf. Plaza 1981).

When there is no identification with the mother-figure, the paradigm can look very different; the ideal, self-sacrificing mother threatens to collapse into the evil phallic one (always seen as evil from the patriarchal viewpoint), who is perhaps defended against in the idealized "sacrifice" image. (For instance, unconscious fear of being devoured by the maternal may lead to fantasies in which the opposite happens, namely where the mother is excessively devoted to the child.)[2] Or the ideal figure may be made object of the text's sadistic urges against her. She is often excessively punished for slight deviation from her maternal role, as, for example in Alexander Bisson's *Madame X*, and the many play and film versions with similar plots (see Viviani 1987 for discussion of the punishment mother-figures suffer in maternal sacrifice narratives). Often, the mother is associated with death and destruction, not only of herself but also of her child. In some of the *East Lynne* versions of the pattern, the mother–son bond is given tremendous power and is also clearly equated with heterosexual romantic love. But the point is that while each specific representation needs to be explored for its unique depiction of constraints and tensions associated with the mother-figure – sometimes so great as to threaten to crack a text open – all versions betray the strong unconscious attraction in the popular imagination of this maternal sacrifice myth.

I will show how the paradigm of maternal sacrifice appeals in different ways to (hypothetical) male and female readers, depending on differences in the way each patriarchally constructed gender deals with the culturally necessary separation from the mother.

Careful examination of the representation of the mother and of pre-Symbolic longings in melodrama may help us to understand not only

get on with it!

some of the discrepancies in male and female fantasies, and how cultural gender ideology inflects unconscious desire, but also the *political* uses of the fallen woman story;[3] in this story, an innocent (often working-class) young girl is sexually abused and destroyed by an unscrupulous, lascivious aristocratic male.

A novel like Ellen Wood's *East Lynne* (1861) is a woman's melodrama enmeshed in pre-Symbolic yearnings and post-Symbolic jealousies and sibling rivalries. The main families involved (the Carlyles and the Hares) are solidly middle class. Isabel Mount Severn is aristocratic, but her family has been virtually erased as a result of decadent indulgence and squandering of wealth. And she quickly joins the middle classes in marrying Carlyle.

The political implications of this narrative have to do with the depiction of the aristocratic class as wasteful, decadent and sometimes immoral. We have here a specific discourse about class: Lord Mount Severn belongs to the old noble aristocracy, but is unable to continue in a noble manner; his sister, Mrs Vane, and Francis Levison, on the other hand, represent the promiscuous, lascivious, impulsive and morally decadent wing of the dwindling aristocracy. The novel's idealization of the middle classes, whose solid families are prey to exploitation from the immoral aristocrats, has to do with the political requirement for a reshuffling of discourses about class as England was becoming more entrenched in the industrial era. Economic realities required that the aristocratic class be dislodged from its privileged status in the political Imaginary, and the middle classes represented as the new source of morality and the Law.

[The psychoanalytic level of the text supports the argument that such a dislodging of the aristocracy is at stake, particularly in relation to the aristocratic heroine's psychic capacity for mothering. *East Lynne* provides evidence for only one of many possible mythic, mother-victim heroines, with its accompanying political implications. But this form, addressing primarily the middle-class reader, was a frequent type. The novel usefully contains, in the sub-plot, a representation of the "bad" mother paradigm in both Carlyle's "surrogate" mother, Cornelia (his sister), and in Mrs Vane, the heroine's Aunt, thus permitting comparison between the two fusional paradigms (i.e. symbiosis with the child through negation of self and through controlling, possessive behaviour) that Monique Plaza (1981) outlines. As in so many nineteenth-century romances by women, the true, "good" mothers are dead, absent or ill. In *East Lynne*, both the heroine and hero, Isabel and Carlyle, are orphaned but only Isabel lacks the protecting surrogate mother-figure. As is frequent in the romance, the heroine's dilemma is presented in explicitly Christian terms, particularly in the imagery that links Isabel to the figure of Eve in the Garden of Eden pursued by the "snake" Levison, and in the imagery in references to Isabel's mother.

The saintly nature of Isabel's dead mother is indicated, first, in the young woman's devoted memories, and second, in the mother's link to holiness through Isabel's cherished cross-adorned necklace. It is this necklace that Levison ominously breaks on his first meeting with Isabel. Isabel's distress comes from the fact that her mother gave her the cross as she was dying, telling the child to let it be a talisman to guide her when in need of counsel (Wood 1984, p. 13). Its breaking signals Isabel's aloneness and vulnerability to the "snake" Levison ready to step into the gap left by her mother's death.

That the breaking of the cross indicates a link between the lover and the mother is clear later on, when we are told that Isabel's thoughts were "running on many things," moving from thoughts of her mother "with whom she was last at East Lynne," via thoughts of her father's illness, to thoughts of Levison ("even as she thought of him, a thrill quickened her veins") (p. 55). Isabel seeks in both a male lover and her children something akin to pre-Oedipal symbiosis with the mother. The novel seems to adhere to psychoanalytic theories showing that in patriarchy women must, like males, reject the mother and turn toward the father so as to enter the Symbolic. Isabel desires the Father because the mother desires him and because it is only in that way that she has a place and a function. But the pre-Symbolic yearning for the mother remains, nevertheless. Thus, Isabel seeks in the male satisfaction both of the desire for symbiosis (the pre-Symbolic mother-relation) and of a place in relation to the Law (the Symbolic Father-relation). The pre-Symbolic desire evokes contradictory responses from the patriarchal system that produces it.

From the start, Isabel experiences a merging sensation with Levison but not with Carlyle. Her marriage to Carlyle, admittedly one of convenience, is nevertheless idyllically happy to begin with, mainly because of Carlyle's stance as protective Father. Upon marrying, Isabel regresses to dependency and childishness, wanting only to be by Carlyle. Bored, listless and empty when without Carlyle, Isabel gives no evidence of a subjectivity outside of him. As the marriage progresses, emptiness becomes her normal state; she still yearns for the embraces and kisses that Carlyle has outgrown, knowing only how to express a desire to be desired. She becomes aware of her own desire only in relation first to the children and then, later, in renewing her relationship with Levison.

Passion for children in the world of *East Lynne* is a "safe" location of female desire, although the text ultimately seeks also to confine such love within suitable bounds. (Child-care discourses of the period, as will be clear below, deplored the over-indulgent mother and praised the one who kept her distance and imposed strict obedience.) The narrating voice manifests sympathy for Isabel's yearnings to merge with her love-objects – be they her mother, Levison or her children – but finally shows that such desire is excessive: the system has no room for this kind of female passion. Like Helene Deutsch (see pp. 80–1), the narrator would turn Isabel toward the Father and away from the Mother: the ego-ideal is "correct" when taking the

79

Father-relationship for the model and "incorrect" (or dangerous) when taking the mother–daughter bonding as the model. But excessive love displaced into the child is socially preferable to taking a lover.

Isabel's realization of this is evident at a crucial juncture, when she is to leave for France. She begs Carlyle to let her take the children, exposing her emotional need for them and her fear of separation, individuation and emotional autonomy. Cornelia's impatience with Isabel's desire suggests that it is seen as excessive; yet the narration makes it clear that Isabel is vulnerable to erotic desire if separated from her children; the text wishes to constrain Isabel's erotic desire, and to reward her attempts to fulfill the proper "maternal function."

Isabel is persuaded not to take the children, and the gap in her emotional life is soon filled by passion for Levison, who steps into the breach. Isabel's desire forces itself upon her *physically*, in a way rare in fictional representations of male characters. Because the novel locates Isabel within the power relations of patriarchy, she cannot consciously accept herself as a desiring subject; desire is thus forced to find expression through her body. "What was it," the narrator asks, "that caused every nerve in her frame to vibrate, every pulse to quicken . . . changing the monotony of her mind into tumult?" (p. 171). The "cause" is Levison's approach.

Both the narrator and Isabel see her desire as evil (Isabel prays for strength to overcome "this dangerous foe that was creeping on in guise so insidious": p. 176). Although the desire for lover and children has similar origins, love for the children provides a kind of defense against the passion for Levison because (despite its symbiotic nature) the former love is to a degree socially sanctioned. Significantly, Isabel asks her husband anxiously about the children as she feels Levison's effects (p. 176).

What Isabel seeks in both the children and the men in her life is the satisfaction of a passionate, merged feeling. This desire for loss of self in the Other images the impossible desire for unity with the Mother left over from childhood. In nineteenth-century patriarchy, women could not sublimate such desire in the public sphere as men did. While Carlyle's calm, distanced, rational style prohibits collusion in this sort of merging, Levison's seductiveness and his own desire to possess makes such projection easy. Just because Carlyle has set himself up as the wise, intimidating Father-figure, Isabel cannot confide in "the strong arm of shelter round her, a powerful pillar of protection, he upon whom she leaned" (p. 188). The text limits its representation of masculinity to these two modes – both unsatisfactory for woman, namely, the good but morally awesome Father, whose standards are so high, and the duplicitous lover, who cannot be loyal.

Significantly, the text cannot accommodate Isabel's *erotic* desire. Although *East Lynne* was written thirty or so years before Freud initiated psychoanalytic discourse, it embodies a conception of woman's psychology that was developed by Freud's female followers. There is no more place in this system than in that of Helene Deutsch for Isabel as subject of erotic desire.

The novel seems to agree with Deutsch that the child ought to become for the Mother the ego-ideal (i.e. the Father) from which a cathexis to the sexual partner has also been drawn. The novel further suggests that the process of sublimation is only affected for the woman in giving birth to the child. In Deutsch's words, in giving birth, the woman "returns to that primal condition . . . in which there was as yet no distinction between ego-libido and object libido" (Deutsch 1926: 414). But, for Deutsch, the woman is supposed to move on from this "primal condition" (a sort of narcissism) to "object-love" (which implies the establishment of proper boundaries), although, as Deutsch notes, the distinction is a difficult one.

It is precisely Isabel's failure to make what the novel (and Helene Deutsch) see as the "correct" kind of sublimation that brings on her tragedy. Instead of displacing the erotic into what Deutsch calls "the maternal function of the vagina," Isabel insists on retaining the cathexis with the sexual partner through her desire for Levison.

This is made slightly more understandable in that even the limited action and power of the maternal domestic role are denied Isabel by class privilege because maids take care of everything, including the children: Isabel is left indeed in the position of lack, object of the male gaze (Levison, Carlyle), and of the jealous female gaze/identification (Barbara, Cornelia). She "completes" Carlyle's world but is herself quite incomplete.

Female jealousy, possessiveness and competition are the product of woman's "incompleteness," her positioning in patriarchy as object, not subject. Cornelia's role runs counter to Barbara Hare and Isabel in terms of her response to this positioning. Surrogate mother to Carlyle, Cornelia, his stepsister, is a mild, semi-comic version of the "bad" mother type – tyrannical, possessive, controlling and not above deceit. But Cornelia's jealousy indicates the incestuous mother–son dynamic that is rarely so explicitly addressed: anticipating Freudian theory again, the text suggests that Cornelia's repressed erotic love for her brother has made her adopt a masculine identification with her brother.

Barbara Hare's story runs parallel to Isabel's, providing another example of a young woman's vulnerabilities and emotional dependencies through lack of a strong mother-figure; the angelic Mother, Mrs Hare, is present, but so sickly and confined as to be unable to help her daughter. Most of the interaction between Mrs Hare and her daughter has to do with the mutually loved son/brother, who is self-described as "spoiled" (essentially "feminized") by his mother. One of the purposes of the Richard Hare plot is to bring Carlyle and Barbara together (around their secret project to redeem Richard from a false murder charge) arousing Isabel's jealousy so intensely that she runs off with Levison on impulse.

Like Isabel, Barbara yearns for Carlyle's love and protection, because Barbara like Isabel lacks the kindliness of the fantasised ideal Father. Although Mr Hare is alive, he is the harsh, domineering Father-type. Arguably, when the Mother provides such nurturing and bonds closely with her daughter, such qualities in the Father are less essential. But in the absence of the autonomous and nurturing Mother, the daughter searches even more for the Father's love and protection. Carlyle emerges as the only Father-figure to carry out his responsibilities in the ideal way that culture requires: Mr Hallijohn is an inarticulate bully; Mr Hare is insensitive and unduly severe; Lord Mount Severn is incapable of running his affairs, and anyway invalided before his death; Levison, not a "literal" Father, cannot live up to the role in any of its forms. And thus, it is left to Carlyle to embody the figure that the Father-husband should be.

It is significant that the experiences of both women are represented in *physical* terms – that is, in relation to the effects of perceptions on their *bodies*. They do not "think" about what they see or even about what they feel. The text implies a bodily sensation direct from the perception, without any mediation. Only when it is all over for her, that is when all her mistakes are made, her situation irreversible, is Isabel granted the capacity to *reflect* on her emotions and her actions.

These representations embody the modern male/female dichotomy that Rousseau first fully articulated in *Emile* (1762) and that informed European and American thought: as I noted in Chapter 2 Rousseau re-inscribes in culture a division of labor necessary for the development of modern capitalism. He theorizes the public (male), private (female) split that structures the separate spheres in the nineteenth and early twentieth centuries. Classic in Rousseau is the ascribing to "nature" what is already cultural, and the assumption that the middle-class ethic is to be taken as the norm. In the new version of the division, as we saw, the very survival of the human race depends on the woman's function in cementing the family through her skills in emotions and relationships, while equally important are the male's capacities for rational thought devoid of unreliable feelings.

Hence in *East Lynne*, woman is shown as delicate, sensitive, prone to jealousy and distrust, easily intimidated, insecure; and the male (in classic Rousseauian style) as uncomplicated, sensible, rational, cautious, moderate, a good citizen, kindly and involved in his work. The narrator almost never describes Carlyle in terms of bodily sensations: the one exception is on his reading of Isabel's farewell note, when, we are told, "Though a calm man, one who had his emotions under control, he was no stoic, and his fingers shook as he broke the seal" (p. 235).

When the seduction finally happens, the text refuses the reader the satisfaction of being witness to the consummation of Isabel's erotic desire for Levison. The two come together now in ugliness, Isabel goaded only by furious feelings of jealousy and revenge on seeing Carlyle and Barbara

Hare together in the dark (in fact, waiting innocently enough to meet with Richard Hare). Her jealousy fueled by Levison, Isabel breaks into bitter sobs: "Alas! Alas!," she moans; but, the narrator tells us, "Francis Levison applied himself to soothe her with all the sweet and dangerous sophistry of his crafty nature" (p. 227).

Once Isabel is repositioned in her own home, incognito, as the Governess, she becomes the voyeur; she is able to look and grieve, but unable to have the gaze of recognition blaze back on her. In the first half of *East Lynne*, Isabel is inside the circle; she is the lucky, successful heroine, whose "sin" makes for a fall, allowing the "good" sister to take her place in the family unit. But Isabel has to endure living out the childhood family romance; she is positioned as governess on the periphery, but is able to watch the goings on, like the child peeking in at the parents through the bedroom keyhole. The narrator ostensibly holds up Barbara as the one to copy, Isabel as the dangerous warning about the results of desire; in reality, however, we are given vicarious satisfaction in the passionate and sensational life that Isabel lives. Her intense emotionality captures our interest, while Barbara ceases to have much appeal once happily married. The device permits all kinds of comparisons between the two heroines.

The two heroines represent different *kinds* of mothering, and point to complexities that child experts of the period were beginning to discuss in the wake of Rousseau. Rousseau's "revolutionary" idea (as we saw in Chapter 2) was to bring attention to the child's needs for special care and attention if proper development were to take place. But as the bourgeois family proliferated itself in the nineteenth century, problems in mother–child relations not envisaged by Rousseau began to appear. In asking that mothers be totally devoted to the child, Rousseau had not envisaged the kind of pleasure that mothers might derive from perpetuating the pre-Oedipal fusional mother–child bonding.

Apparently, some post-Rousseauian child-care experts became aware of the dangers of such excessive bonding, and warned against it, while in a general way revealing their debt to Rousseau. Such experts stressed the mother's disciplinarian role, as yet unhindered by later Freudian interpretations of over-control. John S.C. Abbott, for instance, in his *The Mother at Home* (1834), articulates a discourse of the mother as stern disciplinarian that was to remain basically the same until the 1940s. Abbott's text underscores its religious basis and its belief "that the object of education is to prepare the child for its heavenly home," a task in which the mother is ultimately seen as central. On a very Rousseauian note, Abbott states, "as the Mother is the guardian and guide of the early years of life, from her goes the most powerful influence in the formation of the character of man." An obvious allusion to discourses started by Rousseau is the repeated statement that "the eyes of the community" are now being directed more and more to the nursery and to the issue of the child's education.

The argument of Abbott's first chapter is geared toward proving that if a son "leave not his mother with established principles of virtue and self-control, he will most assuredly fall before . . . temptations" (1834: 8). The girl who falls into sin is also mentioned, but the "sin" is clearly sexual, whereas with the boy alcohol seems to be the main danger. Chapters 2 and 3 deal with Maternal Authority, and here Abbott not only gives tips about disciplining the young child that must have still seemed sensible in the 1940s but also, continuing Juan Luis Vives's early child-rearing discourse, cautions the mother against indulging herself in affection for the child which may not be good for him.

But what is particularly significant, in the light of post-Freudian hysteria about the dominating mother, is the explicit exhortation to mothers to exert their power over their children. Abbott notes that the children are entirely in the mother's hands: "All their enjoyments are at her disposal" (1834: 33). But the following image of the controlling mothers portrays the full force of the mother's power:

> God has thus given [the mother] all the power that she may govern and guide them as she pleases . . . . He has placed in your hands a helpless babe, entirely dependent upon you; so that if it disobeys you, all you have to do is to cut off its source of enjoyment, or inflict bodily pain, so steadily and so invariably, that disobedience and suffering shall be indissolubly connected in the mind of the child. (Abbott 1834: 34)

And in the conclusion, he notes, "Mothers have as powerful an influence over the welfare of future generations as all other causes combined" (1834: 165). It is this power that Abbott is concerned to channel in ways he considers most fit (and religious instruction is, not surprisingly, a large part of the desired way of mothers exerting their "power"). The male voice is concerned to legislate what mothers should do, just because of the enormity of the power she has been given.

Abbott indicates no fear about the mother's power over the child; it is considered a positive and necessary stance – the desired norm. In the pre-Freudian period, there was no question of any negatively valued "phallic" mother; rather the mother was required to assert control through a variety of manipulative means. It was assumed that asserting such power might be a painful duty bought at the expense of "momentary ease;" but not to exercise power over her child was at this time seen as inevitably producing "dissolute sons" and "ungrateful daughters" (Abbott 1834: 34). Abbott also indicates no conception of a "split" mother: the "true womanhood" image, with its submissiveness to the husband/Father, is not set in opposition to the powerful, demanding mother.

Barbara Hare in *East Lynne* (having apparently read all the right child-care manuals) makes it clear first that a mother should not be too much with her children, and second, that being a mother comes second to being a wife. She makes a point of criticizing, not those mothers who neglect their children out of a selfish desire for their own pleasure – such mothers are not worth talking about – but, echoing Abbott, those who dote too much on their children, who "are never but when with their children" (p. 341). Barbara makes a distinction between the physical and mental needs of children, arguing that the former should always be supplied by the nurse, the latter by the mother.

Isabel apparently assents to these views, and indeed, inwardly notes that this was more or less "her system" when first in East Lynne. However, Isabel seems surprised by Barbara's second point about putting wifehood before motherhood. "'You would not stay in-doors for the baby, then?'" she asks; and the round reply is, "'Certainly not. If I and Mr Carlyle have to be out in the evening baby gives way, I should never give up my husband for my baby; never, dearly as I love him'" (p. 343). And indeed, Barbara is mainly described in terms of her desire for Carlyle. The blame here, however, finally rests on Isabel for leaving the children in the first place; no one apparently expects a stepmother to care much. Only at the very end of the novel does Barbara admit that she has harboured jealous feelings for Carlyle's children because Isabel was their mother and had been his wife (p. 525).

Reading against the grain, we can see the contradictory demands that are placed on the patriarchal mother. She has always to be sexually attractive and alluring to the husband; as Barbara points out, if a wife fails in this, her husband will seek amusements elsewhere. At the same time, she must be a devoted mother, taking care of her children's slightest needs. However, she is not to devote *too much* love to them as Isabel ends up doing.

The slippage from erotic energy in the service of husband and in the service of the children seems endemic to the mother's contradiction in patriarchy. Both psychic sets involve a desire to re-experience the original illusory oneness with the mother, and embody a desire for merging, for loss of self in Other. In other words, given their positioning as "lack" in the patriarchal Symbolic order, women are represented as seeking for identity/wholeness either via romantic love or via identification with children – both of which evidence an attempt to re-find the lost mother. Like Isabel, women seek such "wholeness" in the men they marry; but husbands, socialized in Rousseauian manner to perform rationally, in the service of the state, often refuse such symbiosis.

For Isabel on her return only the children are available. Yet it is significant that, on the conscious level, it was longing for the children, not Carlyle, that tempted Isabel to take the dangerous route of returning as Governess to East Lynne. But the children displace by necessity Carlyle, her "correct" love all along, had she but known it. Isabel has more passion for Carlyle once he is unavailable than when they were married. Her passion is perhaps spurred by the Oedipal configuration of her situation, positioned as she is as the child to Carlyle and Barbara. But, more importantly, she has learned the "proper" libidinal relations that culture demands. It is Carlyle's recognition and forgiveness that she now "correctly" (according to the Freudian model outlined by Deutsch) desires and finally receives on her deathbed. Meanwhile, Carlyle's saintly goodness, his protective function, remains until the end. He is capable both of sending Isabel satisfied to her death, and, immediately afterwards, of convincing Barbara of his undying love for her.

East Lynne thus exposes the unconscious "family romance" processes, first articulated as such by Freud in "The Family Romance," that structure cultural relationships in the bourgeois Imaginary. The novel shows Isabel's necessary turning away from the lost mother object toward the Father – a direction she learned only through painful experience. It is significant that the only truly intersubjective figure in the novel is discovered in a male, namely Carlyle. All the mother-figures fail in some way or another: Isabel is too merged with her children, Barbara is too "cool" to them, Cornelia is too controlling. The text exposes the psychic underpinnings of the feminine as constructed in patriarchy, concluding that this "feminine" is not adequate to excellent mothering. It calls in the services of the male to fill the functional gap. The novel's end, however, suggests that Barbara Hare will become the Ideal Mother, once she is secure with Carlyle and has overcome her jealous feelings for Isabel. Barbara thus embodies the "correct" turn from the Mother to the Father that Deutsch outlined.

The novel, thus, underscores women's weaknesses and vulnerabilities, their need of the male. Nevertheless, *East Lynne* earlier problematized Deutsch's model, which, although published later than the novel, it mostly supports: that is, it showed how desire for the mother operates in young girls' sexuality; and how, at least for Isabel, the child does not represent the Father but the Mother. In exposing this, the novel is transgressive. Although Isabel suffers for her transgressions (the novel in that sense supports the patriarchal law), the very articulation of the difficulties of women's lives, of the constraints that hemmed them in, of the lack of any place in the system for female desire, of the contradictory demands made upon women, surely gave some satisfaction to female readers.

Now what of the appeal to the hypothetical male reader? How could a male identify in a text like this, which, judging from the narrator's "lectures" to her addressees, speaks to a female audience? It is possible that males largely "consumed" the narrative via its many play versions (discussed below). But we know something of the response of the male literary establishment to the novel: according to Sally Mitchell (1977) Samuel Lucas loved the novel but felt that he shouldn't, while other critics focused on its literary flaws. Both kinds of response may be useful in theorizing how the novel appealed to the average middle-class male reader.

Both the defensiveness of the critics searching for literary flaws, and the suggestion in Lucas's comment that he experienced some illicit pleasure in the novel, indicate that the novel touched the male unconscious. It is possible that the narrative addressed unresolved Oedipal wishes of some male readers. The longing of the lovely Lady Isabel for her absent children, of whom two are sons, her affection for them when present, her dedicated devotion to the dying William, all address repressed male longings to win the Mother away from the Father, and to possess her love. The second half of the novel, indeed, enacts the male child's fantasy of having "won" the mother from the Father, given that here the children become Isabel's total concern. (The fantasy is somewhat protected by having the children ignorant of the fact that their governess is their mother.) The mythic pattern positions the male both as the one capable of being in control, even when abandoned, and as the focus of the mother's adoring affection and desire. The myth attends to the double-sided male desire for an Ideal Imago while also being object of the maternal gaze.

On a less obvious level, the melodrama may have addressed the powerful, unconscious Father–daughter incest wishes evident in patriarchal discourses. For, once married, Carlyle's feelings are those of a doting Father toward his little girl. When he finds Isabel sleeping on the grass, we are told that "she looked like a lovely child, her lips open, her cheeks flushed and her beautiful hair falling around. It was an exquisite picture, and his heart beat quicker within him *as he felt that it was his own*" (p. 124, emphasis mine). In a rare mention of any physical reactions on the part of Carlyle, it is *possession* that creates the sensations in place of the unmediated desire that thrills Isabel's veins. As the years go on, however, even this level of passion dwindles in Carlyle to a "calmness" which, we are told, "may look like indifference or coldness" (p. 166) but which the narrator warns is inevitable. Already preparing for the later "lectures" about enduring a boring marriage, the narrator tell us that all this is inevitable and in the "nature" of man.

But perhaps there was a more cognitive level on which the novel appealed to men, namely in its political implications. One obvious point of male identification – so obvious that the figure seems constructed largely for that purpose – is Mr Carlyle. In his solid, respectable manliness, his rationality, his calmness in the face of turmoil, his control in the face of loss and crisis, in his dedication to work and his service to the community, Mr Carlyle stands as the epitome of middle-class values of the time – the very bedrock on which the nation could stand. His authoritative position is emphasized (as so often in repetitions of this mythic paradigm) by having the Father also a man of Law on the literal level, thereby doubly inscribed in the Symbolic, doubly in control of the phallic social order. In addition to all this, Carlyle is handsome and wins the ladies' attentions. Every male reader must have wanted to be a Mr Carlyle. The text's focus on women's needs for dependence on the male, their longing for love and protection, permits the male reader to feel strong and needed through identification with Carlyle.

From the start, Carlyle assumes the position of the Law, the Father, toward

Isabel, setting up a distance that alienates her, and yet that establishes precisely his Rousseau-defined "manliness." In an early discussion with Lord Mount Severn we see the sort of discourse about marriage in which men engage, focusing on Carlyle's financial capabilities and on how well he can take care of Isabel. When Severn mentions love, Carlyle at first refuses to answer since "Those are feelings that man rarely acknowledges to man," but finally agrees that he loves Isabel passionately (p. 117). The reader, however, knows that it was Isabel's abandoned situation that provoked the marriage proposal, perhaps out of a desire for a power and dominance over a woman he had allowed Cornelia to usurp. Although Cornelia continues to live with Carlyle and his wife, the power relations are reversed, as becomes increasingly obvious. This is something that a male reader might enjoy.

Further, Carlyle is not only the morally correct hero, but also the one who gains upward class mobility through the marriage. On the political level, Isabel's transgressions symbolize the failure of the aristocracy. Although the novel speaks from her point of view, and the narrator empathizes with her sufferings, Isabel nevertheless has to give way to the middle-class Barbara Hare. Sensible and solidly grounded, Barbara Hare, as we saw, has a more healthy understanding of marital and parental relations than has the aristocratic Isabel.

The narrator serves as a device for articulating the new discourses, which look back to Rousseau's *Emile*. This is significant in that, as a (presumed) female voice addressing a female reader, the narrator endorses the new middle-class family. She serves the patriarchy, further, in her severe critique of female erotic desire. The voice can vividly appreciate the attractions of desire, but self-righteously sets itself against it in the "lectures" to the reader quoted earlier. Like Ellen Wood herself, the narrator cannot think outside of the discourses available within the fictive world and thus cannot conceive of a world in which female desire would not destabilize the entire system. Yet, paradoxically in this novel by a woman author, the narrator registers the power of what has to be repressed in order to secure male dominance.

To the narrator, Carlyle embodies a highly valued puritanical type of middle-class male. Part of this type's values arises precisely from its asceticism. While Carlyle's caution may make him a flat, boring character, the novel sees his as a necessary mode. The new professional middle classes could only prosper and obtain solid ground if they stood opposed to aristocratic waste and self-indulgence.

The novel looks back to *Emile* also in the adoption of the discourse of sentimental individualism that Rousseau articulated. The sentimental discourse of the family replaced the hedonistic type of individualism reflected in the behavior of the declining European aristocracy. Rousseau's text develops a *political* concept of individualism in the sense that the boy's education is specifically to train him to take his part as a responsible citizen. It is a *moral* education, since the boy is to think in terms not only of himself but also of the society as a whole; he is part of a political community in which he has particular responsibilities.

In *East Lynne*, the thriller sub-plot provides an opportunity for articulating middle-class responsibilities. This plot centers on the working-class Hallijohn family, whose promiscuous, sexy daughter, Affy, anxious to upgrade herself, seduces the middle-class Richard Hare and is seduced in turn by a Captain "Thorn," really Francis Levison. Richard Hare is falsely accused of murdering Affy's father; the murderer was in fact the lascivious Francis Levison whose aristocratic degeneracy knows no bounds. Barbara Hare convinces Carlyle of Richard's innocence, and Carlyle becomes the major investigator into the crime.

The sub-plot, then, positions the working class as open to temptation and as requiring the middle-class liberal humanist to keep unsuitable passions in control. Carlyle, in true liberal fashion, does not condescend to the working classes, treating them rather with dignity and respect. This is obvious in all his dealings with the working classes in the novel, but a good example is a short interchange between Affy and Carlyle toward the end of the novel when Affy is to marry the petty-bourgeois Mr Jiffin, owner of the local grocery. Affy thinks herself far above the man, and sets out to be the "kept" middle-class lady; but Carlyle insists that Mr Jiffin is "a very civil, respectable man" (p. 474). He cautions Affy not to spend all Mr Jiffin's hard-earned money.

The novel shows that the only class capable of the correct balance between desire and its release is the middle class. The classes at either end of the spectrum display excess and an inability to control desire that leads to their downfall. Middle-class members, like Richard Hare, who fall prey to seduction or give in to desire inappropriately, also require the services of the liberal humanist for unravelling the disasters contingent upon such behavior. Thus, the thriller sub-plot provides the opportunity for both excoriation of passionate excesses, and for demonstration of the liberal humanist Carlyle's rationality, decorum, moderation and dedication to the larger social community.

Working-class victim-mothers are evidently infrequent in the 1860s, although the seduction of the young innocent working-class girl is a familiar figure in literary and, as Judith Walkowitz has shown, also in extra-literary discourses.[4] When the victimized working-class mother did appear, it was in the context of "temperance" melodramas – didactic polemics against the evil effects of alcohol on the family. Focus on working-class mother paradigms in North America arises only toward the end of the century with the social purity and eugenics movements, when the middle classes were suddenly concerned about the so-called "degeneration" of the race through poverty and the growing slum conditions that began to parallel those long familiar from Europe. These movements coincided with the invention of film, and thus we find in early film a focus on working-class subjects as a way both of addressing working-class spectators (always a large part of the film audience) and of educating the middle-class film audience (increasingly being appealed to as the 1910s wore on) about their social responsibilities (Hansen 1983).

Before the social purity and eugenics movements, there would presumably have been little appeal in the surface narrative figuring the working class; readers were presumed to be largely female and middle class, and plots were shaped accordingly. The working-class plot in *East Lynne* is merely a device for underscoring the political discourse. Unlike many middle-class figures (who are given a certain psychic depth), the working-class characters are one-dimensional stereotypes.

Aside from the specific political implications of the mother-victim pattern in *East Lynne*, the repetition of this pattern, more or less in its basic Victorian and Christian form over at least one hundred years, suggests that it had enormous appeal. It is precisely the basis for that appeal, which could be utilized for multiple political purposes, that I have illuminated through a psychoanalytic reading of the text. In *East Lynne*, it is the double-pronged unconscious desire for the lost-mother object combined with sadistic urges toward the same object, along with unconscious fantasies about father–daughter incest that the text articulates as a powerful field to engage the reader.

East Lynne stands interestingly at the juncture of the melodramatic pattern that showed the family as threatened from the outside (by dangerous, usually male, figures, often aristocrats or men in authority abusing their power) and the later melodramas that explore the sexual dangers and problems *within* the nuclear family – a trend that accelerates after Freud's "discoveries" of sexual desire between parents and children. The previous focus on the evil seducer from outside the family may then be seen as a displacement of what was all the time an internal problem.

Nevertheless, the shift in focus has important political ramifications since where the blame for destabilization is placed depends on what social re-orderings are either economically necessary or are underway for other reasons (e.g. new technological discoveries necessitating changes in work patterns; or the demands of a war situation requiring new gender arrangements).

We can now begin to see the interconnections between the psychoanalytic and the social levels of the novel: the novel's overall project is to show the necessity for control of a socially inscribed desire – a desire that has to do with the very formation of the social order, or Lacan's Symbolic. We see that the text offers a multiplicity of possible positions for reader-identification in satisfying unconscious desire; but ultimately the discourses are hierarchically ordered in the fictional resolution of ideological, patriarchal and political tensions. It is specifically female desire that is the problem and that must be brought under control; in the case of both Isabel and Affy Hallijohn – situated as each is at either end of the class spectrum – desire brings about disaster: Levison is merely the willing and available vessel for evoking and then receiving their sexual desire. The middle-class Barbara Hare is impervious to such an excess as both Isabel and Affy engage in. The ideology of the family in its class relations is to repress and control threats to its security from above and below – an alliance against illicit passions and excessive, "degenerate," desire.[5]

East Lynne is particularly interesting in that it moves from the romance to the maternal sacrifice pattern, and exposes similarities between the psychic aspects of romance and of mothering. Fascinating here is the tension between a view of woman's psychology strikingly similar to the constructs of Helene Deutsch, and the excess desire remaining from the pre-Symbolic mother–child relation that breaks through the narrative and must be contained in the end. Isabel learns painfully that literal fulfillment of erotic desire is impossible (Levison cannot match her fantasies), but she still does not understand "object-love" or the sublimation that culture demands. Instead, she displaces her erotic desire into the boy-child, for which she must be further punished. In contrast to Isabel, the text exhibits the middle-class Barbara Hare as the ideal-model – as the one embodying the correct relation to husband and child.

The novel demonstrates that erotic fantasy, particularly that which arises from desire for the lost mother object, displaced into passionate heterosexual romance, threatens the new capitalist and patriarchal social order and must be severely curtailed. The ego-ideal for both sexes must be the Father, not the Mother, if desire is to be properly subject to the patriarchal Law. The new liberal humanist couple – Barbara Hare and Carlyle – emerge as the ideal toward which the reader should aspire. They embody the new middle class, envisaged already by Rousseau, that will enable the proper functioning of the industrial order. Although this order is barely evident in the novel, it hovers on the margins of the small world of East Lynne. For industrial capitalism to get fully underway, the old aristocratic social order has to be dismantled, and political discourses changed: this is the central, underlying theme of Ellen Wood's novel.

That the political and psychoanalytic patterns outlined in the novel touched something deep in the cultural unconscious may be seen in its instantaneous success as a popular novel. According to Sally Mitchell,

> by the end of the century, it had sold almost half a million copies in England, was pirated by two dozen American publishers and was so popular on the stage that its title became a watchword: "Next Week – East Lynne!" the posters promised, whenever receipts were down and the stock company needed surefire revenue. (Mitchell, S. 1984: xiv)

At the time of Wood's death, Mitchell notes, the play version of *East Lynne* was acted almost constantly in London and the provinces, and "at least nine different adaptations by unknown authors were presented between 1866 and

Mrs. Henry Wood's

E A S T L Y N N E

Sally Mitchell, editor

Figure 3   cover from Rutgers edition of *East Lynne*
Reproduction of a theatrical poster advertising the ever-popular *East Lynne* drama.
Now a governess in what was once her own home, Isabel and her son recognize
each other – the playwright's alteration of the novel.

1899" (1984: xvi), these not counting other plays with different titles that essentially plagiarized the story.

According to Robert Liston (1962), it was an American actress, Lucille Western, who first thought of a play version of Wood's novel. In 1861 she commissioned Clifton W. Tayleure (actor, manager and sometime playwright, as Liston puts it), actually to write the script, which was first performed in America in January 1862 at the Brooklyn Academy of Music. One can find *East Lynne* programs and reviews from 1865 to 1940 continuously, but there are also materials for performances as late as 1950, 1953 and 1961.[6]

The reviews consistently demonstrate the critics' distaste for the play and its sentimental, melodramatic qualities – a distaste often carried over to the actresses who made their fortunes from the pay – and also their amazement at the continuing appeal of the play to audiences. One critic begins his review in 1871, "The lovers of pathetic plays will learn with much pleasure that Miss Lucille Western commenced an engagement" (*New York Times* 6 June 1871); while another, with lethal irony, lambastes Miss Ada Gray for permitting falsely idealized pictures of herself to be "liberally posted upon the walls and fences of this town," and then proceeds to affect "surprise" that she has performed *East Lynne* over 2,000 times before relegating her to the class of "incompetent and pretentious actresses" (*New York Times* 11 June 1882).

The relentless audience fascination with the play made it "perhaps the greatest box-office hit of all time" (Liston 1962: 14). Liston notes that only "'Uncle Tom's Cabin,' first produced in 1852, compares with it as a commercial success in American theater." Liston also notes that entire theatres were constructed on the profits from *East Lynne*, and, further, attributes the development of theatre in North America largely to the play's ability to interest the Victorian middle classes with its mixture of high-flown morality and erotic titillation.

As late as 1909, serious versions of *East Lynne* were still being performed. One critic writes about an old woman so deeply moved by the play because of its reference to her own life that she fainted during the performance. This same critic notes that "more millions have witnessed *East Lynne* than have seen any other play that was ever written" (*Pictorial Leader* 2 May 1909). A poster for the play advertises "Jos. King's New Version" with the sentence: "It touches the heart of all." Further words talk about the great moral lesson the play has to offer women, namely that "A woman is happier rearing a large family and comforting a husband than if she were a College President."

But as the century got underway, the narrative was clearly creaking at the joints: ingenious playwrights and producers, however, found ways to continue the life of the drama through "modernizations" (whatever that might actually mean), parody, or at least a gentle satire. One critic records a new version of *East Lynne*, performed at the Harlem Opera House in 1901, being hissed off the stage. One can only wonder whether this was because the audience resented changes in their beloved melodrama, or because it was played too straight. Another reviewer records in 1905 a "revamped" version of the play (unfortunately not available) that audiences warmed to (it is hard to say how far this version satirized the original), but by 1926 reviewers were expecting that *East Lynne* would be performed as "an amusing echo of the last century" (*New York Times* 11 March 1926). Eugene O'Neill's 1920s realism first made inroads on melodrama, and, in fact, O'Neill was part of a group producing a burlesque of *East Lynne* in 1926 at the Greenwich Village Theater (Liston 1962: 15). Another full-fledged comic version that plays with old Victorian theatrical and acting codes is reviewed in the *New York Times* in 1931, and presumably, with the Depression, the drama's original appeal was over.

The play versions are important not only as testimony to the enduring popularity of the *East Lynne* mythic pattern but also as they look toward the various film versions. According to Michael Kilgarriff (1966), "the first stage adaptation . . . of what can perhaps be called the first High Society melodrama was by W. Archer . . . and produced at the Effingham Saloon, Whitechapel, in 1864 under the title of *The Marriage Bells; or The Cottage on the Cliff*."[7] The change from the original novel to the film versions is mediated through the play versions, where most alterations first occur. John Oxenford's 1866 version (reprinted in Kilgariff's anthology), remains quite close to the tone of the novel, although naturally only a few scenes can be dealt with. By the time of Ned Alpert's 1941 version, it is evidently difficult for audiences to take *East Lynne* "straight" any more: clearly, the pathos and Victorian sentimental moralizing were no longer appropriate unless rendered with some comic relief. The film versions that I will discuss in fact combine elements from Oxenford's version with elements from a version that must have preceded the one I found in print, namely Ned Alpert's 1941 play. Emmett Flynn's 1925 film relies partly on Oxenford, partly on a version like Alpert's; Bracken's earlier 1916 film, on the other hand, must have relied almost completely on a comic play version after which Alpert fashioned his 1941 play and that was available for Bracken's scriptwriter.

Although Alpert's play was published long after the last film versions, it has much in common with the earlier film versions. Alpert does not mention the films in his Preface, but talks of basing his version directly on the novel, which, of course, he does not do. But it is unlikely that Alpert would have gone back to the 1916 film – which his version most resembles. To begin with, the play leans in the comic direction particularly in the figure of Cornelia; the comedy surrounding the figure is exacerbated by the addition of the pursuit of Cornelia – an unlikely object of desire – by Carlyle's legal assistant, Dill. The play reduces the significance of Cornelia's masculinity in the novel – her positioning as a phallic mother surrogate to Carlyle – to a comic caricature of the old maid.

Indeed, the play deliberately parodies well-worn dramatic stereotypes.

Alpert – presumably addressing would-be producers – tries to sell his version of *East Lynne* on the paradoxical basis of its being

> a brand new, sparkling and streamlined play that was dramatized from the novel with one thought in mind – to preserve the spirit of the old play and . . . to provide the audience with more laughs than any other old-fashioned "meller" has ever done. (Alpert 1941)

These "laughs" will come, we are assured, from the pleasure of watching "the most tearful heroine to ever weep into a repertoire of hankies" and "that rogue of all rogues, Sir Francis Levison, that heavily moustached villain with the mocking laugh who has furnished the pattern for all the stage villains who have followed him" (Alpert 1941: 3). We are told that "When Archibald starts spouting speeches you'll be convulsed! He's really some Archie!" There is significantly no mention of "truth to life," or "real-life situations," it being presumed that we are in a terrain where figures are presented only to be laughed at for their absurd, exaggerated plights and emotions. The tone of Ned Alpert's Preface suggests that his play culminates a long line of versions with which he can expect his audience to be familiar.

It is perhaps surprising to find stage versions as late as 1941 (although the 1965 version is equally astonishing).[8] However that might be, the reasons for the excessive mockery in 1941 may differ somewhat from those in versions written about the time of Bracken's film. By 1941, the Second World War was already devastating Europe, and the United States had gone through the Depression, making the sentiments of the original novel difficult to appreciate. The characters had become mere stereotypes deemed too "old-fashioned" to be taken seriously. By 1916, comic caricature had been a long-established way in which to entertain the audiences who flocked to melodramas. (This would account for the changes in Cornelia's character, for the invention of a romance between Dill and Cornelia, and for the ensuing development of Dill's role.) It is also possible that comedy was a way to render the maternal-sacrifice myth "entertaining," since it lacked the basically salacious ingredients of the Richardsonian mythic pattern, namely that of the working-class heroine seduced by a lascivious upper-class male. A male-oriented fantasy, laden with erotic material, the pattern perfectly suited unconscious father–daughter incest wishes. The maternal sacrifice myth, on the other hand, required feminine identification and, after the "fall," namely, the seduction, is hardly erotic.

The maternal-sacrifice pattern was made interesting on the stage, however, through the lure of the upper-class mother's fall; this figure moved from a social paradise to deadly lower-class desolation as a result of a sexual transgression. The appeal of the story to the middle classes is clear, particularly since this group comes to represent the Ideal between two undesirable entities; and the broadening of some lower-class roles together with the introduction of farcical elements ensured that lower classes would also be entertained.

But it is also possible that comedy was a device to mitigate the distance between British class and gender relations, and the specificity of the North American historical context in which the play was being seen. Aside from the novel's length and breadth that has to be reduced to a two-hour play, there is an inherent problem of adapting a mid-nineteenth-century work, dealing with the political discourses specific to Britain, for American audiences in quite a different historical moment and political context. We might well ask what the attraction of such European myths is for North Americans, but this question takes me too far from my project: let me only suggest that, as discussion of the political implications of the American films will show, an attraction to the historic splendour and the traditions of England is combined with a gleeful distaste for the unequal class structures in Europe that jibe with North America's self-professed adherence to a democratic, classless ideal.

When film replaced the theatre as the site of exhibition of the melodrama, North America was the site of massive immigration. It had weathered the first-stage eruptions and dislocations of industrialism, and prided itself on having refashioned the liberal humanist ideal – founding concept of the young nation – anticipated by Ellen Wood's novel. However, since the political implications of the original lacked referents in the North American scene, they were eliminated in the play and film versions; instead, the story focused on romantic and family relationships, and the characters were reduced to comic allegorical stereotypes.

But while the stage versions account for some of the changes found in the two film versions I will discuss, another important influence is surely that of Griffith. Indeed, the revitalization of the mother-sacrifice pattern first in the 1910s (with its suffragette sub-text), and then in the moment of the so-called "flapper girl," may itself be a result of Griffith's *The Mothering Heart*, (1913) his *The Mother and the Law* (1915), and his particularly successful *Way Down East* (1921). A brief look at his simultaneous revitalization and Americanization of the mother-sacrifice myth may account further for some of the changes in the pattern that we will find in the two *East Lynne* film versions.

Griffith's Americanization of the mythic pattern is partly motivated by the need to include (in his very broad repertoire) stories more closely related to contemporary problems of a second-stage industrialism than those traditional ones common on the stage, which were often of European origin (Vardac 1977: 20–67). Such plots, as indicated earlier, addressed both the working classes that were often the center of the stories and the middle classes now being asked to show moral leadership for the lower classes (Hansen 1991). Some stories (although not those treated here) concern the effects of waves of immigrants around the turn of the century, which had produced the severe problems of industrialism long evident in England.

Griffith is well known as one of the initiators of films about current issues, but Lois Weber also made important contributions in this area. As a concerned, socially conscious middle-class citizen, Weber was anxious to provoke a middle-class sense of responsibility for those less fortunate than themselves, and to stimulate moral reforms. Griffith had a similar moralizing concern, but he also saw the dangers of middle-class meddling in the lives of the poor, and the complexities of any plan for social reform (viz. *The Mother and the Law*). Both Weber and Griffith succumb to sentimentalizing the American democratic ideal, but their work is important in Americanizing and shifting elements in the originally European maternal sacrifice pattern.

Since I deal with select Weber films in another chapter, let me here focus briefly on Griffith's Americanization of the mother-sacrifice myth. Griffith still adhered to the premises of the sacrifice pattern as they existed before the First World War and before the introduction of a popularized Freudian discourse. That is, he portrays a "holy" family infiltrated from without, rather than harmed from within. It is not intra-familial relations that usually rock the boat, as will be the case later on, but an outsider, or an "outside" in the sense of impossible environmental conditions that force people into crimes that harm the family. (*Broken Blossoms*, where the father Battling Burrows abuses and finally kills his daughter, would be an example of the latter.) Here, Griffith's *The Mothering Heart* and *The Mother and the Law* will provide respective examples of the types.

In *The Mothering Heart*, the outsider is still a class enemy. The seducer comes from a pleasure-loving upper class that all the self-righteous moralizing directors – especially Lois Weber – vehemently opposed. However, a female seductress, familiar from the European Romantic tradition and to be re-introduced in the cinema in Frank Powell's *A Fool There Was* (1914), replaces the more usual Victorian *male* one.[9] The opening shots of Gish cuddling the puppies codes her as the all-giving mother who against her better judgement gives in to her lover's pleas for marriage. She puts her husband's needs first and helps the family along by doubling her labour within the home, only to find, as the film's inter-title tells us, that "With prosperity comes rejection of homely joys." The husband becomes impatient for entertainment. This could be a sign of an intra-familial problem, suggesting that Gish is not sufficiently exciting any more, but it seems that the need arises from external temptations and social forms. The husband drags Gish to a fancy café with a floor-show; there he is seduced by an upper-class woman. The liaison drives Gish home to her mother, where she gives birth to her baby and temporarily finds joy. The baby's sudden death coincides with the husband's rejection by his mistress, and the couple are reconciled in their joint loss.

Gish consistently subordinates her desires and needs to those of her husband and baby. Her one moment of self-expression is the powerful scene toward the end of the film where, distraught over the baby's death, she hacks down the roses in the garden. Otherwise, she maintains the saintly, nurturing, all-forgiving position, and remains pure throughout.

97

In *The Mother and the Law*, the central female figure likewise remains unsullied and innocent, but here the causes for threat to the "holy" family arise from a complex interaction of social and economic forces. The heroine's near collapse into a street-woman like the Friendless One, and her near rape, from which she is ironically saved by the jealousy of the Friendless One, dramatize the fragility of purity in such an environment. Although it is important that Mae Marsh in *The Mother and the Law* has a degree of mischievousness – usually the only avenue for expression of female subjectivity – the problem is never female desire per se, but how to preserve the pure woman, who is given an inviolable essence.

How are we to account for this variation from the European form of the maternal sacrifice pattern? On the level of *political* discourses, the change may be part of the different political implications of the fallen woman story in North America. America represented the victory of the Liberal Humanist Ideal anticipated in *East Lynne*. Or to put it differently, North America's entire self-image depended on the figure of the rational, beneficent, liberal male hero, represented in the Founding Fathers and in the Declaration of Independence. There was no aristocracy per se (though there was the largely self-made upper class), and thus no political need to depict that class as evil. As will be clear in the 1925 *East Lynne* film, the main fear seemed to be the instability of the *masculine*. North American culture, as Leslie Fiedler (1966) has argued, had long tended toward excessive fear of the feminine (particularly the phallic mother) perhaps as a result of there being no aristocratic enemy. That is, castration fears were displaced into the figure of the seductive upper-class female, the *femme fatale*, who will re-emerge in film noir in the post-war period, when she is no longer necessarily upper-class. The figures in Griffith's *The Mothering Heart* and *The Mother and the Law* are minor versions of the full-blown vamp figure, most graphically represented by Theda Bara in Frank Powell's *A Fool There Was* (noted above).

The upper-class male seducer does continue in film representations, and in fact is the main cause of the heroine's dilemma in Griffith's own *Way Down East*. That narrative, however, is closer to the poor-girl-as-victim pattern than to the proper mother-sacrifice myth as Griffith treats it in the other films mentioned. Gish's seduction as a young girl, and the resulting baby, are the causes of her problems rather than, as in the mother-sacrifice myth, problems arising from the mother's sexual transgression after a happy marriage. Nevertheless, Griffith manages to Americanize this pattern as well: for example, one inter-title, "Motherhood: Woman's Gethesemane," empathizes with the burden of motherhood for the heroine, instead of identifying such suffering with her deserved lot as in *East Lynne*. At the end of the film, the heroine bursts forth in defense of herself, and publicly names her male oppressor: "Suppose they found out about your past life?", she says to Sanderson. Sanderson's reply, "O, it's different with a *man*; he's supposed to sow his wild oats," only underscores the sexual double standard. Although

Gish, more in keeping with earlier traditions, then rushes self-destructively out into the storm, no nineteenth-century heroine would have turned on her seducer in such a bold manner. We find then a strange intermixing of elements of the "new woman," and old, sentimental, sacrifice traditions.

In the case of Griffith's *The Mothering Heart*, the European maternal-sacrifice figure, in which the mother's loss is linked explicitly to sexuality and to seduction by the upper-class male, has been split into two. There is the victim-mother, whose plight results from the fallen male's sexual crime, and then the evil seductress, whose sexuality has lured the male and who, although not *literally* a mother, betrays elements of the feared castrating mother.

In all the films, however, the idealized mother remains pure and unsullied, heroic in her undying loyalty and often ultimate forgiveness, while the transgressing male, of whatever class, must suffer for his sins and be redeemed through her. But the two female figures threaten to collapse into one another; the idealized figure seems an elaborate defense against the phallic mother (Hansen 1991). The system, in any case, neatly splits women into virgins and whores, in a way not true in the European paradigm. This is evident in the American reworkings of *East Lynne*. Isabel's sexual desire for Levison, which played a central role in the original novel, is all but eradicated in an attempt to minimize the link of the ideal virgin-mother to evil and retain her mythic purity. She is instead made to suffer a lack of good judgement from misplaced emotions, resulting in her excessive, irrational jealousy.

In the case of *The Mother and the Law*, there are dangerous social forces of various kinds (crime groups, prostitutes, meddling middle-class reformers), who threaten the heroine's purity and goodness. In a sense, this latter type embodies the Thoreauvian notion of the city or the "crowd" as leading to evils like poverty, crime, dishonesty, moral corruption. It is this anti-city position that Vidor takes up in his 1928 film, *The Crowd* (see Chapter 7), and it stands in contrast to the European preoccupation with class prejudices and rivalries instead of gender and city-versus-nature themes.

Griffith, then, was one conduit for the entry into film of the sentimental tradition, still prevalent on the American stage at the turn of the century. Like some other directors (such as Weber), he focused his gaze on the contemporary American scene as well as on the standard stage melodramas, like *The Clansman*, that treated events in America's past. Breaking with the traditions of stage melodrama that included many European stories in their standard fare, Griffith took pains to adhere to the North American scene and to contemporary issues facing working-class and lower-middle-class people. There were exceptions, such as his ground-breaking four-reel *Judith of Bethulia* (1914) or dramas taken from sentimental British poetry by Browning or Tennyson. His Americanization of the maternal-sacrifice melodrama, along with other directors like Lois Weber working in the early 1910s, provides part of the context for representations in the *East Lynne* film versions, to which I will now turn.

If the *East Lynne* film versions manifest some strain in their effort to integrate the original European story into the contemporary American version of nineteenth-century sentimentalism, and also seem anachronistic in their historical period, why did the studios return to this form of the mother-sacrifice myth? One could say that the recourse to this mythic pattern, even on Griffith's part, was precisely a reaction to events (such as suffragettism, or the rise of the New Woman) in the social formation. But that suggests too simplistic a relationship between the terrain of the Imaginary and that of the social formation. Certainly, in the case of *East Lynne*, a complex set of processes is at work such that the revitalization of the mythic pattern in its European form at once produced a kind of self-congratulatory feeling for Americans not living in a rigidly hierarchized class society, and satisfied sadistic urges toward woman, exacerbated by women's increasing political and social demands. Recourse to the European setting enabled the displacement of such sadistic urges safely into a terrain far removed from North America.

There are at least six proper US films of *East Lynne* from 1913 to 1931, a seventh being called *East Lynne With Variations* (1919). While all versions vary in their degree of patterning on play versions like Ned Alpert's, all clearly derive from stage scripts rather than directly from the novel.

The 1916 version, directed by Bertram Bracken and starring Theda Bara, is interesting as presenting Bara in a role quite the reverse of her carefully cultivated vamp (Frank Powell's Fox film launching the image, *A Fool There Was*, was released in 1914). But in a strange way, the vamp image is pasted over what the script attempts to show as a blameless Isabel. Bara's coaled, black eyes, her dark hair and haunted look contradict the Hollywood stereotype of a happily married wife and mother that the text calls for. More than either the novel or the 1925 film version, Bracken's script depicts the tragedy as the sole result of Levison, the evil seducer outside of the family. The concept of the snake in the Garden of Eden, suggested in the original but tempered in favor of a more complex analysis of subjectivity and desire, is here literalized: when Levison is planting the seeds of jealousy in Isabel's mind, we cut to an image of a snake slithering through the grass. This is one of the places where Mary Murillo's scenario follows Ned Alpert's play, in which, indeed, Levison actually forges a note to Carlyle that he feigns comes from Barbara!

Bracken updates the story to contemporary settings and clothes (as I assume play versions did), and again presents many of the characters as semi-comic caricatures: Lord Mount Severn is a bad-tempered, drunken invalid; Archibald is over-earnest; Levison is evil incarnate – he is seen kicking a dog needlessly; Isabel is sad-faced and over-dramatic. However, this version does not exploit the Cornelia–Dill comedy, since Cornelia's role is much reduced and Dill absent.

Bracken's film manages to tell its story only in a rather clumsy manner, and the state of the art then was barely equipped to deal with the complexities and multiple plot lines of a five-hundred-page novel in one hour of film time. Events happen so rapidly and by chance in the film that the spectator often has no time to become any more involved with the characters than was possible in the context of late-nineteenth-century theatrical melodrama. As Nicolas Vardac (1977) notes, by that time stage plots were so well-worn, so mechanical and fixed, so allegorical, that audience interest was taken up in the elaborate stage spectacle. The insistent audience demand for realism taxed stage facilities to their utmost, and, according to Vardac, partly determined the invention of the moving picture to satisfy a demand no longer able to be fulfilled on the stage. But while film was perfectly fitted to providing realism, it was at first sometimes limited by its own devotion to stage-like scripts and to filming stage plays.

Nevertheless, in some hands, it was beginning to realize its unique possibilities for the inscription of subjectivity in the screen–spectator relationship. Indeed, Bracken and his photographer, Rial Schellinger, at times use the camera and editing to convey the subtleties of relationships. The Hare family here come closer than the later version to Ellen Wood's characterization; Mrs Hare is sickly and devoted to her son, Barbara Hare a sensible, rather staid young woman, who does what she must, and who is not above being jealous of Isabel's remaining presence in her children, even when she is presumed dead.

The film gains dramatic power in the scenes of Isabel's blind jealousy through Levison's artful manipulations. Theda Bara, as actress, is clearly more suited to representing jealousy than joy, and her brooding face and body are effective here and in the following scenes of her destruction and fateful return to East Lynne. While the play already de-emphasized Isabel's desire for Levison and her unhappiness in marriage, the 1916 film version eliminates what made Isabel's situation all but tragic and subversive in the novel – namely her marital unhappiness and her erotic desire for Levison. The film thus aims to preserve the concept of the "holy" family, unsullied from within and merely destroyed by evil external forces. Already miserable as she leaves with Levison, Isabel is not party to her destruction (as she was slightly in the novel), and marital relations are cleared of blame. As we will see later on, this change is part of the Americanization of an essentially European mother-sacrifice myth.

However, within its prescribed limits, the film does at times exploit its special resources to convey subtle emotions. For instance, in a key scene early on, all the complexities of two sets of triangular desire are efficiently conveyed through a combination of framing (using front-frame for one couple, the rear for another), and of carefully inserted facial close-ups. The two sets of misplaced desire (Mrs Vane–Levison–Isabel; Barbara Hare–Archibald–Isabel) both lead to Isabel as object of desire. Judiciously placed close-ups of both Barbara Hare and Mrs Vane expose their emotions on seeing the men they love fascinated by Isabel's dark, soulful beauty. She, meanwhile, avoids looks, gives misleading looks, or stares confusedly out of the frame, thus leaving ambiguity about what she *does* desire. At first she seems interested in Carlyle, then in Levison; when the latter is drawn aside by Mrs Vane, Isabel turns back to Carlyle; she then apparently sizes up the two men (at one point each is on either side of her, and her eyes are seen to dart glances each way, in turn), and decides for Carlyle, whom she calls "the most decent of men."

Later on the film again manages to elicit spectator identification with a character, as in the poignant moment when Isabel says goodbye to her children, a scene that can hardly fail to be pathetic. In a later scene, when Isabel is already in disguise, we have a shot of her intense longing for her children that leads her to accept the East Lynne post as Governess. Towards the end we get a glimmering of some of the symbiotic Isabel–William and Isabel–Carlyle bonding when the camera displays the three of them linked together as the child dies. Isabel strokes her son's head, her arm stretched toward him, while Carlyle similarly leans with out-stretched arm toward Isabel. But this is only too soon interrupted with the histrionics of first William's, and then immediately afterwards Isabel's, death. The 1916 film follows the Alpert play in having Isabel reveal herself to her dying son, when he calls for his mother, with the words: "Look at me! I am your mother," whereas, in the novel, Isabel holds out to the end. In this case, as we saw, the child dies anyway. In the 1916 film version, the Carlyle–Isabel relationship is privileged at the end, rather than the Carlyle–Barbara one, as in the novel and the 1925 film. As she dies in Carlyle's arms, Isabel whispers "Until Eternity!", and Carlyle repeats her words in evident pain, as the shot fades. The film thus seals the fantasy of an undying, idyllic love.

The 1925 version of the film stands somewhere in between the original novel and the Ned Albert play. Directed this time by Emmett Flynn (again for William Fox), the film stars Alma Rubens as a haunting Lady Isabel, and Edmund Lowe as Archibald Carlyle. Longer than the 1916 version, this one includes more of the Hare family sub-plot, all but dropped from the earlier film, which in any case serves mainly to provide the reason for Barbara Hare's and Carlyle's secret meetings. (However, in the book it also importantly echoes gender issues in revealing the close mother–son bonding between Richard Hare and Mrs Hare; part of the work of the novel is to remedy the boy's "feminization" resulting from that closeness, but this is all absent from the film.)

The film exaggerates the patriarchal nature of the Hare family, making Judge Hare into a kind of semi-comic monster, Mrs Hare the frail, sickly and dominated ideal mother, and the children healthy and lively but intimidated by their father. There are many scenes showing Mrs Hare and Barbara cowering in the corner or half-way up the stairs while Judge Hare rants on below. Barbara Hare's one aim in life, from the start, is to make herself into the ideal mother-housewife so that Carlyle will marry her, while her brother is consumed with desire for the inappropriate, loose and lower-class Affy Hallijohn, taking great risks to see her.

This more or less happy and conforming middle-class family is contrasted to the unhappy and broken aristocratic Severn family. Not only is Lord Mount Severn seriously ill, but also he has squandered his wealth, and, penniless, is forced to sell East Lynne to Archibald Carlyle. In addition, his motherless daughter, Lady Isabel, is seen flirting with an obviously unsuitable rake, Levison.

These scenes are important in at least permitting some expression of Isabel's erotic desire. She is seen in a romantic nature setting, perched on a tree branch, while Levison woos her. Levison's evil is signified by his constantly eating apples, sign of the snake in the Garden of Eden, who tempted first Eve and then Adam to bite the forbidden fruit. But Isabel is clearly infatuated, gazing up at Levison with her big, dark eyes, visibly moved when they kiss. It is only her father's severe disapproval, his extracting a promise that she will not marry Levison should he die that induces her to quench her desire and agree to marry Carlyle, who fell in love with Isabel at first sight.

While in the novel, Carlyle represented the Ideal Liberal Humanist, mediating between these two families separated by class, and creating the ideal middle-class family as the synthesis of the two, this film version, even more than the earlier one, presents a very different kind of Carlyle, as part of the Americanization of the mother-sacrifice myth. Carlyle is interestingly "feminized," as we see at once in the opening scene when he arrives at the Hare's from London replete with female-looking packages for the women. More so than the figure in the novel, Carlyle here is soft, playful, accessible and emotional. He does not represent the Law Man, cover for the Law of the Father, as in the novel; he is, rather, playful with Barbara Hare, and then, after falling in love with and marrying Lady Isabel, happy to exist on her child-like, funloving plane. The scene in which we watch Isabel and Archibald putting their children to bed and playing with them is a wonderful example of affectionate parenting, but is especially unusual in showing the father playing so fondly and so childishly. This Carlyle, unlike the novelistic one, is also far more obviously emotional when Isabel leaves and again when she returns, and stands in stark contrast to Judge Hare, the supremely authoritarian father who wields total control over his family members. This text apparently argues for a masculine ideal on the level of gender-role rather than on the level of the political formation: the ideal father, it seems to say, would be a cross between the too-fond and therefore vulnerable Carlyle, and the rigid, over-controlling Judge.

Isabel's mothering in the scene mentioned above has particular diegetic importance, bringing emotional resonance to the scene much later on when William dies. In the early scene, when the boy is in robust health and romping happily with his mother, Isabel lovingly plays "This Little Piggy Went To Market" with him, putting the child's toes in her mouth as she plays and indicating her passionate involvement with him. In this film version, unlike others, it is this very passionate symbiosis that will save William from death. When William calls for his mother as he is dying, Isabel simply begins to play "This Little Piggy," putting now the child's fingers in her mouth. The sick child, recognizing his mother unconsciously through this action, is given the strength to recover.

But this version also permits articulation of even more unconscious Oedipal fantasies in the secret bond between Isabel and Carlyle immediately after William recovers. Carlyle peeks into the room as Isabel is playing "Little Piggy" with William, and recognizes her. He agrees not to divulge her identity, and then, when she becomes ill, he comes regularly to her, in secret. Barbara never knows who the governess her husband visits really is. In this way, Isabel wins the Father from the Mother, in the current household set up. But she also rewins her husband from the woman who threatened her marriage in Isabel's mind. Finally, she regains her literal father, Mount Severn, whom she possessed in a certain sense as her mother was dead, and who in the first place handed her over to Carlyle.

Differences between these two adaptations arise in part from their emergence in different decades and at different points in Hollywood's institutional history. The 1916 version stays close to the late nineteenth-century play version and appears to cope with the difference between the political discourses in the original, and those prevalent in North America at the time of the film's production, largely through mockery and exaggeration. Since the novel's preoccupation with changing images of the British aristocratic and middle classes was irrelevant in early twentieth century North America, that dimension is dropped and the plot transformed into the problem of "good" versus "evil."

The 1925 version, on the other hand, displaces the original political discourses about class into the area of gender, and here the contrasts are fascinating. For, instead of Carlyle representing the rational, puritanical and controlled ideal middle-class male figure found in the novel, the Fox Carlyle is effeminized. The 1925 text is more concerned with addressing American masculine than feminine ideals; the film may be seen as a warning against the male abrogation of his rational, distanced role, for Carlyle's lack of strictness is seen to produce Isabel's fall. In a parallel move, Mrs Hare's over-affectionate relationship to her son Richard may be viewed as causing *his* sexual lapse. Addressing a specifically American concern (Douglas 1977), the film warns of a male feminization perhaps provoked, as in our own period, by challenges to traditional gender roles in the various women's movements of the time. Meanwhile, the working-class thriller plot is reduced in both film versions, possibly because those particular forms of class relations were not germane to early-twentieth-century North America.

On the psychoanalytic level, it is striking how both versions divert the original story in a phallocentric direction that the novel tentatively challenged. First, Isabel's mother, not mentioned once, is totally repressed in both versions. These Hollywood Isabels have heeded Helene Deutsch's advice before it was given, and turned themselves towards the Father: both are living alone with the Father as the film opens, and the relationship is portrayed as incestuously close in the later version. There is no indication of Isabel's fond memories of her mother or of the cross symbol that keeps reminding the reader of the mother in the novel. Neither film suggests any slippage from desire for the lost mother to desire for the seductive male. On the contrary, the strong mother–son bond is represented as replacing heterosexuality – as a desire for the Father, as in the Freudian and Lacanian systems. In the 1925 film alone, this mother-love is so all-powerful that it *cures* the dying William. And once this supreme act of love is accomplished – an act which drains Isabel of all her remaining life – her libidinal energy is turned toward Carlyle; in this version, Isabel ekes out a final satisfaction in his illicit (because he is now remarried) love before she dies.

Second, Isabel's status as object of exchange between men is clearly marked in the 1925 film. Here, Lord Mount Severn, deeply disturbed by his daughter's developing sexuality, and in particular her attraction to Levison, willingly hands her over to Carlyle, whom Isabel admits she does not love. As in the novel, Carlyle assures her she will grow to love him in time.

Third, unlike the novel, neither film indicates any unhappiness in the marriage, despite Isabel's original lack of love. On the contrary, the marriage is miraculously happy, and we have many shots of parents and children playing joyfully. In the film Isabel's mind, it is Carlyle who forces her into Levison's hands through his apparent infidelity with Barbara Hare. The Hollywood Isabel, then, is not imaged as following her desire, but rather motivated by what appears to be her husband's desire. The note she leaves in both versions explains that she was driven away by Carlyle's love for Barbara.

Thus unlike the nineteenth-century British novel, which was written by a woman primarily addressing a female audience, the twentieth-century American films, directed and adapted within the Hollywood system, construct a cleanly sealed phallocentric discourse. Ellen Wood also wrote within the constraints of a patriarchal discourse; her gender does not free her to speak the female position in any unmediated way; nor does it position her that differently from the male film directors. But her text has some potentially subversive elements in its exposure of women's sufferings, frustrations and oppressions within the male system. The films apparently accept the moralizing voice of the novel's narrator as the position of the text as a whole; in fact, as we saw, that voice is often a cover for subversive elements spoken through the gaps in the patriarchal system. It is in such "gaps" that the text addresses the problem of excess female desire, the boredom and emptiness of most bourgeois marriages, and in so doing it articulates repressed needs, wishes and fantasies. Although the novel recuperates these desires through Isabel's long punishment for daring to transgress given codes, something remains for the female reader in having such fantasies articulated.

In replacing a struggling feminine voice by a phallocentric discourse, the films address male Oedipal fantasies rather than female ones. Carlyle's feminine identification is portrayed rather than Isabel's. While one might argue that this identification is also often repressed, it is very evident in the woman's melodrama. Indeed, as Laura Mulvey (1977–8) noted, the genre arises at least in part as a correction of the misogyny in the dominant male genres. The films speak the traditional male yearning for the lost mother object evident also in the novel, showing both Carlyle and Richard Hare closely bonded with a mother or a mother surrogate. A male viewer could identify both with the young William, showered with love and affection by the beautiful Alma Rubens, and with the handsome Carlyle who first wins Isabel and then the almost equally beautiful Barbara Hare; and who regains the dying Isabel's love as well! At the same time, the male viewer is warned against an excessive feminine identification; the common sense, autonomous Barbara of the 1925 version is preferred over the passionate, soulful Isabel partly because she prohibits any over-identification on Carlyle's part. She will make sure that the masculine retains its needed place, thus allaying the specifically American fear of males becoming too "soft."

We thus see how dominant representations, even in the forms that specifically address women, satisfy unconscious male desire more than any possible unconscious female ones. In the films in particular, the female spectator can receive pleasure only through the fantasy of surrendering all for the phallus. Isabel's "mistake" in the films is not a desire that the system cannot accommodate, but rather misplaced, revengeful jealousy. Since Isabel has Carlyle, the films seem to say, what more can she need? In positing this as the question, the Hollywood versions of *East Lynne* recuperate even the mildly subversive aspects of Ellen Wood's novel.

6

THE MATERNAL MELODRAMA: THE "PHALLIC" MOTHER PARADIGM

Now Voyager (1942) and *Marnie* (1964)

Freud's contribution in relation to the mother is his discovery of the mother in the unconscious. While the phallocentric aspects of his theories are a problem for feminists, this should not be confused with a second problem, namely the neo-Freudian collapsing of the level of the social (the historical mother) and the psychic (the mother in the unconscious). (See discussions in Chapter 3.) Helene Deutsch's theories of the woman psychically satisfied only in mothering buttressed images of the saintly "angel" mother-figure, like those in *East Lynne*, abounding in fiction and film; Karen Horney's study of maternal narcissism – that is of the mother's projecting on to the child her own unfulfilled desires, or of her use of the child to play out problems with her own mother – were reduced in the post-Freud period to notions of masculine identity and penis envy inhibiting successful mothering. Melanie Klein's important theory of the two internalized unconscious (imaginary) mothers arising from the child's experience at the breast was later literalized in the alternate "idealized" nurturing mother and the dominating "phallic" one that popular materials featured.

I want to discuss Klein's and Horney's theories since their scenarios, reduced and simplified, are echoed in 1940s films like *Now Voyager*. Kristeva's recent development of such theories, in turn, illuminates Hitchcock's 1960s film, *Marnie*, which I will compare to *Now Voyager*. These two films together are representative of the many films with "phallic" mothers (or their surrogates), including *Rebecca, Little Foxes, The Snake Pit, Secret Beyond the Door, Psycho* and *The Birds*.

In developing Freud's theories while working in Britain in the mid-1920s, Melanie Klein stressed the child's unconscious fantasies of being devoured by the mother. Klein's work is important since she theorized the centrality of symbol-formation in ego-development; this enabled her to make a clear distinction between the mother in the unconscious and the "real" or historical mother. The fantasy of the attacking mother arises, according to Klein, out of earlier fantasies of parental coitus in which the father "attacks" the mother.

107

This leads to the child's sadistic fantasies of biting, tearing or stamping the parents to bits (Klein 1930: 24). These in turn produce fantasies of the devouring parent in punishment for what the *child* has done.

Klein also theorized that early on the child has two internalized unconscious mothers which emerge from its experience in relation to the breast; the child first symbolizes a "good" and a "bad" breast (according to whether the breast is present and providing milk, or absent and leaving the child in need), which are transferred to the whole body of the mother once the child reaches that level of cognition. It is easy to see how these two unconscious mothers later become the alternate "ideal" nurturing and evil "phallic," denying mothers. It is also clear that, from this psychoanalytic perspective, the mother in the social cannot hope to satisfy the infant, no matter what she does or how nurturing she is.

As Sylvia Brody (1956) has shown, other psychoanalysts in the 1920s tended to focus on whether or not a mother accepted or rejected the child. Inevitably, given that people were writing out of their clinical experience, focus was on neurotic mothers, and on the degree to which a woman's own unresolved problems with her mother in turn affected her mothering. Work was done on maternal narcissism (which Freud had previously raised), on the mother's projecting on to the child her own unfulfilled desires, on the mother's use of the child to satisfy needs for mothering that remained from her own childhood; and finally (and what is most relevant to the "phallic" mother representation), on the degree to which a woman's masculine identity – her penis envy – would inhibit successful mothering.

It is not accidental that it is Freud's female followers who developed theories about the child's conception of the mother in the unconscious and about what mothering involved for women. I discussed the importance of Helene Deutsch's theories in buttressing and continuing images of the woman psychically satisfied in mothering; in relation to the "phallic" mother it is again the female analysts who are most relevant. But their reasons for working on mothering issues are not necessarily those that Freud gives;[1] Freud tried to slip out of responsibility for not focusing on the pre-Oedipal period, which is where the mother is central, by arguing that it was the female analyst's *gender* that permitted a mother-transference and thereby access to data on this early phase. It is now clear that transference is not tied in that literal way to gender and thus Freud could have worked with the early mother–child phase had he been interested in it. Most likely, it was because of their own conflicts as mothers and daughters that female analysts wrote about those relationships.

Karen Horney exemplifies the type of work Brody notes as characteristic of the 1920s. Writing in the wake of both Deutsch and Klein, Horney (1967b) focuses mainly on the way "in which the relation of the mother to her own parents is reflected in her attitude toward her children." She shows how an unconscious father fixation was displaced first onto a mother's son, and then onto her young male pupils; in both cases, the woman inverted the predictable attraction to older men (like her father) through the mechanism of wishing to reverse the actual childhood situation in which she could win the love of her unattainable father. If she could be "big," Horney notes, and him "small," then she could be in control. The patient in question had married a man younger than herself, with a weaker personality, and their relationship had a mother–son quality prior to the birth of her son, when her interest in her husband declined. Her obsessive overprotectiveness toward her son, according to Horney, resulted in the son developing obsessional neurosis and states of extreme anxiety (1967b: 176).

Citing another case, Horney turns to the problems in mothering caused by an unconscious mother-fixation. Horney adheres to Freud's notion of the "feminine" as embodying a proper position of passivity in relation to the male, although she is very aware of the social reasons for a woman rejecting such a position (1967b: 179). Acquiring for whatever reasons a dislike for her own female world, Horney notes, such a girl "emotionally turns away from her innate sexual role and develops masculine tendencies and fantasies." Such women, Horney continues, "are frigid and dissatisfied and their masculine tendencies will show, for instance, in the wish to be domineering" (1967b: 180). These masculine tendencies may result in the mother desiring to have absolute control over her children, or, in defense against such wishes, to be too lax with them.

Perhaps most important for my concerns is Horney's representation of "masculine mothers" – representations that are duplicated and literalized in the films under study here. Horney observes that such mothers often develop an over-attachment to the *daughter* similar to that which other mothers feel toward their *sons* (1967b: 180). The result may cripple the daughter's capacity to establish normal relations with men, since she in turn has developed an overattachment to *her* mother. Horney tells us that such mothers desire to control the girl-child absolutely by prying into her affairs relentlessly.

> The resentment against the female role [Horney says] comes out in teaching the children that men are brutes and women are suffering creatures, that the female role is distasteful and pitiable, that menstruation is a disease ("curse") and sexual intercourse is a sacrifice to the lusts of the husband.
>
> (Horney 1967b: 180)

Such mothers will be particularly disapproving of any evidence of sexual interests on the part of their daughters.

Horney's work, like that of Deutsch, shows the collapsing of the unconscious and the social mothers that Klein had tried to keep separate: for Horney attributes a direct cause–effect relationship between the mother's unconscious and the child's problems, without taking into account the child's Imaginary mothers, about which the social mother can do very little. This trend was developed by later Freudian psychoanalysts who betray extreme concern for the child's emotional health. They stress the literal level of maternal behaviour to the exclusion of the level of fantasy or the role of the child's "Imaginary points of identification" in the mother–child relationship so poignantly discussed by Maud Mannoni (1970) (see pp. 54–5).

Film is perhaps more guilty than other art forms of performing a similar collapsing of the unconscious and social mothers, and in the process, again literalizing and reducing Freudian motherhood theory. But the desire to confine the mother within restricted pop-Freudian stereotypes is itself a symptom of the mother's increasing cultural threat in the post-war period. The 1940s arguably represent a transitional phase between a cultural motherhood role that prescribed a stern presence, and the Freudian "attentive" mother, whose image was to evoke the polar opposite, an hysterical "phallic" mother. If we compare a film like *Now Voyager* (1942) with Hitchcock's *Marnie* (1964) the change will be clear: significantly, however, we are talking about degrees of difference rather than substantive change. On some levels, *Now Voyager* and *Marnie* are only too similar in their representations of mother–daughter relations. But shifts in the cultural motherhood discourse resulting from the films' different historical contexts and cinematic genres produce significant alterations in emphasis and point of view.

In between *Now Voyager* and *Marnie* are the immediately post Second World War films – *The Locket* (1946), *Secret Beyond the Door* (1948), *The Snake Pit* (1948) – where the evil mother has less prominence or where the stress is not so much on the mother's specific damage to the child's psyche. These films, however, mark the first impact of women's move into the work-force during the war. The increased level of women's threat to returning veterans began to stimulate a deeper kind of reaction for which Freud's theories became a convenient conduit.

It is the uses of the new popularized Freudian discourse that I will analyze in looking first at *Now Voyager*. I will argue for its status as a text transitional between a cultural-role theory of the mother and later "hysterical" texts like Hitchcock's *Marnie*. *Now Voyager* arguably still works with the nineteenth-century concept of the mother as educator, teacher, purveyor of Christian moral values, but it combines this stance with the new Freudian awareness of Oedipality and of the psychic damage that mothers may inflict. Because Freudian theory is only just being assimilated culturally, the text does not yet *embody* the level of the psychoanalytic; it rather *uses* psychoanalysis as a narrative discourse, as a means for producing character-change and explaining mother–daughter interaction. Generically a "woman's melodrama," the text asks the spectator to identify with, and to appreciate, the daughter's, Charlotte Vale's, development to maturity and autonomy – her triumphing over her oppressive mother.

Marnie rejects this cognitive-constructive level and rather positions the spectator between identifying with the heroine's terrifying mother-related

Figure 4a   Rapper's *Now Voyager* (1942)
Dr Jaquith establishes a relationship with Charlotte Vale, driven into herself by
her mother's aggression.

neurosis and the hero's self-confident analysis and mastery of Marnie's
neurosis (a "mastery" also of both Marnie and her mother). Although the
film pays lip-service to a popularized Freudian discourse in its analysis of the
mother's impact on the girl-child, the text has more to do with a deeper level of
reaction to the mother described by Kristeva in *Powers of Horror*. Generically a
thriller of sorts, *Marnie* speaks mainly from the patriarchal position.

Most analyses of *Now Voyager* focus, naturally enough, on the heroine,
Charlotte Vale (Bette Davis). While there are issues relevant to mother-
images in the Bette Davis figure, Mrs Vale, Charlotte's mother (Gladys
Young), is more pertinent to my immediate concerns since she exemplifies the
negative (possessive, controlling) pole of the split-mother in the popularized
Freudian discourse of the time. Charlotte herself comes to embody the other
"positive" mother-pole in her self-denying nurturing of her lover's child, Tina.

111

Figure 4b   Rapper's *Now Voyager* (1942)
Dr Jaquith berates Mrs Vale, Charlotte's mother, for what she has done to her
daughter.

In this way, the film sets up the mother-duality (phallic/angelic) of Freudian
theory that was not evident in earlier films.

In the first part, the text (relying on psychoanalysis as a discourse)
presents as "true" the notion of the possessive mother as unmediated
cause of her daughter's, Charlotte's, mental illness. The representation of
Mrs Vale in the opening sequence mimics one of Karen Horney's "masculine"
mothers, suffering from penis envy and an unconscious over-attachment to
her daughter. Her figure is harsh, rigid, severe; her hair is scraped back from
her face, highlighting the long thin nose and high cheekbones, while her dress
is pulled tightly up to the neck. Her loud, dominating voice with its sharp,
clipped tone seals the image of a non-nurturing, unyielding mother-figure,
far from the idealized patriarchal feminine.

The confrontation with the psychiatrist, Dr Jaquith (one of a long line of such Hollywood figures to follow),[2] who has been called in by her sister-in-law to help Charlotte, merely authorizes the "reading" of Mrs Vale for the spectator. Jaquith quickly makes a bond with Charlotte and turns his "medical" gaze on to Mrs Vale as well; only now this gaze is thoroughly negative: "If you had deliberately and maliciously planned to destroy your daughter's life, you couldn't have done it more completely," he tells her. This statement supports images provided the spectator in a flashback sequence to a shipboard romance Charlotte had when on vacation with her mother. Mrs Vale's icy manner and unrelenting demands on Charlotte climax in her brutal severing of Charlotte's affair with a petty officer.

Unlike Charlotte, Mrs Vale refuses to surrender to Dr Jaquith and to accept his power to help and cure her daughter. For this refusal, she must be punished, just as, in a parallel move, Charlotte will flourish because of her submission to Dr Jaquith, her entry into the (repressed) erotic relationship that will act as a lever to pry her from her mother. It is only through the text's dehumanization of Mrs Vale – its refusal of any sympathy or sensitivity to her subjectivity, her unconscious, her history/memory – that the text makes possible Charlotte's "freedom." The text insists on the central relationships being those of Charlotte and the surrogate Fathers (the psychiatrist, the lovers); only by punishing Mrs Vale sadistically, and forcing the spectator to hate her, can the narrative pry Charlotte and her mother apart, sever the mother–daughter bonding.

As in Freud's famous case history of Dora, the mother becomes not an entity to be *worked through* in the "proper" psychoanalytic sense, but rather a figure in the background who is dismissed as an object, positioned as an obstacle that must be gotten around rather than as part of a central and dual relationship.

Here psychoanalysis is used as a discourse to repress any feminine that refuses to submit to patriarchal law. For, reading against the grain of the film, Mrs Vale's oppressive behavior arguably arises, in the first place, from her own oppressive positioning in patriarchy. In accord with Monique Plaza's (1981) analysis, Mrs Vale's possessiveness could be seen as her only way of getting something for herself. Her distaste for the patriarchal feminine (and her desire to keep Charlotte away from it), may have legitimately given Mrs Vale's possible knowledge of its oppressive function. The text itself, however, cannot see Mrs Vale's behavior in this manner, and is not interested in its origins. It is precisely such constraints that enable us to see the force of patriarchal law, even in films made for the female spectator and focusing on women's issues.

To this extent, *Now Voyager* would seem to address the popularized Freudian type of mother. Mrs Vale's possessive, controlling behavior serves as a displacement for social anxiety at the very moment (1942) when the United States' entry into the Second World War entailed women's entry into the work-force in large numbers. The fear of the mother's power, spilling out into the public sphere and not safely confined within the home, that such a social situation re-evokes on the unconscious level feeds into the production of the hated, controlling figure. Further, for a short space during the opening sequence, the film touches on deeper psychoanalytic (even Lacanian) levels, showing Mrs Vale as a mother who tries to keep her daughter down with her in the Imaginary – who refuses to release her child into the patriarchal Symbolic. In the first scene, Charlotte, although technically adult, barely has access to language, especially when in the presence of her overpowering mother. The psychiatrist's role is to represent the Third Term (the Father, the Law) that has to come between mother and daughter. This achieved, Charlotte is able to separate and to form an adult sexual relationship of her own.

It is significant that *Now Voyager* represses any attention to the mother, Mrs Vale's, experience of the releasing of Charlotte into the patriarchal symbolic. This shows the patriarchal bias of the film: instead of showing the pathos of our human condition (that the separation from the mother is necessary) – something that Kristeva and other French feminists in particular have begun to explore – the text rather behaves sadistically toward Mrs Vale, acting out a child-like hatred rather than empathizing with both parties in the dyad.

It is precisely the refusal to address the poignancy of Mrs Vale's (and any mother's) position which allows us to see that patriarchal fear of the mother remains; this suggests an arrested desire for the mother – a desire for subjection to her masked as fear. At the start particularly, the film speaks from a position of incomplete entry into the Symbolic, which, if smoothly accomplished, should eliminate any need to fear the mother.

But the film does not continue to function on this level: it quickly accomplishes Charlotte's separation from her mother, and works to distance not only the mother but also the psychoanalytic terrain: first, the film uses the Freudian discourse to "psychoanalyze" the prior nineteenth-century "stern" mother, showing the negative aspects of this sort of command over the child. In this way, the text positions the mother safely for us: it explains her behavior as wrong and as deserving the punishment it gets.

Second, since it is a woman's melodrama, the film situates itself in Charlotte's point of view and grants her increasing subjectivity (in the sense of controlling the narrative, making things happen and forming her own decisions). The film allows us to follow Charlotte's triumph over her mother through her increasing autonomy. We see Charlotte overcoming her fears, and achieving a degree of independence with the help of the various "Fathers" referred to. The fearsome mother is reduced to a whining, bedridden, almost comic object. And meanwhile the text replaces her outmoded mothering with Charlotte's new, self-consciously

Freudian "attentive" surrogate mothering, which has positive and "strong" aspects to it.

Nevertheless, this mothering involves (as required in the paradigm) personal sacrifices in that Charlotte cannot have both the child and the man she loves: in this way, if Charlotte can be seen as maturing into an increasingly self-reliant woman, it is important to note that it is a "maturing" into a predictable patriarchal feminine which exposes the absence of any alternate tradition or perspective with which to identify. The film does, however, raise the problem of female independence – it allow us perhaps to glimpse its parameters, its constraints – in a way quite impossible in a film like *Marnie*.

Here, *Now Voyager* follows the conventions of most women's melodramas: these films allow exploration of woman's desires, wishes, conflicts and often involve a struggle between the male and the female discourse, as here Charlotte contests the discourses of all three men in her life to some degree. (The struggle between mother and daughter, however, involves a patriarchal construction of these relations and thus functions on a more complicit level.) But while these narrative aspects provide some satisfaction to the female viewer, narrative resolutions usually insist on the woman being positioned as subservient to the male. *Now Voyager* provides Charlotte with slightly more autonomy than usual, but her desires are still conventionally patriarchal.

Now Voyager is, then, a transitional film in that it keeps fear about the mother under control through its "analysis" and "placing" of her, and through introducing Charlotte as a counter-balancing figure. This ability to control fears about the mother is increasingly rare in the next decade when films manifest what can be described only as a kind of hysteria in relation to the phallic mother.

Hysteria about the mother – evident in the "monstrous" mother image – was perhaps foreshadowed already in a book written in the same year that *Now Voyager* was released, namely Philip Wylie's *A Generation of Vipers* (1942). Wylie's book betrays the sort of slippage from the unconscious to the social mother that prevails in Hollywood images: that is, he purports to be writing about the social scene (just as films *pretend* to be mimicking "reality"), when the book's language indicates the transferring of unconscious hostility to the mother into a generalized depiction of a *social* mother-figure. Although Wylie is remembered as the one to conceptualize "momism," the virulence of his attack may be forgotten.[3]

After a brief genuflection to Freud's interpretation of "mother-love-in-action" as "an incestuous perversion of a normal instinct," Wylie proceeds, at first relatively gently, to note that "megaloid momworship has got completely out of hand" in North America (1942: 185). Subjectively mapped, he says, our land would have more silver cords and apron strings crisscrossing it than railroads and telephone wires. Mom is everywhere and everything and damned near everybody, and on her depends all the rest of the U.S. Disguised as good old mom, dear old mom, sweet old mom, your loving mom, and so on, she is the bride at every funeral and the corpse at every wedding. Men live for her and die for her, dote upon her and whisper her name as they pass away.

(Wylie 1942: 185)

But Wylie's animosity gradually increases, as he dehumanizes "Mom" by using animal and machine imagery to describe her destructive career.

There follows an elaboration of "Mom's" nefarious doings, leading up to the hysterical comparison of Mom to Hitler: "Like Hitler," Wylie says, Mom

betrays the people who would give her a battle before she brings up her troops . . . . Traitors are shot, yellow stars are slapped on those beneath notice, the good-looking men and boys are rounded up and beaten or sucked into pliability, a new slave population continually goes to work at making more munitions for momism, and mom herself sticks up her head, or maybe the periscope of the woman next door, to find some new region that needs taking over. This technique pervades all she does.

(Wylie 1942: 193–4)

Wylie ends with an excoriation of the radio (he presumably has Soaps in mind) for its "goo, slop, hidden cruelty, and the foreshadowing of national death" (1942: 202). He concludes that "We must face the dynasty of the dames at once, . . . take back our dreams which, without the perfidious materialism of mom, were shaping up a new and braver world" (1942: 203).

One can appreciate that Wylie, writing in the midst of the Second World War, was concerned about the moral state of the world (a concern evident in the rest of the book); to be fair to Wylie, he is also hard on men for their greed and materialism, although he sees their main problem as weakness, succumbing to what are really *female* desires for the accumulation of objects.) But such a rhetorical excoriation of "Mom" for all the United States' ills is obviously hysterical from a contemporary perspective. One can only speculate on how widespread such a stance was, and on its immediate social causes. Presumably women's entry en masse into the labour force to replace the men going to war must have represented an unconscious threat that could be displaced into such a tirade against, note, not the working mother, but the greedy, stay-at-home moms. But obviously, in Wylie legitimate social anxiety is confused with a deeper cultural problem regarding the mother – perhaps the dread of her body that Horney had discussed already in 1932, or

116

what Kristeva has called the "abject" associated with the mother. Kristeva's theory of the abject (Kristeva 1982: 13) illuminates the kind of horror toward the mother that we find in Hitchcock – and particularly his 1964 film *Marnie* – by delineating the place that the mother occupies in patriarchal culture as that which "disturbs identity, system, order. What does not respect borders, positions, rules. The in-between, the ambiguous, the composite."

Kristeva links the phenomenon of abject being to "our earliest attempts to release the hold of *maternal* entity even before existing outside of her" (Kristeva 1982: 13). The mother becomes for the child the realm of the abject that must constantly be struggled against through identification with the Father in the Symbolic. Kristeva notes that one can hardly expect the mother to help the child "become authentic and autonomous in its turn," given her own problems with the phallus that her husband represents (1982: 13). Important for my project is Kristeva's noting that the breaking away from the maternal (the abject) is violent and clumsy "with the constant risk of falling back under the sway of a power as securing as it is stifling" (1982: 13).

The mother, then, becomes a sort of phobic object: a form of the abject, the phobic object has to do with uncertainty over boundaries ("all the more determining as the paternal function was weak or even nonexistent" – 1982: 63), and with the tenuousness of the Symbolic. The cross-cultural importance of the mother, socially and symbolically, results in the need to separate the sexes (a need which is often expressed through rituals of defilement); this means giving men rights over women (Kristeva 1982: 70). But the very victorious masculine, Kristeva notes, "confesses through its very relentlessness against the other, the feminine, that it is threatened by an asymmetrical, irrational, wily, uncontrollable power . . . . That other sex, the feminine, becomes synonymous with a radical evil that is to be suppressed" (1982: 70).

In addition to this already awesome fear of the mother, the mother is the authority that maps out the bodily areas and impresses "differentiation of a proper-clean and improper-dirty, possible and impossible" (1982: 72). Kristeva importantly distinguishes this "maternal authority" of bodily "mapping" from the paternal laws, within which, "with the phallic phase and acquisition of language, the destiny of man will take shape" (1982: 72). It is precisely this repressed maternal authority from the pre-Oedipal, early moment, that is responsible for the culturally pervasive, and for Kristeva, universal, phenomenon of the mother as "abject" (1982: 68).

Kristeva's analysis moves far beyond the classical Freudian formulations found in theorists like Deutsch and Horney; nevertheless, these formulations are important not only because of the use that Hollywood made of them in the war and post Second World War period, but because of their continued use to conceal the deeper horror to do with the abject. In other words, Freudian psychoanalysis, as a discourse, was a means through which culture attempted

Figure 5   Hitchcock's *Marnie* (1956)
Marnie surprises jealous Liz and passive but friendly Mr Rutland by
appropriating the 'wifely' role.

to articulate and defray fears regarding the abject maternal. The angel and
evil mother paradigms that Freud articulated were an easy and useful tool
for re-presenting deep unconscious fears of falling back into the horror of the
mother's being, where boundaries are elided.

I will argue that this pull toward the abject maternal underlies representations of the mother in film; it cannot be made conscious yet constantly
threatens the subject. Perhaps Irigaray (1985c) describes this pull in her
haunting essay "This Sex Which Is Not One;" and it is the horror of the
abject maternal that perhaps accounts for the "monstrous" mother image so
prevalent in Hollywood films like *Marnie*.

The comparison with *Now Voyager* interestingly exposes the new hysteria
toward the mother evident in the genre differences between the films. *Now
Voyager*, as we saw, was a maternal melodrama, the form explicitly addressing

the female spectator and permitting the insertion of female subjectivity in however tenuous a form. *Marnie* significantly legitimizes the horror that it is dealing with by situating itself partly within the thriller genre that is associated with the male look.[4] In fact, the film intermixes the stuff of melodrama (Marnie's family history) with the thriller (Marnie as the criminal whose deeds must be investigated) so as to permit a patriarchal investigation into the very mystery of woman herself. The film then, unlike the woman's melodrama, speaks from the male position, very much as does most film noir. Indeed, the intermixture of melodrama and thriller evokes *Mildred Pierce* and Fritz Lang's *The Blue Gardenia*.[5]

In *Marnie*, the real horror displaced into the thriller genre is produced by Kristeva's "phobic object" which in turn (as noted above) involves early pulsations in the mother–child relationship. One could see the film as constructed precisely as an attempt to articulate and then control the terror of the mother via a clever narrative structure. That is, the actual experience of terror/love in relation to the mother – that duality whereby the child at once desires the mother *and* fears being swamped by the dual relationship which risks, in Kristeva's words, "the loss not of a part (castration) but of the totality of his living being" (Kristeva 1982: 64) – is (as in *Now Voyager*) located in the figure of the heroine, not the hero. Here, however, the film dwells far longer on the daughter's hysterical, panic reaction, to her mother. Whereas the institution of psychoanalysis quickly "saves" the daughter from the mother in *Now Voyager*, in *Marnie* this "saving" constitutes the film's *aporia*, its climax and resolution.

Marnie's relationship to her mother, Mrs Edgar, is then the one that involves terror/love; Mark Rutland's mother is, usefully, dead, and he is fully in control of his relationship with his father. In this way, the depiction of the mother as abject does not implicate the hero. On the contrary, the hero (played by Sean Connery) appropriates the role of the Law/the Father/the Symbolic – the sphere through which the mother can be overcome, or in which such a conquest can *appear* to have been made. Indeed, Rutland's function, like that of Jaquith in the earlier film, is to exorcise the heroine's terror of the mother. But, unlike *Now Voyager*, Mrs Edgar is never actually controlled or rendered harmless as is Mrs Vale: in the climactic final scene, *Marnie* still longs for her mother, still wants something from her (perhaps the illusory oneness?), and is still refused. The spectator is denied the satisfaction of the mother's emotional acceptance of Marnie; Marnie has rather to be pulled brutally away from the mother by Mark Rutland. His tool, the *discourse* of psychoanalysis, has not "worked" for Marnie, as it did so easily and smoothly for Charlotte Vale. Mrs Edgar resists *total* control – something in excess remains, and it is the threat of that excess that brings Mark to brusquely drag Marnie away.

In terms of *genre*, the film's combination of the woman's melodrama and the thriller is, like the psychoanalytic discourse, a device that attempts to erase

119

the trouble that the mother causes in the narrative. For the introduction of the thriller plot into the melodrama usually results in the repression of the female discourse and of female subjectivity; it legitimizes the ultimate control of the narrative by a male protagonist, who is responsible for unraveling the mystery, which (as noted above) turns out to be the mystery of woman herself. It is through assuming the function of investigator of both Marnie and her mother – through his interference in their relationship – that the two women are finally brought under Rutland's control: or, more accurately, the device brings Marnie under his control, and ensures Marnie's separation from her mother; but the mother as noted is not entirely defeated.

The cinematic devices used in relation to Mrs Edgar indicate that the text itself is working on a primal level in relation to her figure. She is an unattractive, awesome and negative presence from the start – the deliberate antithesis, it would seem, to any dominant ideal-mother code. And yet she does not fall neatly into the usual mythic opposite of the "evil" or "possessive" mother, like Mrs Vale; or, in Hitchcock's own oeuvre, the surrogate-mother figure Mrs Danvers in *Rebecca*. She rather occupies some other terrain – more mysterious, more ambiguous and contradictory. The spectator is torn between hatred toward her, for her rejection of Marnie who adores her, and pity for her: this pity emerges once we understand her tragic life; her taking upon herself the murder Marnie accidentally committed as a child, and – on some level – her love for Marnie. And it leaves us confused as to how we are to position her – it means that the question about the mother is never satisfactorily resolved, never quite closed.

We experience Mrs Edgar through Marnie's consciousness (including her unconscious, dream images). Marnie's recurring dream and day-time hallucination (set off whenever she sees the color red) revolves around the traumatic, primal scene of her mother's lovemaking with a sailor, which the child innocently interrupts when a thunderstorm frightens her; the drunken sailor begins to fondle the child, and the mother, taking it for rape, beats him with a poker. When the mother is overcome, Marnie picks up the poker to protect her, and the sailor dies of the child's blows.

The beloved mother is, then, associated with primal terror, sex, blood and death. And the text itself takes Marnie's stance toward her: the screen is suffused with red whenever Marnie has her hallucination; the mother's image is sinister – back-lit, silhouetted and shot from a low-angle; the eerie, rhythmic banging in Marnie's dreams always refers to the walking stick which represents her "castration" in the fight with the sailor (literally, her leg was broken and never properly healed).

At the same time, Marnie loves her mother with a pathetic, slave-like longing that betrays her uncertainty about boundaries and that exposes the tenuousness of the Symbolic which precisely strives to establish clear boundaries. The tenuousness of the Symbolic is underscored in another frequently posited binary opposition in the film – that between "nature" and "civilization." Rutland, a part-time zoologist, is attracted to Marnie precisely because she represents the wild animal in the jungle that always threatens to overwhelm society. (This analogy is made literal in the scene in Rutland's office when the thunderstorm brings on one of Marnie's hallucinations and transforms the place into a temporary "jungle.")

It is this danger of lack of boundaries that Mark Rutland eradicates through his use of a popularized Freudian discourse: Rutland, on the one hand, acts like the zoologist with a wild animal, hunting Marnie down, following her tracks until he captures her; on the other, he reads psychoanalytic books, like *Sexual Aberrations of the Criminal Female*: he interrogates Marnie in the manner of the psychoanalyst searching for psychic clues to her disorder, piecing together bits of the puzzle, despite Marnie's aptly ironic refusals; "You Freud, me Jane?" she says, after one such attempt by Mark at psychoanalyzing her. Finally, Mark locates the mother as the "criminal" who has "ruined" Marnie. In order to "free" Marnie of her, Rutland orchestrates a confrontation, under his supportive, analyst presence. Rutland is waiting in the wings to "possess" Marnie, once the mother is dislodged from her dangerously close position. He thereby restores a patriarchal order that Marnie had severely challenged.

The film works with a simplistic and reductive Freudian scheme of revelation of the "trauma" followed by the instant "catharsis" and "cure" – a pattern familiar from many Hollywood films of the post-war period. Once again, the Hollywood-style psychoanalytic discourse simplifies and refuses any understanding of the mother–daughter relationship in all its pathos and difficulty for the mother as well as the child.[6] It brings under control the dangerously independent stance of both mother and daughter, who articulate hatred of men, who despise sex, and who want to live without men. Indeed, Marnie defends herself well against Rutland's controlling attempts, until he finally brings on her neurotic panic and elicits her cry for help. Theoretically, had Mrs Edgar been able to return Marnie's love openly (she loves her child but cannot express it, for reasons that remain unclear), the two would form a unit unto themselves.[7] The potential for this is enough to cause the "trouble" in the film that must be eradicated: it is an option that is interestingly also refused in *Now Voyager*, but within a different configuration. There it is Charlotte's love for Jerry that remains unfulfilled. She and Tina do not constitute a threat because the *child* is not what Charlotte *really* wants, she substitutes for Jerry. But Marnie does want her mother, and it is the hope of fulfilling this desire that the film wrenches away from her.

Marnie's terror has to do with her fear of losing her mother – either through sex with a man, through her being hurt by a man, or through not being lovable herself. Her terror is linked to need of the mother on a primal level that precedes the entry into language. This is evidently a culturally pervasive fear, as Kristeva (1982) has argued.

121

In this connection, then, it is significant that the historical Hitchcock betrayed this sort of fear of losing the Mother, if we can believe the material in Donald Spoto's biography of the film director. Spoto (1983) quotes Hitchcock as saying, when questioned about his interest in fear:

> Fear? It has influenced my life and my career. I remember when I was five or six. It was a Sunday evening, the only time my parents did not have to work. They put me to bed and went to Hyde Park for a stroll . . . . They were sure I would be asleep until their return. But I woke up, called out, and no one answered. Nothing but night all around me. Shaking, I got up and wandered around the empty, dark house, and finally arriving at the kitchen, found a piece of cold meat which I ate while drying my tears.

This passage is interesting in several ways: that Hitchcock would automatically link a question about fear to this episode is itself important, since fear is directly linked to missing the parents. The phrase "Nothing but night all around me" suggests how the mother fills in the gap in identity indicated here – enables the child to be a subject. Without this mirroring, the child is caught in the terror of loss of subjectivity ("Shaking, I got up and wandered around the empty, dark house"), and significantly, he moves toward the kitchen (the mother's place) and replaces her with food. One might argue that the fascination with horror on the part both of film directors and audiences has to do with this primal fear of losing the mother.

One of cinema's functions is to address specific anxieties that prevail in particular cultures and historical moments. In twentieth-century North America, scholars have argued that desire for the cinema is a desire for repeating Oedipal anxieties in a controlled (or "safe") situation (Barthes 1984; MacCabe 1974). The cinematic apparatus provides the plenitude, the fullness that the child experienced pre-Oedipally and he/she lost with the entry into language. Via the cinematic apparatus, Oedipal anxieties can be vicariously "worked through" in the identification with screen figures, like those in *Now Voyager* and *Marnie*. The narratives move the conflicts toward a resolution, so that the arousal of anxiety is followed by its containment. The heroines are "saved" from the bad mother by being securely ensconced in heterosexual relationships.

It is the ideological underpinnings of the way Oedipal anxieties are resolved that is often overlooked: both *Now Voyager* and *Marnie* are important, ideologically, in dealing with the mother from the point of view of the *female* child so often neglected. Nevertheless, the repetition of negative mother fantasies, and of the need for a male savior, perpetuates mythic stereotypes that tell only one of many possible mother stories. The problem is Freudian theory's fixation on "correct" Oedipal resolution for the woman (meaning her subordination to the male, her entry into motherhood), and its neglect of the desire for the mother, a desire aroused pre-Oedipally.

In the final chapters of this book, I turn to films that try to show other mother–child psychic dynamics – films that resist repeating the two, limited stereotypes focused on so far.

7

THE "RESISTING" TEXT WITHIN THE PATRIARCHAL "FEMININE"

Nineteenth-century women's writing and the "maternal woman's film" in the silent era: *Uncle Tom's Cabin; Herland; The Blot; The Crowd; Applause*

In the previous chapters, I examined both the pattern of maternal sacrifice and its flip side, the phallic mother fantasy, as present within the Maternal Melodrama or "complicit" texts. As was clear, these texts are normally narrated from an implicit male perspective, even when the narrational voice places itself within a female figure; it is for this reason that the two dominant motherhood paradigms threaten to collapse into one another, for both arise from similar castration fears expressed in opposite ways. The mother-sacrifice pattern uncritically embodies the patriarchal unconscious and represents woman's positioning as lack, absence, signifier of passivity. The pattern is often set within the mother's point of view, since for most of the narrative she has accepted her patriarchal positioning and is suffering for her transgression. Or, in the American version, she is blameless and heroic, and thus can be made a central figure. In both cases, she has ceased to be a threat in the male unconscious.

The phallic mother paradigm, on the other hand, is most often narrated from the *child's* point of view since texts are geared toward moralistic condemnation of the (feared) possessive mother-figure. This can be most easily achieved through focus on the mother's negative impact on the child. Occasionally, as in a text like *Little Foxes* when the evil phallic mother is central, judgement of her emerges in the pathetic emptiness of her pyrrhic victory.

However, we saw that in some versions of these mythic patterns, the unconscious contradictions within the narrative surface permit "the 'beneath' or 'behind' – the unthinkable and repressed – to achieve material status" (Gledhill 1986). In other words, the narrational voice, close to the heroine's unconscious, inadvertently reveals repressed resentments about woman's oppressive placement within the nuclear family, particularly her repressed longing for the lost Mother object, or her unmet needs for power and self-fulfillment that may originally have caused the transgressions. At least,

124

such texts can be shown to foreground repressions on the level of the psychoanalytic, and thus to violate the easy "good"/"bad" mother categories of male-identified texts when read by feminists "against the grain."

The "resisting" text, however, goes further than this: it situates itself more fully than the complicit one in the level of the social formation. Its voice places itself within cognitive, secondary-process thinking as against the primary process mode of the complicit text. It is this deliberately rational/cognitive stance – a stance often associated with the explicitly political text – rather than any specific aesthetic strategies, that differentiates these works from the complicit ones. As I noted in Chapter 1, it is the psychodynamic/conscious-rational polarity that governs spectator positioning rather than textual devices per se. Within mainstream fiction and film, resisting texts use realistic strategies not unlike those of the melodramatic/complicit texts, although differing in terms of overall narrational stance. Strategies, that is, open up a space between text and spectator: they interrupt the complete narrative identification elicited by the "cliff-hanger" suspense mode typical of most complicit melodrama.

My distinction here should not be confused with the condemnation of the emotional/irrational realm (read, the feminine) discussed in Chapter 4 in relation to male *Screen* critics, and to Ann Douglas and Alfred Habegger in literary criticism. My whole project stands on suspending the terrain of the popular, and specifically judging the hitherto scorned melodrama genre geared to female audiences. The project hopes to contribute to understanding in what ways patriarchally defined "femaleness" is appealed to in such texts, what pleasures the texts provide. But I am also interested in the function these discourses themselves serve *politically*, *economically*. A political perspective considers the impact on women of repeated victim scenarios, now in relation to social institutions as well as to individual psyches. Economic needs have to be taken into account in each specific instance as constructing women in particular ways in culture. Victim scenarios may ultimately be useful for a particular society's economic needs, but a disservice to the female spectators involved.

The resisting maternal woman's film, on the other hand, may serve women better in terms of opening up a space for critical appraisal of *how* women are constructed or positioned in a particular scenario. The distinction, then, has nothing to do with condemning "femaleness," the terrain of the emotional, or the particular *aesthetic* of the melodrama. It has nothing to do with valuing the *masculine* sphere over the *feminine*: rather, it distinguishes texts in relation to how far they serve to better woman's situations on all levels, in a specific historical context. The male/female bi-polar structure is itself constitutive of the qualities then called "masculine" or "feminine." Even "resisting" texts do not question or challenge this bi-polar structure. It is a matter of distinguishing some texts that at least recognize certain discursively constituted female positions as *oppressive* as against those that simply validate the structure.

The resisting text raises moral/political issues in its very narrative – in the discourses between characters or through disembodied commentary – that are simply not introduced in the complicit text. The melodrama sub-text often remains in passionate identification with heroines – an identification which permits the unconscious of the one writing to flow into the text – but it is balanced by a more detached judgement that brings the discourse into the terrain of the social – relations of power, institutional structures, politics. But these "resisting" texts shift the balance between realism and melodrama in the direction of the cognitive voice not heard in melodrama texts. There is here, as with the complicit text, a range within the grouping, from more weakly to more strongly resisting texts as we shall see.

I found nineteenth-century domestic fictional strategies useful for conceptualizing the resisting film text. It is for this reason that I return to fiction in this chapter. *East Lynne* in Chapter 5 proved useful in allowing a historical accounting for images in the later Hollywood films taken from the story. In this case, different nineteenth-century fictional paradigms provide a similar opportunity for accounting for forms in twentieth-century films, even if the actual stories are not taken from the novels that I analyze. Early film stood in close relationship to literary models, often theatrical melodramas taken from popular nineteenth-century fiction. These film narratives then established the archetypes on which Hollywood created genres that were constantly repeated in the ensuing decades because continually successful. Returning to the fictional forms ultimately behind Hollywood narratives and genres illuminates specific films.

What is important about the nineteenth-century fiction explored briefly here is that these novels established certain strategies through which women demand equal access to the symbolic order: that is, women writers implicitly demand equality rather than subjection in the kinds of figures they construct in their fiction.

Although the strategy is associated largely with the nineteenth century, it was actually Mary Wollstonecraft (1975) who first argued in her 1792 *A Vindication of the Rights of Woman* for woman's right to the sphere of the "rational" (basically the male Symbolic order) from which Rousseau excluded her (E.A. Kaplan 1988). As I argued in Chapter 2, according to Wollstonecraft, if woman's reason were developed, she would stand alongside, and not different from, men. But while I was preoccupied in Chapter 2 with the medical and clerical establishment, and with non-fictional address such as that of Mrs Sigourney, let me now deal briefly with a few representative nineteenth-century fictional women writers before going on to show how this "liberal" or "domestic" feminism persists in twentieth-century film, at least up through the 1930s. It was precisely linking women's melodramas back to nineteenth-century fiction like the ones to be discussed that provided clarity about distinctions between such melodramas.

Nineteenth-century domestic feminism produces fiction which manages to articulate woman's oppressive positioning in such a way that that positioning is exposed, even though the text does not usually consciously critique it.[1] Some texts do more than express female resentment at their positions, and valorize the patriarchally constructed feminine in order to dignify women and to elevate their given status. Often narrated from the feminine perspective, texts such as Harriet Beecher Stowe's *Uncle Tom's Cabin* manage to expose male codes and uses of social power while remaining basically within sentimental traditions of the popular woman's novel. A more explicitly resisting text, such as Charlotte Perkins Gilman's *Herland* (1915), while influenced by those traditions moves beyond them by resorting to the genre of utopian fiction: as a result, her text situates itself primarily within the conscious-rational mode that is present but weaker in Stowe's novel. Gilman's text actually looks toward a later stage of Feminism, in which women see men as the enemy and attempt to construct separate communities. I will look briefly at these two representative examples of mid-nineteenth-century/early-twentieth-century women's writing before turning to the issue of film narratives that seem to continue the fictional tradition, even without Hollywood consciously being influenced by it. It is possible that some of the many play and then film versions of *Uncle Tom's Cabin* helped bring some of Stowe's strategies to writers' awareness.

As Jane Tompkins (1981; 1986) has eloquently shown, *Uncle Tom's Cabin* is primarily concerned with establishing the higher morality of woman's domestic realm. But Stowe does more than this, revealing the falsity of the patriarchal polarity between the "Angel in the House" and the evil phallic mother-figure explored in Chapters 5 and 6. The refusal to categorize mothers in the mythic patriarchal manner arises from the text's close identification with the mother position, as against the distancing that is evident when a text looks with patriarchal eyes. Her text, thus, avoids playing out usual defense mechanisms that are exemplified in Ellen Wood's novel. *East Lynne* begins with a close identification with Isabel as a young romantic woman; but as she becomes a wife and mother, so the narrating voice distances itself from the heroine and increasingly situates itself in patriarchal ideology, articulating (unconsciously) the images that the culture required at the time.

Stowe's text is important precisely because it shatters the easy polarizations of male fantasy. It does this despite its given historical constraints, namely the prevailing constitution of the "feminine" and additional constraints imposed by the context of production and dissemination. The novel appeared as a serial in a woman's magazine, and thus had to conform to certain demands of the serial and its intended female audience. For my purposes here, what is amazing for its time is the novel's way of foregrounding its varied mother-figures as speaking subjects rather than as passive sufferers or evil manipulators.

Once so situated, the mother-figures in the text are seen to defy the mythic paradigms and to refuse easy categorization. In the case of all the women who dominate the text – Rachel Halliday, Aunt Chloe, Mrs Shelby, Mrs Bird, Eliza, Miss Ophelia, Marie St Clare, Little Eva (as child-mother), Simon Legree's mother Cassy – the *context* for their speech and actions is clear, their constraints and limitations obvious. The very plethora of different mother-figures attests to the multiple positions available to mothers as they struggled in various ways to create spaces for themselves within the controlling patriarchal ideology.

From this perspective, Stowe does far more than merely transvalue the subordinate position traditionally assigned Motherhood in patriarchy. That this is an important part of her project is reflected in the much-discussed figure of Rachel Halliday, wielding a beneficent power over her ideal, mother-centered community; it is also reflected in the transformation of the socially constructed, self-sacrificing feminine value into a political agenda involving the Christian "change-of-heart" outlined so well by Jane Tompkins.

More transgressive is the way mothers are shown involved in conflicts and contradictions, and as speaking out strongly in defense of what they know to be right. Mrs Shelby and Mrs Bird, for instance, both severely criticize their husbands' actions in direct confrontations. Mrs Shelby early on tries to dissuade her husband from selling Eliza's child, pitting her nurturing, other-centered values against Mr Shelby's abstract, instrumental morality.[2] Mrs Bird shortly after takes on Senator Bird for having endorsed a new Senate Bill outlawing aid to slaves. While Senator Bird insists that "we musn't suffer our feelings to run away with our judgement" (p. 93), Mrs Bird claims that true morality can arise only from empathic identification with the slaves. She views moral principles arrived by other (usually expedient) means as dangerous, while upholding abstract principles arrived at through passionate involvement.

In a similar manner, less educated slave mothers, like Eliza and later on Cassy, are seen confronting the awesome moral dilemma of being torn between self-preservation and love of child; or their powerlessness is tragically demonstrated by their positioning as passive observers of a child's victimization.

On the psychoanalytic level, equally transgressive is how the body of the text positions itself within the *mother's* fears of loss and separation: this differs from the usual text-position as the abandoned child looking out on a motherless world and blaming the (absent) mother for its woes. Close mother–daughter bondings abound in the text, demonstrating that mother–son bondings (such as that between Eliza and the boy) are not given their usual privileged status. The Oedipal fantasy of eliminating the Father that underlies much nineteenth-century female-bonding (and that arises out of the repressive authoritarian Victorian family) is evident throughout the text, and has led some male critics to read the text as "emasculating" (e.g. Habegger). Such a fantasy is perhaps most touchingly imaged in

128

the surrogate mother–daughter relationship between Cassy and Emmeline towards the end of the novel. Partly spurred by her desire to save Emmeline, but also by revenge for her own earlier intolerable abuse at male hands, Cassy becomes the powerful phallic mother so feared in patriarchal narratives. In Stowe's text, this figure is, however, positively, not negatively, valued: Cassy saves the day by bringing about Simon Legree's mental derangement and death. In the novel, the women gain enough power to undermine the male business of making profit out of non-white human bodies.

From a contemporary and feminist point of view, Stowe's text does have severe limitations, which arise inevitably from the constraints that bind its author. The tradition of sentimental individualism within which Stowe worked made it impossible for her to transcend an essentializing feminism: it was inevitable that her text would argue for a transvalued bourgeois nuclear family as the social form whose discourse could save humanity. Likewise inevitable is the reifying of motherliness as woman's true destiny: Black or white, her figures are rated on a scale according to motherliness.[3]

Significantly, Stowe's male figures are also made moral to the degree that they embody the feminine mother-ideal. Christ as the emblem of the sacrificial Mother represents Stowe's ideal male type as embodied in Uncle Tom, the supreme mother-figure in the text. Women rate high on the scale of spirituality as measured in relation to self-sacrifice and suffering, but biological males, following Christ, can attain the status also. Stowe's text provides a persuasive argument for a society built on the caring ethic.

However, Stowe's essentially millennialist brand of Christianity resulted in a limited social analysis; the text's reversion to an (albeit transvalued) family discourse as what can save humanity is utopian. If Stowe seems aware of the economic issues in her treatment of slavery as a capitalist institution, the work pits morality against capitalism, and evidences no vision of possible alternate and more humane economic relations.

But perhaps most interesting is the intertwining of psychodynamic and conscious/rational elements, and the text's alternation between social criticism and melodrama. Mythic, unconscious elements are evident in the text's passionate identification with the heroines, in the sentimentalizing, and in the obvious fantasies and wish-fulfillments that weigh down the text, especially in the characters of Uncle Tom himself, Oliver St Clare and Little Eva. In the manner of the classical realist text, including the melodrama, the authorial persona assumes an omnipotent stance toward the fictional world, raising no questions about the authority and validity of the text itself. The voice assumes a transparency; it assumes that signifying practices directly present the referent, and does not recognize how the inherently patriarchal language carries with it race and gender stereotypes far from "true" or "natural."

It is partly because Stowe does not raise questions about language, and about woman's special relationship to it, that her black figures end up as stereotypes. Speaking from the privileged white Christian position,

129

Stowe's positioning prevented her from seeing the condescension inscribed in dominant white language about blacks.[4] It is significant that it is the mulatto women, Eliza and especially Cassy, who are the most active and effective; the mulatto, as signifier, is white enough to permit identification on the part of white readers, and she can therefore carry repressed desires (such as the erotic) that would not fit into the white model that must equate sexuality with evil. The mulatto stands between the white woman and the savage dark type, represented by Bertha in *Jane Eyre* and Antoinette in *Wide Sargasso Sea*, who is too black for identification and in any case, whose way leads to an undesirable madness.

But as a result of her historical and class positioning, Stowe's female figures, including the mulattos, are defined solely in terms of their "motherliness." This will be significant in illuminating both Hollywood versions of Fannie Hurst's (1933) novel *Imitation of life* (1934; 1959). The mulatto in both versions refuses the oppressive black female "Mother" position society demands of her, opting to be sexual and to "pass" as white, and in so doing brings about a crisis. Stowe rather adheres to a socially constructed notion of the "feminine," which, in embodying only partial womanhood, leaves out sexuality and fulfillment in intellectual and public spheres. In this way, Stowe's novel does not challenge the bi-polar western constitution of "feminine" and "masculine."

Although Charlotte Perkins Gilman's *Herland* suffers from similar limitations in relation to sexuality, it is in many ways revolutionary and manifests a greater degree of resistance than does Stowe's work. The novel abandons melodramatic devices in the service of its chosen utopian genre, and firmly situates itself in the cognitive-constructive domain. Writing at the turn of the century, Perkins Gilman was one of the first to theorize that a different social organization was essential for more humane interpersonal relations, and to base the new ethic specifically around motherly qualities. *Herland* projects an all-female society based on a caring ethic, itself premissed on mothering. The loving mother–daughter relationship provides the model for all bonding in the community. Only a few women literally mother. Others give birth to parthenogenetically conceived children since there are no men in the community, and then pursue intellectual and physical tasks in an atmosphere of collectivity and democratic functioning.

Herland sets up female representations that are still extraordinary: the women are all gentle, nurturing and yet not boring; the young women that the male intruders pursue are lively and mischievous, and smart enough most of the time to elude their would-be seducers. Along with the senior members of the community who are officially interrogating the intruders, the women engage the men in debates and in so doing reveal their alert intelligence. These women are not ascetics or prudes, but full-bodied and healthy, while still embodying the motherly qualities made passive and boring in dominant patriarchal texts.

Like contemporary feminist utopian fiction (see Chapter 9), *Herland* is important in projecting mythic female representations that alert women readers to other possibilities – that stretch our imaginations and make us see the world we live in (and ourselves) differently. But even as a utopia, Perkins Gilman's world is limited by her nineteenth-century semiotic constraints: first, sexuality is eliminated from the all-female community in the novel, perhaps because Perkins Gilman does not dare to introduce images of sexual relations between women. Motherliness ("goodness") and sexuality, then, are still polarized. Second, the novel subscribes to the problematic eugenic theories of the time, which, as Ann Lane (in Gilman 1915) notes, are far more explicit in a sequel to *Herland*. These theories were part of the drive for social purity defined according to race and sex which emerged as the twentieth century got underway and as immigrants poured into North America. The theories are prevalent in early films, like that by Lois Weber discussed in Chapter 7, which also reflects tensions about race and sex.[5]

This brief discussion of *Uncle Tom's Cabin* and *Herland* has shown that long before film replaced the novel as the dominant popular narrative form, women writers had developed certain strategies for avoiding the complicity of many melodramatic traditions in regard specifically to mother-figures. The articulation of these strategies illuminates some early twentieth-century films, still tied closely to prior popular narrational forms, and enables perception of similar strategies at work in popular film, even though now most of the directors are *male*. Significantly, though, the novels used as sources for "resisting" films like *Imitation of Life* or *Stella Dallas* (which are discussed in Chapter 8) are written by women.

For all its limitations, then, *Herland* (published in 1915) stands ideologically far ahead of any "resisting" film melodramas that Hollywood produced at around the same time. Nevertheless, films from the 1910s and early 1920s in hindsight offer a surprising variety of female images, and a high degree of sensitivity to gender issues compared to films in the classical period. Arguably, it was the closeness to representative nineteenth-century models explored in Stowe and Perkins Gilman that made this possible. Some films take a conscious-rational look at motherhood as an institutional form, exposing some of the semiotic constraints imposed on the "mother" as a social function – namely, a term in a specific set of hierarchically organized discourses. No doubt the eruption into dominant culture of feminist demands through the suffragette movement, and the need to give women traditionally male work during the First World War, had something to do with this, as also the related phenomenon of the existence of a number of feisty female directors, like Lois Weber, or producers, like Mary Pickford.

The "resisting" films from the period are those which deliberately fore-ground the public/male – domestic/female split, making it central to their narrative strategies – a way to make a social comment as against the mere acceptance of such a split in the complicit text. Texts, that is, manifest *some* awareness of gender as a socially constructed institution, rather than simply playing out such constructions. This is true of Lois Weber's *The Blot*, Harold Brennon's *Dancing Mothers*, and King Vidor's *The Crowd*, which will be considered here (some only briefly). Other films, like Mamoulian's *Applause*, explore subtle emotional mother–daughter bondings, and the constraints that patriarchy imposes on such relations.

Lois Weber is significant as an unusually prolific early woman film director – the only female director of the period for whom a substantial body of films remain, and whose films can be seen as in some ways "resisting." Weber first gained notoriety through her daring 1914 film, *Where Are My Children?*, which, in addressing the controversial issues of abortion, eugenics and birth control, stirred up enormous debate (see Degler 1980). *Where Are My Children?* contains contradictory discourses arising from the context of the film's production, cultural preoccupations of the period, and Weber's idiosyncratic concerns. Hollywood's sensitivity to scandal in the 1910s as the cinema aimed for respectability is well known, and accounts for some of the film's conservatism. But this period was one of ferment and debate about the so-called "Woman Question" and the film reflects this. Weber's own puritanical Christian values account for her strong identification with a familiar construction – that of the virtuous working classes, and a wasteful, idle upper class.

The film is split between a conservative, male-identified address in the upper-class story that is the main plot, and a female-identified and more radical address in the sub-plot concerning a working-class mother and child. The question of the title is the question of the *husband* in the upper-class plot concerning wives who deliberately eschew the "duty" of bearing children because they prefer to lounge about drinking, smoking and playing cards. The film condemns these women for this attitude, and even more for going so far as to have illegal abortions.

Here Weber echoes the discourses of medical experts of her time, who also condemned wives who did not immediately rush to bear children. August K. Gardiner's *Conjugal Sins Against the Laws of Life and Health* (1974, originally published 1870) for instance, is a self-conscious polemic against contraception, abortion and infanticide that represents the sort of semiotic, early-modernist (Darwinian) climate in which Weber was working. Indeed, Gardiner's discourse mimics melodrama in its style, which is closer to story-telling than to medical writing per se. He provides short, fictional examples to support broader points, sketching in character types not unlike those that Weber images in her film. For example, Gardiner creates a "poor, deluded girl – seduced, betrayed, abandoned – who, in her wild frenzy destroys the mute evidence of her guilt" (1974: 112), a figure close to the maid's daughter in Weber's film; and he pits the child against "the married woman, who disregards her divinely-ordained duty" to bear children. For her, Gardiner has only contempt, "even if she be the lordly woman of fashion, clothed in purple and fine linen. If glittering gems adorn her person, within there is foulness and squalor" (1974: 112). In a statement that again is relevant to Weber's drama, Gardiner condemns particularly the way that such women

> persistently and continually [endeavor] by every means in their power to avoid the great object of married life – an object which was the special design of Providence in creating the sexes – love, parental feeling, and all the higher and nobler emotions of the soul – the begetting of children.
>
> (Gardiner 1974: 177)

And he ends by imploring women to be true mothers, "instinct with all the holy attributes of maternity." This mother stirs "us up with a sweet, soft voice, yet ringing louder than clarion blasts through our inmost souls, to duty" (1974: 235).

These sentiments and images dominate the upper-class plot in Weber's *Where Are My Children?* Here the husband's right to demand and have children is clearly established. Upper-class women, the film argues, owe it to their husbands to provide healthy children. The film also, parenthetically, argues for upper-class women choosing "well-bred" husbands so as to prevent deterioration of the race, such as the film shows happens in lower-class environments. The film's indirect argument for abortion is conservative in its problematic advocacy of eugenics and preventing proliferation of the lower classes. It was, however, a conservatism propped up by the popularizing of Darwin's ideas about survival of the species among the animals, and his followers' application of these principles to man.

However, in the working-class sub-plot, we have a contrasting picture: here, the upper-class rake who seduces and impregnates the innocent working-class daughter is severely condemned, as is also the abortionist who manages to kill her. The film makes an indirect case for birth control or perhaps even for legalized, and safe, abortion. In this plot, the identification is obviously with the mother and the daughter, in contrast to the heavily male identification in the main plot, revealing, perhaps, Weber's complex, contradictory positioning as a woman, shaped by nineteenth-century ideas, but living in a transitional moment, and as a woman working within Hollywood's patriarchal constraints.

If *Where Are My Children?* is indeed "a heavy dinner" – as Weber, looking back in 1918, called it – it embodies a complex set of discourses about social issues. It inaugurates the kind of film-making that Weber was to develop in the 1920s once she had her own company. Left to her own devices and not controlled by a studio, Weber not only continued her interest in female concerns but developed an extremely sensitive and subtle way of handling them. This involved not only presenting issues from a female point of view, but also dealing with the interaction between female and male in ways that

Figure 6   Weber's *Where Are My Children?* (1914)
The heroine tells the abortionist about her pregnant friend's plight. Note the
sinister tone conveyed through the doctor's face, shadows in the office, and the
series of looks, including the terrified young girl behind the heroine.

reveal Weber's understanding of the complexity of gender relations within
the changing codes of her period.

Weber's 1920s films are unusual for their period in their exploration of
female/male emotions from a sensitive, psychologically sophisticated point
of view. In particular, the films explore feelings rather than following formula
plots, and show close attention to domestic detail and texture. Weber stands
out among the women directors of her own period in these ways, as is
evident from comparison with some of the other women at Universal City.
Grace Cunard, for instance, made mainly spy/detective formula films, and
we have little evidence that other women in the teens made films exploring
male–female psychological interactions. Instead, they evidently made the
usual clichéd melodramas, and none survived as directors well into the 1920s,
as did Weber.[6] Weber by and large eschews the one-dimensional, mythic and

melodramatic level of things, searching rather for a realistic style that will satisfy her urge to probe "human nature" as constructed for the middle class at her historical moment.

But Weber does more than this. In fact, it is possible to make an argument for *The Blot* similar to that made for Dorothy Arzner films (see Chapter 8). Like Arzner, Weber does not "sweep aside the existing order of language and found a new one," but she does disturb the established hierarchy of discourses that privileges the male at least to the extent of permitting us self-conscious access to the patriarchal feminine discourse. Unlike Arzner, however, she does not go so far as to position her heroines as the ones that make the narrative happen; her women do not have powerful desires and wills that dislocate the male order, as do some Arzner heroines. But Weber's very retention of the established sex difference codes of her period enables her to expose their constraints and to look toward the new marital patterns developing in the 1920s.

The Blot is significant in that the main narrative line is not ostensibly related to a female issue. The "blot" of the title is society's refusal to offer payment to professors and clergymen commensurate with the worth and respect of their respective professions. And yet Weber chooses to focus on the effect of the deprivation on Mrs Griggs, the professor's wife, rather than on its effect on Mr Griggs directly. The narrative as it were slides away from the discourse of the male to that of his wife, showing us the pain and inner conflicts that poverty induces in her.

What we have then is a sensitive, carefully studied examination of Mrs Griggs's struggle to provide for her husband and sick daughter in the manner to which they are, as gentlepeople, accustomed, on next to no money. Shots are structured predominantly from Mrs Griggs's point-of-view, so that we get inside Mrs Griggs's consciousness and world view, seeing as she sees, suffering as she suffers. Near the start of the film, for instance, we have close-ups of Mrs Griggs's worn face, wearily surveying her house, and then cut in to close-ups of what she sees – namely the worn carpet, threadbare chairs, thin curtains; a little later on, we are made painfully aware of *her* awareness of the lack of food through the device of close-ups of the hungry kittens hovering around their empty plate – there are no scraps for them since the adults have nothing to eat. Later on, the film insists on the lack of money for clothes by several close-ups of the holes in Amelia's, her daughter's, shoes.

All of these deprivations are highlighted by the device of intercutting between this threadbare but educated and genteel all-American family, and the materialist, consumerist and (relatively) wealthy *nouveau riche* immigrants, the Olsens, next door, who are in turn contrasted with the impoverished, but highly moral, preacher, one of Amelia Griggs's many lovers. Class is central to the narrative and world view in the film, and it addresses Weber's historical moment, when, indeed, class tensions resulting from new

Figure 7   Weber's *The Blot* (1921)
Shots are structured predominantly from Mrs Griggs's point of view, presenting her consciousness and pain. Here, the tired housewife is bewildered by the surprise food basket. Attention to domestic details illuminates the mother's plight.

immigrants prevailed. It is the film's constitution of class, if often relying on clichés and xenophobia, that is important.

Mr Olsen is a shoe manufacturer, and this permits a lot of ironic intercutting between the Griggs's hole-ridden footwear and the Olsens' well-leathered feet. The Olsen baby is allowed to play with the fancy shoes while Amelia cannot walk in the rain without catching cold. Olsen does well for himself and his family, although he is imaged as lacking in taste and refinement, and titles indicate a heavy accent. His well-padded wife wants nothing to do with the proud Griggs whom she thinks are snobbish. So determined is Mrs Olsen not to help the Griggs that she even forbids their cat to eat the Olsen's garbage.

There is a gentle sub-plot, focusing on the love affair between Amelia Griggs and the rich Phil West, which gives Weber an excuse to criticize the wasteful rich and to pit the vampish Juanita, also in love with Phil, against the angelic Amelia. This sub-plot is, in itself, not at all "resisting." In fact, it would be perfectly in place in a complicit melodrama. The sub-plot, however, provides the context for Mrs Griggs's dilemma. Resisting plot elements have to do with the camera's identification with Mrs Griggs and her situation: she desperately desires a rich match for Amelia, but she cannot afford little luxuries necessary when Amelia's suitors, who include not only Phil but also the poor clergyman and Peter Olsen, come courting. One of the most powerful scenes in the film is that where Mrs Griggs pawns all that she and her aged mother have left in order to buy tea and cakes for Phil West, who has come to visit. The camera sticks close to Mrs Griggs as she goes about her tasks hoping to impress Phil West, only to find the poor clergyman seated when she brings in the tea-tray.

A second equally powerful scene is that where Mrs Griggs, desperate to have nourishing food for her sick daughter, at first steals, and then replaces, one of Mrs Olsen's chickens. Weber captures the mother's moral dilemma in the editing, complicating matters by cuts to Amelia seeing her mother steal, but not replace, the chicken. This produces a crisis in their close mother–daughter relationship that seems far more intimate and central than the relationships between heterosexual couples.

But the question is the degree to which such a portrayal may be said to offer a "resisting" image. Weber clearly keeps safely within the semiotic patriarchal codes, dividing her female characters into good/bad images in the familiar Hollywood manner. Obviously, the image is not "resisting" in the feminist sense of a whole critique of the assumptions of a society that positions women in this way. Weber has no vision of any alternative to the positioning of woman as the unquestioning nurturer and general care-taker, nor does the film take issue with the assigning of woman to that role. Its discourses accept the sex-role division as socially constructed.

Nevertheless, that ideology was the only one available to Weber at the time. Even the suffragettes by and large were not questioning the division of labor, or the burdens placed on wives and mothers. In this ideological context, the film is important in allowing access to the specificity of the mother's emotions, conflicts and desires. The mother is not assigned to silence, absence and marginality as in the maternal melodrama that we studied in Chapter 5, where the heroine is constructed completely by the male discourses in which she is embedded, and only "permitted" the dubious release from constructing herself for the male gaze.

By contrast, in *The Blot*, Mrs Griggs is at the center of the action for most of the film. We see her struggle against her plight, figuring out ways to get what she needs for those she loves. The cut-ins to her emotional reactions allow spectator identification with her, while the Professor figure remains a shadowy, absent one, sunk deep in his books.

Ultimately and probably "inevitably," however, it is a male discourse that brings about the solutions. Phil West has been the male figure "opposite" Mrs Griggs in the sense of perceiving her struggles and wanting to help out of his love for Amelia. It is, then, Phil who finally brings the needed food and who ultimately "saves" the family by convincing his father, head of the College Board that controls Mr Griggs's salary, to get higher pay for professors; and of course Phil marries Amelia for the requisite happy ending.

Nevertheless, we must honor Weber's achievement at such an early date in exposing the codes that constrain Mrs Griggs. We are able to see the burdens that the codes place on Mrs Griggs, and the difficulty for her to obtain pleasure. She is a "poor thing," as it were, and the film allows the female spectator to experience and pity that all too familiar positioning. We are also made keenly aware of Amelia's positioning as object of the male gaze. If Mrs Griggs is not set up for the male gaze, this is because Weber has constructed an unattractive image for the mother. Here, Weber sticks to the Hollywood conventions for representing middle- and lower-class mothers as physically plain, usually tired and over-burdened. Mrs Griggs is de-specularized partly so that Amelia can be the central spectacle: early on, there is a sequence where Peter Olsen, sitting on his door-steps, gazes with longing at the fairy-like, ethereal Amelia (an effect created by the soft-focus and back-lighting) sitting next door on her steps. Amelia gazes straight forward, and we have cuts to Peter's gaze at her.

At the end of the film, a scene occurs in which Amelia is embracing Phil West in the Griggs's house; both Peter Olsen and the clergyman enter, and gaze with envy at the couple, but focus their longing on Amelia. This longing gaze is privileged at the end of the film as the clergyman walks sadly away. He turns to gaze back at Amelia standing at her door, unavailable, transcendent, the camera holding on his look.

Weber is clearly sorry to let her clergyman go home without the prize, but Hollywood codes demand that Amelia marry the rich boy. And Phil has earned his prize, in the film's eyes, by befriending the clergyman and "doing good" for the Griggs. He has redeemed himself by rejecting Juanita and the fast, wasteful life of the rich so distasteful to Weber. Weber's basically Christian ethos shines clearly through this plot: the text disapproves of both the new consumerist immigrant class, and the old aristocratic one. Weber is on the side of learning, asceticism and service to the needy – values that the Church has often held dear.

As the 1920s got underway, Weber's values became increasingly archaic; her moralizing, propagandistic tone was unsuited to the era of the "flapper" girl and a hedonism that seemed all the more urgent because so long held at bay. But perhaps just because of the construction of the so-called "New Woman" out of all the disruption, later 1920s films offer a more explicit exposure of gender roles; that is, young females' departures from traditions created a new level of debate about "the woman question," including mothering, on lines more directly linked to ongoing sex-role changes than was evident in the Weber films discussed.

Mothering was the last female role, historically, to be questioned; the nineteenth century, as we saw, dared not suggest that women choose not to mother, or raise complaints explicitly about the role, preferring rather to valorize it and extend the role into the public sphere; while the 1920s focused on the right of the young, upper-class woman to freedoms routinely granted men, like promiscuity, smoking, dancing and partying all night. In this context, Harold Brennon's *Dancing Mothers* (1926), produced toward the end of the decade, is interesting. The film might be said to mark the transition from early to high modernism, since it already parodies the famed "flapper girl," played enchantingly by Clara Bow, and shows how it is the daughter's new freedoms that eventually open the mother's eyes to her own repressive situation.

The film reveals the generational imbalance in relation to the new freedoms: as the film opens, father and daughter are coming to the end of a European trip. The absence of the wife and mother, Ethel, is unclear, although it is implied that she is simply too dull to undertake such pleasure trips. During the voyage home, both father and daughter have fallen in love with people with whom they will continue to carry on affairs on their return. Ethel has waited passively and in boredom at home.

The narrative proceeds to offer a surprising violation of the dominant mother paradigms discussed earlier in that the hitherto passively victimized mother-figure not only moves out of the home to enter a night-life considered inappropriate for her, but also falls in love with the daughter's boyfriend.

In keeping with the drawing-room drama style of the play, of which the film is an adaptation, and its conscious-rational stance, the film is not interested in the obvious Oedipal issues: father and daughter, for instance, are incestuously involved in each other's love affairs, while mother and daughter enter into erotic competition for McNaughton, the surrogate father/son figure. A complicit melodrama would have seized on this level of things and made it central. *Dancing Mothers* rather explores issues on the individual level, looking at the mother's evaluation of her husband's and daughter's behaviour, at her own needs, and whether or not her upper-class family setting is able to satisfy her.

In a reversal of expected imaging, the mother who seeks autonomy is not seen as "bad"; rather, it is the father and daughter who are shown to be morally "lacking" in the way that they relate to Ethel. Dismayed by the revelation of love between Ethel and McNaughton, father and daughter try to prevent Ethel from leaving, as she intends to do following her insights about them. But Ethel, whose duty, she has realized, "is now to herself," understands that father and daughter are still thinking only of themselves in needing her. The last shot of the film shows Ethel's car leaving the house – whether to join McNaughton or not is unclear; the point is that she leaves her victimized position, refuses any longer to be the silent figure in the background, keeping things together by

Figure 8   Brennon's *Dancing Mothers* (1926)
Mother and daughter enter into erotic competition for McNaughton. If Ethel is
liberated by the love affair, the film endorses mother/daughter rivalry, the man
coming in between them as so often in following films.

her passivity and self-abnegation, and begins to function as a speaking
subject.

Despite the somewhat superficial treatment of its subject, which arises
partly from the limitations of its comic drawing-room genre, Brennon's film
addresses issues about sex-roles in its historical moment, in a forthright and
occasionally poignant way. But by 1928, the effects of industrialism on the
family could no longer be ignored. The sort of elegant play in a narrative
about the upper classes like *Dancing Mothers* no longer satisfied everyone. Just
as Weber's moralizing made no sense in the heady 1920s, so stories about
elegant upper-class dilemmas in turn began to be complemented by socially
conscious statements as the Depression loomed and the stresses of increasing
industrialization became clear. King Vidor's *The Crowd* (1928), made just
before the Depression, explores the impact of industrialism on the family.
For industrialism demanded a particular sort of human being, closer to the
machine – a being at least accustomed to discipline and regularity (Degler

140

1980; Filene 1986). "In the interests of industrial regularity," Ehrenreich *et al.* (1978) point out, "spontaneity would have to be strangled in the cradle." A new and different burden was imposed on the mother – namely, that of the "industrial" approach to child-rearing that required a mother's full-time attention. Although single women were already working in their late 'teens, work had to be automatically abandoned once a woman married. It was assumed that children would follow marriage, and that caring for these was an involved task (Ehrenreich *et al.* 1978: 182–3). It was the era of John B. Watson and behaviorism, in which "the problem in child raising was simply to program the little machines to fit into the larger industrial world" (Ehrenreich *et al.* 1978: 184).

Advanced industrialism, then, put an even greater strain on the family asked to live up to the new version of the nineteenth-century mother-sacrifice paradigm, than had the First World War or its "new woman" aftermath. In exploring this strain, Vidor uses a bitter irony: *The Crowd* is constructed like a mathematical equation in which the "givens" lead inevitably to certain conclusions. The allegorical couple, John and Mary, set out on their only too familiar and predictable path: like the good girl she is, Mary adopts the codes of her time, and sets out to be an uncomplaining obedient wife. But John is a dreamer/poet type, impulsive, spontaneous, full of fun and games. These are qualities unsuited to industrialism. John's inability to adapt to the requirements of the machine society, or to raise his children with suitable qualities, is the snag in their fulfilling the American dream.

Because of his lackadaisical mode, the marriage almost breaks up prior to Mary's pregnancy: Mary, in fact, packs her bags one morning, but decides first to tell John about her condition. The idea of having a child transforms John, and it also transforms his view of Mary. Vidor exposes how the myth of motherhood's mystery still functions, and how motherhood codes include special treatment of the woman. From being criticized, neglected and berated, Mary is suddenly showered with as much love and attention as if she were indeed carrying Jesus Christ. But the film stresses the burden of child-bearing, as it will later stress the woman's labor in the home. Vidor not only manages to have us identify with John's fantasies and innocent pleasures but also makes clear the bitter realities of the couple's lives – realities which Mary shoulders and protects John from, as self-sacrificing mothers have always done. At a disastrous picnic, where Mary is doing all the work of producing a meal on the beach while John fiddles away and romps with the children, Mary finally bursts out that this is no holiday for her since she is doing what she always does at home!

Part of the film's purpose is to explore the constraints on women of being confined to the home. Social codes construct Mary as the home-maker, and thus unable to fulfill herself in any other way. Yet the film makes clear that Mary is smarter than John, and would, possibly, have been a more suitable breadwinner. Indeed, Mary helps John win an advertising jingle. But the money only creates more tensions: Mary wants to spend it on practical things, while John impulsively buys frivolous treats – toys and luxuries. Worse, it is the desire for consumer goods, for the pleasure of *things*, that causes their little girl's death, and the family's subsequent decline. John is so heartbroken by the tragedy that he cannot function at all at work. Vidor's ending, however, is ambiguous, since the family are seen coming back together and enjoying a show. Clearly this is no solution to anything, but it possibly suggests that the family has now transcended the personally destructive bourgeois values of the machine age, emblematized in Mary's mother and brothers. But the questions nag: what is the alternative? How will they live?

A very different, but equally significant, sort of exploration is carried out by Mamoulian in *Applause*, made the year after Vidor's film and about a different sector of the working classes. This film explores a complicated mother–daughter relationship that has elements in common with the story of *Stella Dallas*, originally published by Olive Prouty Higgins in 1923, and first made into a film in 1927 (see Chapter 8). Like both versions of *Stella Dallas, Applause* may be seen as a "resisting" text only in the degree to which it, first, alters the basic mother-sacrifice pattern by figuring a close mother–daughter, as against mother–son, bonding; and second introduces the element of the teen-age daughter's love of, and willingness to sacrifice herself for, the mother. In fact, the story focuses more than *Stella Dallas* on the daughter's poignant attachment to her mother, and in this sense deals with the mother mainly from the daughter's perspective. *Applause*, in addition, adds to an already strong female identification the exposure of male abuse of women. Nevertheless, like the versions of *Stella Dallas*, the film insists on separating the loving mother and daughter, and on introducing a thoroughly decent young man to whom the daughter can be safely married at the film's end.

Mamoulian's film is able to transcend the sentimentality of its maternal melodrama genre through the sheer virtuosity of its cinematic strategies; presumably Mamoulian's Russian origins and European education played a role here, introducing him to expressionism and futurism. Although already a sound film, the film's techniques are closer to the silent era because Mamoulian put his camera on wheels to restore the mobility of which early sound deprived films. The use of camera movement and camera angles, together with the sensitivity to *mise-en-scène* and subtle editing techniques, provide a level of meaning beyond that expressed through the rather banal narration alone. Because of these devices, the text is able to convey in an unusual way the complexities of April's relationship to her mother, Kitty, the aging performer in a sleazy vaudeville.

The opening sequences of the film leading up to April's birth establish the sleazy environment in which Kitty lives and works. Using a shot that will become a hallmark of the film's style, the camera pans along the line of legs belonging to the aging chorus girls in the show, revealing their baggy stockings and unshapeliness that match the women's homely faces. The

Figure 9   King Vidor's *The Crowd* (1928)
It is the desire for consumer goods that causes John and Mary's little girl's death.
Here, the couple hold out new toys to the children across the road. The girl is
knocked down in running for the toy. A grim lesson in materialism.

camera pans left, so that we can see the upper-class men "slumming" in the boxes with their prostitutes, before returning to the stage without a cut. It thus establishes an ironic contrast, while also helping narrative probability: the doctor later called to Kitty's birthing backstage will emerge from just such a box as we have been shown. We are then given a disorienting bird's eye view of the stage – a distancing device, perhaps – followed by an extreme face-on long shot, where a man's silhouette appears in the foreground, suggesting the voyeurism inherent in the context. The show goes on as Kitty gives birth, and we again have high-angle shots of the stage that separate us from the action. We then cut to the birthing room and an extreme close-up of Kitty's absurdly made-up face, with tear lines in the thick powder. The troupe file in to congratulate her, but the high-angle shot makes it look more like a funeral. Especially disorienting is the low-angle shot from the point of view of Kitty lying down and looking up at the grotesque faces peering down on her.

We cut to the feet of a young girl dancing, and from the voice-off realize that time has gone by and Kitty is teaching her daughter to dance. This second part of the film exposes Kitty's pathetically weak character, her alcoholism, her inability to take any stance of her own, her vulnerability, especially to manipulation by men who want to use her for their own ends. Her first lover insists that she send April away to a convent, and although Kitty loves the child and wants to keep her, she agrees to the plan. We then see the child receiving a religious education in idyllic surroundings. Kitty's next lover, Hitch, is thoroughly evil – a fact emphasized by the frequent image showing his blown-up shadow looming in a sinister manner behind Kitty. He insists that she bring home the young girl, now 17 years old, to work in the company and make money for Hitch. Against her better judgement, Kitty agrees. She is presented as a mere pawn in male hands, as totally dependent on male love – as unable therefore to resist male demands.

The third and central portion of the film traces April's gradual awakening to the realities of the world outside the convent, and in particular to those of her mother's world. She is rudely introduced to the voyeuristic, lustful mode of the vaudeville world when she first sees her mother perform there. The camera picks up in close-up one lustful male face after another, and makes clear the mother's position as passive object of this erotic gaze. The positioning horrifies April, who cries and insists, against Hitch's contrary urgings, that she will never go into vaudeville.

We cut to April's first night at home, and a scene that reveals the difficulty of communication between mother and daughter. Kitty has no way of understanding April's responses that emerge from her training in sensitivity and religion; but she tries in her pathetic way to comfort April by telling her "It ain't what you do so much as what you are," and by spelling out her hopeless dream of one day having a role on Broadway, and living alone with April in a regular, middle-class life. But as Kitty gently

Figure 10a   Mamoulian's *Applause* (1929)
Kitty embraces her daugher April lovingly, in a classic maternal pose.

caresses April, the camera pulls back to reveal Hitch's shadow behind the door, indicating his sinister control over both of them.

Because of Kitty's abdication of subjectivity, the issue in the film becomes April's ability to stand up to Hitch. In a sense, the issue becomes Kitty's destiny, and April's role in shaping it. The question of the film has to do

145

first with the possibility for a female discourse to prevail in the face of an overwhelming male one; and second with what strategies woman is driven to as the lesser of two evils in a situation where she is powerless. Mother and daughter have their love for one another, but nothing else; the question is what can that love produce or make happen? Hitch has the power over their jobs and livelihood: he can close Kitty out of the show if he wants, and can manipulate April because of her love for her mother. I see the film as "resisting" in part because it makes very clear issues of male power over women; it insists on demonstrating that male discourse dominates, and subordinates, the female one.

The one element that Hitch had not reckoned on was a decent man falling in love with April: this heterosexual love, in classic fashion, produces the film's climax. Kitty, out of genuine love for April, wants her to be happy, but realizes that if April marries there is nothing left for herself. Kitty prefers to die rather than be a burden to April, and thus commits suicide. April, meanwhile, realizes that without her, Hitch will abandon Kitty, and out of love for her mother she decides to give up Tony, her fiancé, and stay in the show. The two women arrive independently at their ideas of sacrifice for the other, thus producing the tragic denouement whereby Kitty, unbeknownst to April, lies dying to save her daughter from the very fate that April is enacting, namely replacing Kitty as star of the vaudeville act. That anything is saved from this tragic, if ennobling double sacrifice, is due to Tony's unexpected return to rescue April.

But within the constraints of this patriarchal necessity for the male *deus ex machina*, *Applause* is surprisingly female-identified. Tony is totally uninteresting as a character, as are most of the other men, who are reduced to cyphers (evil, good) in contrast to the far more subtle female figurations. We can see once again how *Applause* looks back to nineteenth-century domestic feminism, despite the vastly different cultural milieu, in its creation of a female sphere (moral, nurturing, caring) quite distinct from the instrumental/materialist/ruthless male one. In keeping with nineteenth-century domestic feminism, the ruthless male world is associated with a heartless, restless, noisy and anonymous city (viz. April's arrival by train), while the nurturing female realm, epitomized by the all-female world of April's convent, is linked to nature, peace, idyllic beauty. The contrast is of course a staple of American mythology going back to Thoreau and re-evoked in the films of Griffith and Weber, and also in Vidor's *The Crowd* (1928). It is the nurturing female world of the convent that April evokes to carry her through the trials of her crass, city world; and in their bonding and mutual sacrifice for each other, Kitty and April re-discover an analogous sphere beyond the physical one that constrains them.

Possibly, this nostalgic return to basic North American ideals and paradigms articulated in the nineteenth century reflects the desperation of a period of transition, a period on the verge of collapse. Filmic discourses can

Figure 10b   Mamoulian's *Applause* (1929)
Kitty is torn between love for April and for her manipulative lover. Once again,
the man comes in between mother and daugher.

go only so far: even these "resisting" films avoid addressing the economic crises in play, or their causes. They insist on keeping issues on the level of individualist discourse. The 1929 Depression was to initiate basic changes in the historical family in terms of challenging hitherto unquestioned male and female roles established a century earlier, at least. The inability of males to be secure in their breadwinning roles in the Depression, and again in the post Second World War period was to have devastating psychic consequences (K. Silverman 1990) – consequences which in turn were damaging for women (see discussion of Martin Ritt's *No Down Payment* (1957) in Chapter 8). The Second World War, as was clear in Chapter 6, would exacerbate such challenges, and set in place conditions for explicit confronting of gender roles with the various 1960s women's movements. Since some pre- and post Second World War films anticipate such challenges, I now turn to Hollywood representations of the mother in maternal woman's films in the sound era. I will explore how far the demands emerging from the level of the social are able to become part of Hollywood's representational system.

8

THE "RESISTING" MATERNAL
WOMAN'S FILM 1930–60

Arzner's *Christopher Strong* and *Craig's Wife*; *Imitation of Life* (1934 and 1959); *Stella Dallas* (1937); select Sirk films

Inevitably, the 1929 Depression had an indirect effect on mother representations, just as did the Second World War (see Chapter 6). As an historical event, an irruption of the "real" into the delicate balance between the Lacanian Imaginary and Symbolic, the Depression jostled those terrains even if it could not be represented directly. As in all moments of disturbance, there are reactionary formations: thus the conscious-rational, more socially conscious 1920s films represented in the select examples studied in Chapter 7 give way to a plethora of films repeating a straight version of the *East Lynne* paradigm that one might have thought would be waning in film as in theatre.

The 1930 sound version of *East Lynne* indeed ushers in a decade of look-alikes in what turns out to be the heyday of the *East Lynne* paradigm – Wellman's *So Big* is made in 1932, there is a 1937 version of *Madame X*, and Joe May's poignant *Madame X* remake, *Confession*, is also released in 1937. Meanwhile, *The Old Maid* appears in 1939 (see Viviani 1987) which of all the films mentioned perhaps most closely mimics the poignant *East Lynne* situation. Bette Davis plays a mother, Charlotte, who yearns to nurture her natural child but who is forced into the position of merely observing her daughter's development and her love for another woman whom she knows as "mother."

But in the 1930s (in contrast to the 1940s), partly because the Freudian discourse had not yet entered popular spheres, the disturbance that the Depression represented yielded some resisting paradigms along with the reactionary return toward the maternal sacrifice paradigm exemplified by *East Lynne*. For instance, two very different films by Dorothy Arzner – *Christopher Strong* (1932) and *Craig's Wife* (1936) – manifest a continuing questioning of established patriarchally constructed female positions well into the 1930s. Stahl's *Imitation of Life* (1934) is a maternal woman's film with some interesting resisting elements, and I will argue that *Stella Dallas* in its 1937 Vidor remake situates itself right on the line between a complicit and a resisting maternal melodrama.

149

Arzner's *Christopher Strong* (1932) betrays the legacy of 1920s discourses in its main focus, not on the maternal but on the conflict between female desire for an independent career and an autonomous life-style, and male desire to keep the heroine focused only on himself – to make her exist only for him. The element of maternal sacrifice is present from the start in a negative way, in the figure of Elaine Strong (Billie Burke), who passively endures her husband's infatuation, and then full-blown affair, with the aviatrix, Cynthia Darrington (Katherine Hepburn). But the issue of maternal sacrifice becomes central as the heroine discovers that she is pregnant. I want to explore the way in which the discourse of maternal sacrifice provides the means through which Cynthia is subjugated: the heroine is made to succumb to the sentimental tradition of motherhood which her pursuit of independence, and her adulterous affair, threatened.

Suter (1976) has argued that monogamy and the nuclear family are rendered inviolable institutions, particularly for women, in *Christopher Strong*; but one could also argue that the film takes a critical look at the concept of sacrificial motherhood prevalent in nineteenth-century fiction and early-twentieth-century film. The very possibility of these contrasting arguments suggests a deep ambivalence built into the film's structure that reflects the contradictions of its historical moment. For while North American culture (as we saw) had been persuaded, in the 1920s, to open up codes pertaining to the upper-class, *single* woman, there was still resistance to any loosening of the codes surrounding motherhood and the family. This (as noted) typifies early as against high modernism, where at least tension between women desiring to break out of the home, and patriarchal insistence on the home for women, is felt (see, for example, late 1940s Rosalind Russell films, such as *His Girl Friday*, or the 1950s Hepburn/Tracy films, like *Adam's Rib* or *Pat and Mike*).

Indeed, as historical subject/author of the film, Arzner evidently accepted resistances to opening up the domestic sphere, and on the cognitive level, shared the values behind them (we know from an interview that she was "sympathetic" with her hero – Peary and Kay 1975). But I will argue that the text itself, albeit unconsciously, contains an ironic subversion of its surface meanings, especially in its ambiguous final section and ending.

Following the pioneering work of Johnston and Cook (1975) and of Peary and Kay, critics of this film have mainly discussed Cynthia Darrington's transgression of accepted female codes of the time in her extraordinary daring in taking up flying, or focused on Cynthia's transgressions as they ultimately function in the service of monogamy (Suter 1976). Johnston and Cook make perhaps the most extreme case for Arzner's heroines as consistently transgressive; they view the women in Arzner's films determining their "own identity through transgression and desire in a search for an independent existence beyond and outside the discourse of the male" (Johnston and Cook

1975). Johnston and Cook see the attempt of the female protagonist to locate her own discourse as providing each text's structural coherence:

> The central female protagonists react against and thus transgress the male discourse which entraps them . . . . These women do not sweep aside the existing order and found a new, female order of language. Rather, they assert their own discourse in the face of the male one, breaking it up, subverting it and, in a sense, rewriting it. It is this form of rewriting which then becomes the structuring principle of the text, the particular nature of the rewriting depending on what is being rewritten.
>
> (Johnston and Cook 1975: 4)

Jacqueline Suter (1976), arguing in the opposite direction, sees Cynthia's supposed transgressions as all along *ultimately* merely in the service of shoring up monogamy. It is because of Cynthia that Monica Strong and Harry Rawlinson, though at first in an adulterous relationship since Rawlinson is married, are brought into marriage and then into parenting; and also that Strong and his wife are happily reunited as grandparents-to-be. Suter argues that Cynthia simply has no place in this familial system, and once having served her function from outside that structure, can be dispensed with. That is, for Suter, the text never did take Cynthia's transgressions seriously in and of themselves, but only used them for its essential and conservative ends of firming up patriarchal monogamy.

I want to argue that both critics are only partly correct: to begin with, it is unlikely that a text geared toward validating patriarchal monogamy would include as unattractive a married couple as Elaine and Christopher Strong, or such a whining, shrill daughter as their offspring. Elaine is surely a parody of the maternal sacrifice ideal in her whimpering, simpering behavior, her huffs, her unsuccessful manipulations. It is hard then to accept her as a serious spokesman (*sic*) for patriarchy, as Suter argues. Her passive/aggressive mode is matched only by her husband, who is hostile and rejecting beneath his surface adherence to gentlemanly codes. He is in the relationship only out of guilt and duty, and concern for his public status.

Second, the first part of the film sets up several conflicts on the one hand between Cynthia's desire for self-fulfillment in the public sphere and, on the other, cultural codes governing gender, and gender relations, that are treated quite seriously and exist in their own right. There is first the simple fact of Cynthia's deeds being viewed by the dominant culture as "perverse," as, in the words in Mulvey and Wollen's *Amy!*, causing a "rent in the fabric of family and law."[1] This stance grows more strong as the film continues: at first, Cynthia is viewed rather tolerantly by her upper-class group as merely an oddball. This tolerance exists because of the respect accruing to her via her father, a famous establishment figure, now dead, whom Christopher Strong (himself a Member of Parliament) knew and loved. In a sense then, Cynthia's transgressions are condoned only because of the paternal authority behind her, and not in and of themselves.

Underlying attitudes toward her emerge as the film proceeds: for instance, when Monica is upset about Harry's breaking off ties because of Monica's affair in France, she impatiently berates Cynthia for knowing nothing about love, for caring only about flying, for most likely dying up there in the sky without ever having loved. And Elaine Strong, invited by Christopher to join Monica in watching Cynthia take off on a flight around the world, betrays extreme distaste for "that girl's dangerous exploits."

But the *text* apparently delights in the figure: she is seen racing Harry Rawlinson in her car, and then later speeding again when driving Strong (Colin Clive) to the airport; there are scenes of her happily at work at her drawing-board at home or in deep conference with her mechanic and manager. Prior to her involvement with Christopher Strong, Cynthia seems to be happy and self-contained: her interest in flying is not a substitute for love, but embodies her desire. Yet it is precisely this sort of independence that the filmic system cannot permit: the woman not bound by love and/or family represents an intolerable threat and must be brought into the system. Hence the text sees that she falls in love, and thus sets up the conflict between love and career.

But this is only a *conflict* at first because of Strong's patriarchal codes. It fits within upper-class codes for him to have a mistress, but he cannot tolerate his mistress's daring feats. He forces Cynthia to give up flying once they consummate their relationship, superficially out of concern for her safety, while in reality he wants to contain her – because her deeds are "perverse." From Cynthia's point of view, the affair and her career are *not* in conflict: in fact, she eagerly seeks love, and violates traditional female codes for the "good" woman in initiating and sustaining the erotic gaze. For instance, when they first meet in the course of the Treasure Hunt, Cynthia sustains a long gaze at Strong while she speaks about her virginity, her interest in flying taking precedence over love, and praises *his* praise of monogamy. However, this initial privileging of monogamy on which Suter bases so much of her argument does not mean that the film as a whole will retain Strong's position as its own to the end.

Later on, in the scene where she first attracts Strong's erotic gaze, Cynthia appears in an overdetermined moth costume. It is possible that the text is playing with the notion of woman as spectacle in setting up Cynthia so outrageously as object of the gaze. But it is also possible that the film itself subscribes to the notion that Cynthia has to be outrageous in order to permit the transition from masculinized female, in plain leather coat and jodhpurs, to the patriarchal feminine. However that may be, Cynthia is seen as taking control of this first erotic scene. She is intrigued by the idea of being made love to, returns Strong's gaze, offers and lights his cigarette, sits higher than he does, and in general offers a contrast to Strong's obsequious, guilt-ridden behavior.

Again, at the party on the Riviera, Cynthia blatantly and unabashedly

152

exhibits her love for Strong. Dressed now in a soft fluffy gown, a concession to patriarchal codes, finally, Cynthia nevertheless gazes with unflinching adoration at Strong. The camera remains on her gaze, cutting briefly to Strong's, back to hers and then to Strong lowering his gaze, unable to manage the full force of her visual declaration. After the romantic interlude with the fiddlers, with its ominous foreshadowing of doom, Cynthia more or less confronts Strong with her desire to marry him. His cowardice is evident, and having tactfully addressed their differences in relation to risk-taking, Cynthia takes the initiative again in breaking off the affair.

It is here that Johnston is right to see Cynthia's discourse as breaking up and subverting the male one. Cynthia simply refuses at this point to be positioned in passivity, objectivity, negativity; she refuses to go along with the male discourse that would position her as a temporary fling within the monogamous structure. She is unafraid of Elaine's misery, asserting her own desire and right to happiness, and is in every way much more decisive than the mis-named (perhaps ironically named?) "Strong."

But significantly, all this is to change once the relationship is consummated. What interests me here is the symbolic domination of intercourse, its inscription as male "possession," even when the man is clearly morally weak, basically a cad, in a way that even Cynthia dare not challenge. The representation of Cynthia's submission through a single shot of her hand, bedecked in an expensive bracelet, extinguishing a light has multiple meanings, ranging from the symbolic suggestion of Cynthia as the "moth" now drawn to the light that kills, to notions of possession suggested by the bracelet, to its being a signifier of Cynthia's entry into the patriarchal feminine. But most significant is the refusal of any image of Cynthia's erotic *pleasure*. The shot signifies renunciation rather than exhilaration, loss rather than gain.

Within the text, then, intercourse already signals Cynthia's accession to male domination, her subjugation; the visual, as against aural, track arguably represents this negatively, as we have seen. But Cynthia tries once valiantly to regain a lost subjectivity in the secret lunch meeting, when she declares that she must resume flying. She could not put things more fittingly than when she tells Strong, "You have your career, your family, your friends and me; I have only *you*." But she is already changed: her gaze does not confront and challenge Strong's as before, she has lost her energy and enthusiasm, and she easily gives in to Strong's urging not to take up flying again. Her decision to have a physical check-up anyway provides the narrative means for discovering the pregnancy that is to be so fateful.

The last section of the film is most crucial to my arguments about the impact of the traditional, sentimental maternal discourse on Cynthia after she learns she is pregnant. For what we have is a poignant demonstration of the apparently intolerable constraints of motherhood as an institution on a young, would-be career woman. I say "apparently" because the text frustratingly refuses to allow us *inside* Cynthia's turmoil; we can only deduce the conflicts and difficult choices before her through camera-use, lighting, *mise-en-scène* and editing, and secondarily through verbal language.

This occlusion of verbal language – of the level of the Symbolic at this point – is not accidental: Cynthia has hitherto been noted for her articulateness, for her command of the (male) Symbolic, including speech. Suddenly, she is inarticulate, silent. Whereas before she confidently wielded her drawing-board instruments, so concentratedly that her maid had trouble getting her attention, now she cannot even make her pen work for her. She is, as it were, immobilized through her accession to what patriarchy deems the supreme feminine, that is motherhood. Her sudden loss of power now suggests that, far from being woman's most creative activity, motherhood deprives, contracts and reduces woman. This reading supports the earlier pleasure that the text took in this vital, achieving woman.

The change in Cynthia is immediately evident in the afternoon party at Carry's house. It is here that all the constraints on Cynthia bear down on her at the moment when she is most vulnerable because of her newly discovered pregnancy. In a sense, all the contradictory discourses at play in the film and in which Cynthia was central, present themselves at the same time. Each confrontation that Cynthia is engaged in is loaded with irony for the spectator as for Cynthia, since we alone know what she knows. It is for this reason that the entire scene may be viewed as an *exposure* of patriarchal codes and constraints, as against their endorsement, as Suter argued. Let us look at each confrontation involving Cynthia as she moves through the group at Carry's.

But first, in order to appreciate the full irony of Cynthia's encounters for the spectator, it is essential to recall the meetings that take place, and that we are privy to, *before* Cynthia arrives. The scene opens with Monica and Harry informing Elaine of their forthcoming child – information that immediately transforms Elaine's feelings about the marriage. The maternal discourse is responsible for Elaine's reconciliation with her daughter, just as the experience of adultery was responsible for Christopher Strong's reconciliation with his daughter. Only now can Elaine say, "Your Father was right to let you be happy."

We cut to Cynthia arriving outside, where by chance she meets Strong on the steps up to Carry's house. "I've something to say," she tells him, but does not actually *say* it: instead, she asks him to come early for dinner. Cynthia, that is, cannot speak publicly what Monica was just able to speak, because she is outside of the family circle that permits the maternal to be spoken. The double pregnancy is what permits exposure of the contrast in their situations.

Inside, Cynthia once more meets Strong, but because they are in public they must whisper and keep interaction short. Cynthia still cannot disclose her pregnancy, but she makes Strong promise to come to dinner with her. She then moves over to Elaine, Monica and Harry, who form a happy trio

Figure 11   Dorothy Arzner's *Christopher Strong* (1932)
The film takes a critical look as the concept of sacrificial motherhood. Here
Cynthia, whose pregnancy is secret, is snubbed by the friends she helped marry
and who are celebrating imminent parenthood.

now that Monica is pregnant. The coincidence permits a comparison between
legitimate (socially sanctioned) pregnancy and that not sanctioned; Monica's
pregnancy reconciles her and Harry to her hitherto resisting mother, while
Cynthia's puts her beyond the social circle, situated outside in an impossible
manner. Cynthia must forgo all the motherly joy and affection that the
pregnancy inspires in Elaine.

Monica and Harry snub Cynthia, for now that they are married, they
adopt dominant conservative values; they are furiously self-righteous about
Cynthia and Strong's affair which they inadvertently discovered. Ironically,
where Cynthia had been supportive and helpful from her "outside" or
"transgressive" position, they are rejecting and thankless from within the
system. Cynthia manages a brief resurgence of wit and articulateness when
she replies that "they have short memories," to which Monica self-righteously

and resentfully answers that *they* did not pretend to be better than everyone else, meaning presumably chaste/pure, as Cynthia had declared herself to be at the Treasure Hunt.

Elaine then engages Cynthia in discussion, concerned as she is to apologize for Monica's behavior and to thank Cynthia for having brought about Monica's marriage. Only the spectator can appreciate the extreme irony of this interchange for Cynthia, who for the first time sees some of the effects of her transgressions on the very family she really longs to break up. Elaine's patriarchal discourse certainly dominates the interchange, as Suter has clearly shown, but this does not necessarily mean that the *text* supports it; it is rather a discourse positioned *ironically* in relation to what Cynthia and the spectator know and have experienced during the course of the film.

Finally, a young college student reinserts the discourse of Cynthia's heroism, now not as a perversity but as a role model for young women: "You were our heroine; you gave us courage for everything," she says as she gets Cynthia's autograph. The text then reminds us of Cynthia's position at the film's start – of the greatness of her exploits – while at the same time showing the impossibility of these exploits being integrated into ongoing social systems and gender relations. Patriarchy can barely permit the coexistence of female erotic desire and female achievements in the public sphere (that is why Cynthia had to stop flying once she consummated her love with Strong); but even less can it tolerate *motherhood* outside of marriage.

The final scenes of the film deal with Cynthia's reaction to her own pregnancy. Pregnancy has evidently swept aside her prior conflict between desire for self-fulfillment and desire for Strong's love. Now the conflict seems to be between marriage, motherhood and Strong, and death. Why is the choice set up in this particular way? Has Cynthia really forgotten all about flying and those achievements? Why is she suddenly rendered inarticulate, unable to use the realm of the Symbolic to get what she wants? What exactly are the constraints put upon her? Or that she puts upon herself? Is it fair to say that motherhood per se is being critiqued? Or is Cynthia's depression caused merely by her fear that Strong would not divorce Elaine and give her proper access to patriarchal motherhood?

The film does not ultimately provide clear answers to these questions since, as noted above, it refuses us full access to Cynthia's thoughts. Cynthia's immobilization and uncharacteristic uncertainty are obvious, however, in the final scenes. When Strong does not arrive as arranged for dinner, Cynthia becomes more and more depressed. Low-angle shots produce images of her looming forebodingly out of the frame; her previously lively, restless eyes are now locked in a fixed, haunted gaze at the fire, at the empty room; her black dress and shadowed face and hair exacerbate the sense of doom. Death pervades the entire waiting scene in stark contrast to all previous scenes involving Cynthia.

When Strong finally sends a message, Cynthia's immobilization is momentarily released: she goes to her desk and writes a note, telling Strong that she wanted to let him know that she is carrying his child. But she immediately scrunches that one up, and merely invites Strong to come the next night. She cannot any longer speak her desire, and this change is crucial. Once with Strong, Cynthia raises the issue only in a hypothetical fashion: "What would you do if I were pregnant?" she asks. And it is Strong's answer, "It'd be my duty to marry you and to take care of you first," that further silences her. Why has pregnancy had this drastic result of curtailing her subjectivity?

One obvious reason, in an era when illegitimate child-birth was scandalous and abortion unheard of (although certainly illegal private abortions took place) is Cynthia's new vulnerability and dependence. For social reasons, her choices are to get Strong to divorce Elaine and marry her, or to destroy herself. But her refusal to discuss the situation with Strong is what frustrates the modern female spectator. Is it her apparent internalization of patriarchal norms that makes her unable to "bother" Strong with the truth? Or is it perhaps her fear of rejection – of being married only for the "duty" Strong already mentioned – that keeps her quiet and that sends her back to flying? The interchange with Strong frees her to send a telegram to her mechanic, "Going to do altitude flight." This in turn frees her to write her final note to Strong: "I am breaking my promise to take no more risks; you will know why when I don't come back. Courage conquers everything, even love."

This statement is important symbolically in that flying was her first love, and in that she had never fulfilled her ambition to beat the altitude record because Strong argued that the exploit was too dangerous. In returning to flying, then, in a way she is returning to herself and to her desires for achievement. Flying is symbolically her only recourse against the prevailing maternal discourse that threatens to confine and reduce her. The memory-images during the final flight are ambiguous enough for there to be different readings of what goes on: it is possible to argue that if Cynthia at first intended a suicidal mission in challenging existing altitude records, she regretted that decision when it was too late. One's reading depends on how one deals with the sequencing of the memories that Cynthia has as she flies: the note to Strong suggests that she intended suicide in undertaking her mission, but it is possible that the train of her thoughts created a certain ambivalence. Let us look briefly at how the thoughts and images are arranged: it is important that throughout the sequence we are aware of Cynthia in the plane and of her mission: the memory-images are superimposed on an image of her face and head in flying gear, and on an image of the plane's altitude gauge.

The first image presents Cynthia's whole-hearted declaration of love to Strong: "You are my first and my last love." We cut from this to a close-up of Cynthia's eyes. The second image represents the conflict between Cynthia's desire for achievement and the demands of Strong's love for her; we see images of the parade celebrating her successful flight around the world, followed by

157

Strong's words, "I died a thousand times," and the close-up of Cynthia's hand which symbolizes the consummation of their relationship. The next image is of Strong telling Cynthia to give up the altitude flight. Following images recall the contradictory behavior of Monica to Cynthia, contrasting Monica's earlier gratitude for what Cynthia had done for her with her later hostility; this is followed by Elaine's genuine warmth at Carry's party, "I give you a mother's sincerest thanks." The last image, before Cynthia pulls off her mask, is of Strong telling Cynthia that it would be his duty to think of her first if she were pregnant.

What we have gathered together here are all the moments that were particularly significant to Cynthia. But the progression also betrays the way in which romance and then pregnancy successively *silenced* Cynthia. Only the first memory has Cynthia actively declaring her desire: all the rest show her being addressed by the Other – object of an address, not subject. Nevertheless, she is the subject producing the images and engaged in courageous action as she does so. In other words, we have the paradox of the achieving, adventurous woman locked into an Imaginary that reduces her to passive object of the address of the Other; it is evidently Strong's word "duty" that is, on this level, intolerable – Cynthia desires to be unambiguously desired – and that causes her to pull off her oxygen mask. But perhaps it was some unconscious recognition of her own courage (a word that is closely linked to Cynthia throughout the film and that implies subjectivity) that urged her to reach again for the mask; it is as if Cynthia regretted accepting her assigned place of absence – her dispensability now that Monica and Harry are married, and her "excess" in the monogamous system now that she is pregnant.

The final shots of the film suggest the text's possible ironic commentary on itself: there is first the swish-pan from the newspaper item noting the honoring of Cynthia Darrington and the unveiling of a monument to her bravery, to a second item announcing Sir Christopher and Lady Strong's voyage to America. As Suter has noted, the pan links the two items in a special way: it is suggested that Cynthia's death has reunited Sir Christopher and Elaine: but the question is how are we to read this coincidence of events? The pan could indicate irony – that Cynthia had to die to bring the couple together, or it could, as Suter argues (1976: 142), mirror the driving force of the narrative as a whole, recuperating any ironic elements.

The ironic and more subversive reading is perhaps supported by the following shot of the monument to Cynthia, which has a cupid-like image on it. The suggestion here, following my reading of the text, is that heterosexual love leads to death. As Suter notes (1976: 146), dominant discourse, as represented in the motto beneath the statue, "In Memory of Cynthia Darrington whose life and death were a source of inspiration and courage to all," avoids the more revolutionary implications of Cynthia's own motto "Courage Conquers Death." But Cynthia had already changed her motto significantly in her suicide note to Strong, when she said that

"Courage Conquers all, even *love*" (emphasis mine). "Death" and "Love" are thus linked in the two versions of her motto, in which each stands as the predicate for "Courage." In having a monument to the dead Cynthia connote "love," the text seems to be commenting ironically on the end product of such heterosexual romantic "love."

In making these arguments for an ironic undercutting of the text's overt meanings, I am in no way attributing authorial intention to Arzner. We know from the Peary and Kay (1975) interview already referred to that Arzner herself was interested in Strong's dilemma as a husband, devoted to his wife, who nevertheless was fascinated by the daring aviatrix. The text's contradictions and ambiguities (slipping away from Arzner's conscious control) are perhaps a result of a struggle between unconscious and cognitive-constructive elements.

A similar case can be made for Arzner's 1936 film version of George Kelley's successful stage play, *Craig's Wife*. Just as *Christopher Strong* rewrites the maternal melodrama paradigm so as to expose the oppressiveness of that discourse, so in *Craig's Wife* she anticipates, and "rewrites" before it is fully articulated, the phallic mother-figure. It is perhaps significant that Harriet Craig, who resembles a mild version of *Jane Eyre*'s Mrs Reed, is a *surrogate* mother to the young woman she tyrannizes over. The evil, possessive *natural* mother, that much more monstrous in going against "nature", analyzed in *Now Voyager* and *Marnie* in Chapter 6, did not appear until the post Second World War period. The post-war period was the time that Freudian discourses fully entered popular cultural productions, and it was also the period when there was most anxiety (as we saw in Chapter 6) about woman as threat to male dominance. In the films discussed in Chapter 6, the evil phallic mother is looked at from the child position – and appears indeed "monstrous." But in *Craig's Wife*, the narrative is told largely from Harriet's point of view. The film makes her discourse central, as against asking the spectator to stand outside it as in *Now Voyager* and *Marnie*. The spectator is invited to identify with Harriet, while at the same time showing how she *is seen* by Craig (Steven Boles), Mrs Austin (Billie Burke) and by Harriet's niece. We are then given a *double* look again, so that, in the manner of the Gestalt vase/face, we can see the film either way: as a denunciation of the domineering, jealous wife and surrogate mother, or as an exposure of the constraints on women that *produce* such behavior. The latter suggests a denunciation of the social institutions of marriage and motherhood.

The ambiguities of the film are similar to those we explored in *Christopher Strong*. Fascinating once again is the possible bitter irony implied by the title *Craig's Wife*: once again the title displaces the woman, silences her, positions her in relation to a man. She is not the subject "Harriet," but the appendage of her husband, Craig. Nevertheless, the non-subject is, in a further irony, the "subject" of the film, as in the case of *Christopher Strong*, where the subject, Cynthia, was totally absent from the film's title.

We thus have two films in which the social erasure of the female subject's subjectivity is ironically signalled in the film's title. Both films, however, can be read as endorsements of the values I want to argue they undercut: hence, their intrinsic ambiguity, or their genuine ambivalence about the matters with which they deal. On the one hand, we can read Craig as already the object of a "momism" not yet named, and Harriet as a prototype of Wylie's hysterical figures; on the other hand, the film also clearly shows us *why* Harriet needs to assert control over her life – a control symbolized in her obsessive urge to keep her house spotless. The film can be read as explicitly revealing how the woman within oppressive patriarchy may be driven to monstrous behavior through a desperate need to salvage something for herself. Unlike the case of *Now Voyager*, this is not a reading that has to be done "against the grain;" the evidence is there on the film's surfaces.

That the film continues the critique of the self-sacrificing mother paradigm is clear in the representation of Harriet's sister: the traditional, good mother figure is seen near the film's opening as unattractive, aging and in fact dying. She is useless and powerless, and Harriet (smart, beautiful, energetic and articulate) can barely conceal her utter scorn for the figure. Not believing, or choosing not to believe, that her sister is really dying, Harriet drags the tearful daughter, Ethel, away from the needy mother in order to have her in her control. In the process, she aborts the loving farewell that represents an emotionality unbearable to Harriet.

Prior to this scene, we have already encountered Harriet's power over her husband and indeed over her entire household: even in her absence, Craig is afraid to go and play poker with his friend, Fergus. Encouraged by his Aunt, who lives with Craig and Harriet, Craig makes the visit, only to find a depressed, unhappy Fergus, emasculated by the obvious affairs in which his wife Adelaid is engaged. The scene at the Fergus household mimics that of the Craig household, underscoring the theme of domineering, phallic women.

In the case of Harriet, however, the film allows us some glimpse of the needs underlying her domineering behavior. When she and Ethel discuss marriage on the journey home from the hospital, Harriet shows how, for her, marriage meant, as it had for most women prior to the twentieth century, a certain independence and emancipation, given that like most women Harriet had no particular skills. Harriet saw the position as wife as offering the possibility for security and for control over husband and household. Ethel, however, representing the new generation, finds this "dishonest." She believes in romantic love, which Harriet finds absurd.

Later, in the showdown between Craig and Harriet, we learn more about Harriet's needs for control: "What else has a woman but her house?" she asks; and goes on to describe how her mother died in poverty and with a broken heart as a result of her father's affairs. Determined that this would not happen to her, Harriet decided to prevent it by taking control from the

Figure 12   Arzner's *Craig's Wife* (1936)
Harriet drags the tearful daughter, Ethel, away from her needy mother in order
to have Ethel in her control. The film reveals how 'monstrous' female behavior
results from woman's oppressive patriarchal positioning. Here a *woman* stands
between mother and daughter.

start. Her mother's naive romanticism, her pathetic vulnerability, lead only
to her destruction.

On the other hand, the film offers criticism of Harriet through the Aunt,
Mrs Harold. Unable to stand Harriet's obsessional control of the household,
the Aunt decides to leave, noting before she does so that Harriet ultimately
does not want anyone in the house, and warning that she will be left alone as
a result. The Aunt prefers to travel, to *see* things. By implication, the Aunt,
situating Harriet's world as "small" and her values as pretty and trivial,
introduces a critique of the materialism that Harriet values.

As Claire Johnston noted long ago, this critique reaches its height in the
scene where Harriet becomes hysterical upon noting the scratch marks

that the Aunt's trunk has made on her shiny floor. Violating the house equals, for Harriet, violating her*self*. Harriet's reaction marks her hysterical identification with *objects* instead of *people*. This displacement is emphasized throughout the narrative in the contrast with the neighbor, Mrs Austin. Mrs Austin, her small son and Craig are set up early on as constituting the "ideal" family that Harriet will not provide (there is an image, shot from Harriet's point of view, of the three framed within the doorway, happily chatting). It is Mrs Austin who, at the end of the film after Harriet has driven everyone away by her controlling behavior, drops by in a nurturing way to see if Harriet needs anything. Too late, Harriet recognizes her need, as the tears in her eyes confirm.

The text then poses two alternatives, neither of which the spectator can readily identify with. The spectator is forced into a Brechtian-style distanciation: forced to ponder not only the equally unattractive alternative modes of the "feminine" but also the heterosexual dilemma that reveals the incompatibilities of the sexes. Craig loves and needs his wife; but Harriet's returning the love and fulfilling his needs would make her vulnerable to abuse, given the patriarchal system that privileges male needs and desires. Like Cynthia in the earlier film, Harriet is seen confronting two equally unpleasant alternatives: being dominated *by* her husband, or *dominating* her husband. The spectator is left to think through for herself this construction of gender relations. But from my point of view, what is most important about both Arzner films is their rewriting of the familiar bi-polar paradigms that I have explored in earlier chapters – a rewriting that allows us a glimpse behind their facades which enables spectators to grasp something about the functions the paradigms serve. In *Craig's Wife*, the phallic mother, instead of being triumphed over and destroyed as in *Now Voyager*, is demystified. We glimpse the pathetic vulnerability behind Harriet's monstrous surface, and understand this vulnerability as produced through patriarchal institutions.

While Arzner's films deal sensitively with gender issues, they manifest no concern with class or race – this despite their production during the Depression and its aftermath. Both of these narratives concern only the ruling classes (*Christopher Strong* is set in England), and show no awareness about race. In contrast, the two other 1930s films I want to discuss briefly in relation to mother-figures confront problematic class and racial issues. *Imitation of Life* (1934) is particularly avant-garde for its time in its pairing of a white and a black mother–daughter relationship. This "pairing" permits implicit comparisons and contrasts that expose far more about North American attitudes to race and class than the film's surface narrative announces.

The intellectual climate of the 1930s made possible a more sympathetic treatment of race than had been possible earlier in the century. Early film, from Griffith on, is marked by its acceptance of nineteenth-century Darwinian evolutionary ideas. Man (*sic*) was thought to have a series of evolutionary stages, linked to genetic capabilities, culminating in white

European civilization.[2] This now appears as a rampant and unabashed racism. By the 1930s, such Darwinian ideas about evolution and genes were no longer scientifically respectable. With the rise of the social sciences, the concept of social determination of human behavior became dominant. E. Franklin Frazier among others argued that racial differences are not the result of intrinsic physical attributes but caused by different environmental factors.

Nevertheless, North America was by this time sharply divided racially, as historians have detailed.[3] There is no room here for in-depth summary of race relations in this period, but, briefly, W.E.B. Dubois's empirical studies of the conditions under which blacks lived revealed rampant racial discrimination well into the twentieth century. Disagreeing with Booker T. Washington's strategies of accommodation to discrimination, Dubois believed rather that blacks should take a stand. The organizations that Dubois founded (Niagara and NAACP) and the journal *Crisis* that he edited are partly responsible for the more tolerant climate in some parts of North America by the 1930s.

This more tolerant stance provides the background for *Imitation of Life*, taken from Fannie Hurst's 1933 novel with the same name. We shall see, however, that neither the novel nor the book actually confront the dangerous issues they raise.

Despite a general softening of rampant racism, Hurst's novel still marked a brave undertaking – one analogous, indeed, to that of her precursor, Harriet Beecher Stowe, briefly discussed in Chapter 7. But to mention Stowe is to mark at once the distance travelled *and* the common tradition of representing African-American blacks within which both authors worked. The commonality can be found in the figure of Delilah, particularly in the forms of speech given to the black mother. But a courageous difference is to be found in the figure of Peola, who, as Delilah's daughter able to pass for white, exposes and challenges the subtle and not-so-subtle racist codes of North American society.

Hurst's novel, like the drama of *East Lynne*, was condemned by the *New York Times* critic (24 November 1934). Continuing the tradition of excoriating the maternal melodrama, the critic called the film "the most shameless tearjerker of the Fall." In a manner similar to that of the critic talking about actresses playing *East Lynne*, this reviewer casts aspersions on the female author's monetary rewards from her work – as if being "popular" were somehow to be equated with receiving illicit money! Nevertheless, the novel bravely addresses the constraints the business woman labours under – the conflict between motherhood and career on the one hand, romance and career on the other – as well as delving into the intricate issues of female–female bonding, of class and, perhaps most importantly, of race.

Imitation of Life deals with two mother–daughter pairs, one black, one white. The mothers come together when the children are small because, Bea Pullman's husband having died suddenly, she needs someone to take

163

care of her young daughter while she works. Delilah happens to be looking for work as a housekeeper at the same time. Likely employers reject her because she also has a young daughter to care for. Bea and Delilah see their common interest. Bea decides to allow Delilah and Peola to live in her house in return for Delilah's taking care of her daughter, Jessie. Later, the women achieve success in the restaurant business, combining Delilah's pancake skills and Bea's business acumen. The narrative gets complicated when Bea falls in love with a scientist, whom Jessie also desires, and when Peola runs away from home to pass for white.

The novel's narrative strategies, together with the greater time-span than in the film, lead to more focus on the issue of the career woman than on race. The centrality of Bea Pullman over the other characters arises in part because the novel positions itself entirely within Bea's consciousness. We are thus treated to detailed analysis of the heroine's constraints as a girl growing up in this period. We understand the boundaries put upon her self-expression and her desires, the impossibility for such a girl to discover sexual desires, and her oppressive situation as object of exchange between men, epitomized by her father arranging her marriage to his friend.

Suddenly widowed, Bea again has few choices. Since her husband squandered his money, Bea is forced to go to work although not trained to do so. While she gradually succeeds and comes to value the work, the narrational voice never admits that work is self-fulfilling. Like Delilah in the film, the narrational voice believes that Bea needs sexual fulfillment to be whole. While motherhood is shown as deeply satisfying, for some reason that the novel never quite explains, Jessie is reserved with Bea while showering Delilah with affection. For this reason, Bea cannot even satisfy her romantic yearnings via the child:

> Sometimes it seemed to the mother, thwarted and yet adoring, adored yet thwarting, that if literally she could hold the yellow head of this girl close to her for as long as she wanted – and that would be days, weeks; hold it as long as she wanted – that something inside her, the something that hungered, would reach out and draw this child of her being back again into the warmth of the body that yearned for it.
>
> (Hurst 1933: 113)

The description here recalls that in *East Lynne*, where Isabel is described suffering a similar yearning for her children. However, *Imitation* shows that motherhood may not be sufficient for woman's satisfaction, an idea that could not be raised in 1861. Nevertheless, the novel is utterly cruel to Bea Pullman, depriving her, in one blow, of *both* her would-be male lover and her daughter as love object, since they go off together. Bea gets neither of the two loves available to her in 1930s codes. The problem for the feminist critic, however, is that neither code seems sufficient: one wants to locate female satisfaction neither in love with the child nor in love with the male, but somewhere else –

that is, in both and more. But we do not yet have narratives able to articulate anything approaching that "somewhere else."

In relation to the bitter conflict between Delilah and Peola over how to relate to blackness, the novel gives Peola more freedom than does the film. Delilah argues for passive acceptance of blackness, even if it is oppressive, whereas Peola, since she *is* able to pass for white, prefers to leave the black community, including, necessarily, her mother. In both cases, Delilah is victim of her daughter's desire to be white and hence her need to abandon her mother. Having nothing else to live for, Delilah dies of a broken heart. But in the novel, Peola at least gets her freedom. She marries a white man and is never heard from again. The film, however, insists on Peola's return to her black origins – insists that she cannot be white, and also that mothers and daughters bond together if they are black. Dominant North American codes dictated that for blacks, femininity must equal motherliness. As Sandy Flitterman-Lewis (1988) has shown in discussing both versions of *Imitation of Life*, the black *sexual* woman is even more threatening than the white sexual woman, and must be even more severely curtailed. White society will tolerate black females if they stay within the safe boundary of mother-functions – housekeeping, cooking, minding children – both in their own homes and those of whites.

The film *Imitation of Life*, if ultimately more utopian than the novel in the depiction of the relations between the white and black mothers, is also differently resisting. Where the novel bitterly denounced the constraints upon woman, and exposed woman's contradictory positioning, the film is important in at least honoring close mother–daughter bonding, while unable to transcend the patriarchal constructs within which such bonding only can take place. The film violates the master–mother discourse by showing the mother stepping out of her allotted place, and it dramatizes the position of the single, working mother, who also becomes sexual, and who is rarely featured in Hollywood. Though still within patriarchal norms, the film usefully focuses on woman's conflicts between career and love, between mothering and career, and finally between mothering and love. It makes female relationships central and strong. If it ultimately focuses on the daughter's *psychic* health, and on the mother's need to sacrifice herself for it, the film, like the novel, lets us see how complex and contradictory woman's position is.

The film is also important for what it shows about North American society's desire to repress class and race distinctions. Despite its sentimentality, there is a gritty realism to the novel – a realism that 1930s Hollywood perhaps eschewed precisely because of the actual dreariness of many people's lives that it did not want to foreground. The film's participation in the myth of "classlessness" is linked to its involvement in consumerism and the culture of the spectacle: Bea Pullman (Claudette Colbert) has an upper-class "glow" to her, even when she is supposedly down and out. Forced to earn her living to provide for her daughter, Bea is quickly positioned as a glamourous object in a

[marginal handwritten note: dir. by Shahl (1934) [Should be clearer!]]

luxurious upper-class setting. She and her house become (like the department store window, with its idealized mannequins) objects that embody the spectator's desire. Bea Pullman's shimmering gowns and suave business outfits signify her success and are the things that attract the upper-class Stephen to her. As often in Hollywood, the upper-class life-style is assumed as the norm that the heroine must quickly achieve.

On the surface, the film attempts to repress race distinctions also, and the Delilah stereotype angered the black press.[4] But in fact, the racial issues threaten to become central, far more so than in the novel, at least in part because of the convincing acting of Fredi Washington as the mulatto daughter (Peola), and of Louise Beavers (Delilah). The Delilah–Peola narrative takes center stage both because it is ultimately more heart-rending than the Bea–Jessie story, and because of Bea Pullman's disinterested involvement in Delilah's trouble. While the *film* believes that the Bea–Jessie story is the main plot, for the contemporary spectator at least, the black mother–daughter conflict, bitterly tied in as it is to intense racial and sexual concerns, is absorbing. Indeed, the *Variety* review (27 November 1934) calls the film's plot "unusual," and claims that the subject of the mulatto "has never been treated upon the screen before."

Peola's intense desire to be white exposes, by implication, how terrible it is to be black in North America. But this "terribleness" is something that the film refuses to confront directly. Peola's intense emotions are simply *there*, insistently there, but the narrative cannot say anything about them. The black and white mothers embrace, while simultaneously denying their class and race differences. Both collude in repressing difference by agreeing that black is terrible, as in Beatrice's admonition to Jessie when she names Peola black, "How could you say such a thing to her [Peola]?" But, having said that, both pretend that the difference does not exist. Peola, however, keeps inserting the issue and disrupting the complicity of Bea and Delilah. Delilah's answer that it is Peola's *fate* to be black, God's Will, and that she should accept and suffer it quietly is essentially Booker T. Washington's line. Peola, representing a position closer to Dubois's, sees that she can get far more for herself by pretending to be white and cannot see why that is wrong.

Within the film's discourses, there is no way for Peola to be black and sexual, since blackness relegates her to an asexual maternal feminine identity (see Flitterman–Lewis 1988). It is this maternal identification that she is rejecting along with rejecting blackness. Delilah, on the other hand, totally accepts established constructs and thus colludes in the repression of racial and sexual difference.

Delilah sees no humiliation in "mothering" Beatrice, as is evident in the foot-massaging scenes, and no discrepancy in being concerned about Bea's need for love while ignoring her own deprivations. Delilah never complains directly about not having a lover, or about living only through Bea and Jessie. The pain of Peola's departure is written on her body – she becomes grey, thinner, her face lined – but it is never articulated. Even Bea notices the changes in Delilah only when it is too late.

It is interesting that, despite the women's situations as single, working mothers, there is no lessening of the master–mother discourse. Both are supposed to fulfill the ideal-mother position despite full-time working. The film insists on reconstituting as "normal" a nuclear family as is possible in the circumstances. Delilah takes the mother position, while Bea plays "father" by earning money in the public sphere. Both mothers ultimately fail their daughters at least in part because of the inadequacy of the nuclear family they have tried to reconstitute, as if to remind spectators that the traditional way is the better one.

If Delilah's "mistake" was in allowing her mulatto daughter to see at close hand what whiteness would win for her, Bea's error is in unintentionally creating the conditions for Jessie to undergo a female Oedipal crisis. While normally a daughter knows that her mother's husband, namely the child's father, is not a real available love object, whatever fantasies a child may have, in this case, Jessie did not know that Steven, Bea's attractive younger lover, was not such a love object. Not telling Jessie that she and Steven are lovers, Bea asks Steven to "take care" of Jessie when she is away with Delilah. Jessie falls in love with Steven, creating a complex problem for the adults. (Here the film reverses the Oedipal problem in the novel, where the daughter unknowingly takes the lover from the mother.) In the film, Bea temporarily breaks off her relationship with Steven for the sake of Jessie's happiness, and the film ends with harmonious bonding between the two women.

As with *Now Voyager* (which ends interestingly enough in a similar manner), there is a certain ambiguity as to whether or not this ending is transgressive. The answer to the question depends on how one reads mother–daughter bonding. Is mother–daughter bonding always a (negative) narcissistic symbiosis? Or is that merely how classical (male) psychoanalytic theory speaks the relationship, as I have argued in Chapter 4? While the psychic health of both mother and daughter arguably rely on the introduction of the Third Term, the Father, is it also true that there is something transgressive in woman seizing something for herself in engaging in symbiotic bonding, as Monique Plaza (1981) argued? As was clear in the case of *East Lynne*, patriarchy does not mean to advocate mother–child symbiosis. Indeed, texts usually find ways to separate such symbiotic pairs, as in the films studied here or as in May's *Confession* or any of the *Madame X* versions of the paradigm. The ideal mother, at least as conceptualized by classical Freudian theorists discussed earlier, while devoted to the children, at heart subordinates herself to her husband, who should take first place.

In the case of *Imitation of Life*, the white mother–daughter bonding is "safe" for patriarchy because Bea Pullman really desires something else, namely Steven Archer, unlike *Stella Dallas*, who only *pretends* to want something else. The white woman is required to shoulder the burdens of motherhood as a

Figure 13a   Stahl's *Imitation of Life* (1934)
Bea Pullman shows Steven, her new lover, a photo of her daughter Jessie. Jessie's
later love for Steven will come in between mother and Steven. As in *Now Voyager*,
here the *daughter* separates heterosexual love; or requires the privileging of
mother/daughter bonding.

kind of duty. Indeed, the whole concept of the maternal *sacrifice* depends on
women having other desires that they subordinate to this "higher" calling.

No such tension adheres to the black mother, who, as we have seen, is
maternity personified. Whether or not she was working – and the black
woman usually was working – she occupied the "maternal" position, taking
care of white people's children, bodies and houses as well as her own. What
else was there for the black woman to be in the 1930s and beyond? Delilah
is thus not seen as in a position to sacrifice anything in the same way as Bea.
Since archetypal motherhood is the only role that society offers her (she takes
this position no matter what her ostensible labour may be), there is no need to
"bring her into line," as is arguably the case with Bea. The film is forced by its
own discourse of race, that takes precedence over the patriarchal distaste for
a symbiotic mother–child link, to bring the mother and daughter together.

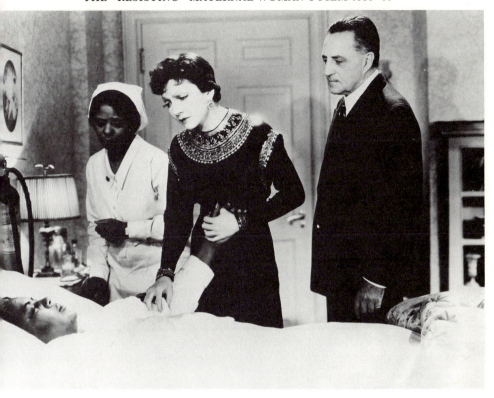

Figure 13b   Stahl's *Imitation of Life* (1934)
Hollywood codes *require* that Peola return to her mother and fully accept her
blackness. Within the film's discourse, there is no way for Peola to be black *and*
sexual. Here Delilah begs Bea to find Peola before Delilah dies!

The film cannot allow Peola to continue rejecting her mother and passing for
white (as happens in the novel). Hollywood codes *require* that Peola return
to her mother and accept fully her blackness. In so doing, she brings about
the film's climax: Delilah's death and the elaborate funeral produce what is
needed, namely Peola's rescinding her demand to be white.

A comparison with *Stella Dallas* emphasizes how the introduction of racial
issues produces differences in the mother–daughter discourse. Since there is
no overt race problem in *Stella Dallas*, the film puts the white mother in the
sacrifice position by privileging upward mobility over close mother–daughter
bonding. Laurel is allowed to move up the social ladder, using her Father for
legitimacy, but this privilege is denied Peola, who cannot use her white Father
in a similar way. *Stella Dallas* uses the idea that it is better to be upper class
than working class to keep mother and daughter separate, while *Imitation of
Life* uses race to insist on keeping mother and daughter together.

Nevertheless, *Stella Dallas* offers an image of a mother in a more deliberately resisting position than *Imitation of Life*, while, paradoxically, it contains perhaps more elements of the maternal melodrama, in its sentimental appeal, than other women's films discussed. It is for this reason that I situate the film on the line between the resisting and complicit types. If the strong mother–daughter relationship in the film, and Stella's refusal of the "classic" patriarchal mother position would seem to signal resistance, Stella's final succumbing to what patriarchy deems best for Laurel pushes the film into complicity.

Stella's resistance takes the forms, first, of literally objecting to mothering because of the personal sacrifices involved (mainly sensual pleasures); second, of expressing herself freely in her eccentric style of dress and being unabashedly sexual; finally, of growing too attached and needful of her daughter. All of these "resistances," interestingly enough, are represented as linked to Stella's being working class: the film assumes that class is an *essential* property of the person and cannot be eradicated. For most the film, Stella never learns the middle-class physical elegance, manners and mode of speech that might make her acceptable to her daughter's upper-class friends (Kaplan 1983a). She is in addition insensitive to her daughter's embarrassment until the end of the film. Further, the film assumes that "working class" equals "undesirable."

The film punishes Stella first by turning her into a "spectacle" produced by the upper-class, disapproving gaze (a gaze that the audience is made to share through camera work and editing), but second, and more devastatingly, by bringing Stella to the recognition that she is an unfit mother for her daughter. It is here that once again the issue of consumer culture intrudes: Stella has to learn that her values are not adequate for her daughter who awaits insertion into the upper-class "department store window," surrounded by the appropriate *mise-en-scène*, in contrast to the inappropriate one of Stella's untidy, unaesthetic and tasteless home. Within the film's value system, the daughter cannot get the nurturing, care and opportunities for material advancement if she stays with Stella. Looking from outside the system, however, it appears that the mother–daughter separation was necessary, first because it was enjoyed too much by the participants, second because it was outside of male control, and finally because being upper class is better than being working class.

I want to examine these theses a bit more, distinguishing the psychoanalytic postulates from those relating to class. In previous chapters, we have seen that filmic representations mimic psychoanalytic theory in assuming that close pre-Oedipal mother–child bonding requires the insertion of the Third Term, the Father, for healthy individuation of the developing child. Both the classical film and psychoanalytic theory assume that what was necessary pre-Oedipally remains necessary in the post-Oedipal period. But does the initial necessary interruption of the mother–child dyad prohibit later bonding within the Symbolic on a different level? What is to prevent a healthy, more mature inter-subjective mother–child bonding, outside of male control – a bonding that would develop non-symbiotic inter-subjective tendencies in the infant, and that some feminist psychoanalytic theorists have postulated? (See Chapter 3.) Do Laurel and Stella have to be separated for psychoanalytic or for class reasons? Or both?

On the psychoanalytic level, there would not seem to be any need for the mother and child to separate. By the time that the issue of separation emerges, Laurel is a young adult. The father's necessary function has long been served, and Laurel has developed into a sensitive person. Indeed, it is perhaps the very mature, mutually aware nature of the mother–child bonding towards the end of the film that threatens patriarchy. At this point, both Laurel and Stella want to do what pleases the other. Each is ready to put the other's desire before her own. Aside from the social question about Laurel's future if she stays with Stella, there would seem to be little need for the separation.

Turning then to the social issue, what do we find? Stella is the one who finally manoeuvers Laurel into leaving her, believing that it is best for Laurel to have the opportunities that upper-class life offers. She also knows that Laurel loves Helen and Stephen, as well as the upper-class young man destined to be her husband. But two other matters enter in: first, given the way that the film represents the working-class and the upper-class ways of life, it is inconceivable that anyone would not desire the latter. Stella's home repeats the crudities of her working-class original home, as if being working class automatically entailed vulgarity. But there is, second, the matter of Stella's own desire for the upper-class way of being marked early on in the film in the scene at the movies. There, Stella as spectator is seen to be moved by the pathos of the melodrama about the rich that she and Stephen are watching: outside, she tells Stephen that she wants to be like the women in the movies – as suave and elegant, and possessing as many lovely things.[5]

In fact, Stella is unable to "be like the women in the movies" because the film assumes that her working-class "nature" gets in the way. But she still desires this for her daughter, betraying her internalization of upward mobility and her love of material things. Her maternal "sacrifice" is then partly in the service of obtaining vicariously through Laurel what she had originally desired for herself in the earlier scene at the movies. The parallelism is obvious in the composition and framing of the final scene where Stella gazes up at her daughter's wedding doubly framed by the wrought iron stakes of the fence behind which Stella is made to stand, and by the window through which she sees the wedding taking place in Helen Morrison's lavish home (i.e. the upper-class, "department store window"). Stella's triumphant, if tearful, face, then, mirrors her (perhaps ambiguous) pleasure in seeing her daughter obtain what she herself never could.

But where does this leave us, ideologically? Does the female spectator also identify with her and experience this as some sort of "happy" ending?

Figure 14   King Vidor's *Stella Dallas* (1937)
Stella's triumphant, if tearful, face mirrors her pleasure in seeing her daughter –
framed as if in a movie – obtain what she never could. The film insists on closure
of the contradiction it had opened up.

Or does she cry because mother and daughter are separated? Must the
spectator accede to the film's values? Or can she appreciate "how they got
us to consent to our own eradication" (Williams 1984)? If indeed, as Linda
Williams has argued, the female spectator of *Stella Dallas* is made to identify
"with contradiction itself – with contradictions located at the heart of the
socially constructed roles of daughter, wife *and* mother – rather than with
the single person of the mother" (Williams 1984: 23), this does not in itself
warrant the claim that the film as a whole does not insist upon a closure of
the contradictions that accords with patriarchal assumptions. It is possible
that the contemporary female spectator, reading the film within the semiotic
frame of the recent women's liberation movement, sees its strategies for what
they are: but I doubt that the 1937 female spectator had available codes for
such a "reading against the grain."

In other words, *Stella Dallas* is a film that has resisting elements, but

172

whose closure pulls the spectator toward dominant patriarchal class and gender ideology. This then is not, taken as a whole, one of those women's films which, in Williams's words, "present a recognizable picture of woman's ambivalent position under patriarchy that has been an important source of realistic reflection of women's lives" (1984: 15). In my terms, the film is not a fully "resisting" film, as are some of the films discussed above.

Both *Imitation of Life* and *Stella Dallas* offer endings that are pathetic because the mother has to give up something: in the first case, Bea gets her daughter but not her lover; in the second, Stella loses her daughter but gets vicarious pleasure in her daughter's achievement of an upper-class perfection she has herself desired. Made in the 1930s, neither of these films betray any traces of the Freudian discourse that entered film narratives in the early 1940s, coming into its own in the post Second World War period, when the evil, phallic mother was blamed for her child's neurosis. Nevertheless, these 1930s films, if less than the later ones, show Hollywood's propensity to displace the level of the social (especially issues of class, race and gender) into the level of the psychological. Or, in Jacques Donzelot's words, "through the roles it assigns to parental images in the formation of the individual and consequently in that of his of her existential or social failures, psychoanalysis makes it possible to displace the question of responsibility into the 'imaginary'" (Donzelot 1979). It is precisely through such displacement that both *Imitation of Life* and *Stella Dallas* manage to repress the race and class issues central to their narratives into the relatively "innocent" terrain of individual, familial relations. Indeed, part of what characterizes the maternal melodrama in the first place is its foregrounding of the familial, the domestic. Its contradictory impulses emerge (as Chapter 4 argued) from the tension between a progressive social function – that of permitting expression of sufferings, contradictions, frustrations endured mainly by women within the constraints of the bourgeois family – and a reactionary impulse that has to do with allowing the level of familial relations to mask political/economic/racial conflicts.

It is precisely the links between the psyche viewed as "individual" and the level of the state, the law, that this book aims to explore. I have shown that such links are routinely repressed in film narratives because they are too threatening of the status quo to be confronted directly. It is striking that even in the films selected for their conscious-rational orientation that involves some explicit attention to the social level we find displacement of political issues into matters of individual desire.

Such displacement (as Chapter 6 showed) reached its height in the post Second World War period, when the need for North America to reconstitute itself after the deep disruptions of the war lead to a stifling of critical positions most marked by McCarthyism. In such a period, representations more than ever embody unconscious fears and desires produced through repressed economic/political/racial and gender conflicts.

Nevertheless, let me mention a few 1940s films that have some resisting elements. My examples come from the start and end of the decade: George Stevens's 1941 *Penny Serenade*, not yet reflecting the Freudian discourse that was soon to become central, inadvertently subverts the usual maternal/paternal codes because it addresses an unusual topic for the Hollywood film, namely that of adoption. That this topic is unusual is in itself fascinating: it suggests the bias toward the biological family that prevailed in the period being studied here, and the distaste for adoption on a whole series of levels (disapproval of pre-marital intercourse and the illegitimate child; concerns about "origins," particularly in terms of race and class; the notion that "blood" ought to beget "blood," etc.). (The degree to which this attitude still prevails today will be explored in Chapter 9.) This film's sensitive treatment of the subject is then quite remarkable in itself.

But for my purposes it was interesting to see how that which the film viewed as "abnormal" (i.e. adoption) released the repressive codes usually brought into play for the "normal" (i.e. biological) family. These codes insist that mothering is totally "natural" – that a woman on giving birth becomes instantly maternal, nurturing, competent and confident at mothering. Such releasing of the codes permitted a more realistic and detailed representation of what in fact goes on in biological families with a first child (fears of being adequate to parent, fears regarding the baby's health and safety, lack of knowledge about how to care for a baby, etc.). The adoptive mother in *Penny Serenade* is clumsy, anxious and hardly nurturing.

But changes in the representation of the father are even more dramatic: having originally been the one most adamant about adopting a boy, this father (played by Cary Grant in an uncharacteristic performance) quickly cathects to his daughter and becomes the most involved parent emotionally. He takes responsibility for the child's welfare, and in general makes her the point of his life. But if this role-reversal is ahead of its time, the psychological discourse is surprisingly nineteenth-century: in this film, neither parents nor social worker show any awareness of concepts now commonplace in any adoption as elsewhere (e.g. bonding, separation/individuation, ideas about attachment), since these became current only in the post-war period, largely (as we saw) through the work of John Bowlby. The film thus provides evidence for the enormous change in thinking that Freud's discourse initiated in the years following its release.

Two other films deserve brief mention: Walter Lang's 1947 *Mother Wore Tights* (starring Betty Grable) is a light-hearted film about a vaudeville mother that avoids the complex subversiveness of Mamoulian's *Applause* (see Chapter 7), while nevertheless confronting tensions produced by the working-mother situation. Lloyd Bacon's *Mother was a Freshman* (1949) meanwhile presents an intriguing situation (mother and daughter both attend the same college and fall in love with the same professor). If the film seems to build on Brennon's 1926 *Dancing Mothers*, it does not have the same ultimate subversiveness: in the 1949 film, the mother ends up happily marrying her professor, while the daughter drowns her sorrows in a man her own age.

These last two films anticipate changes in mother representations that took place as the post Second World War period became the 1950s "Cold War" era. The dominant 1940s phallic mother is no longer prevalent, perhaps because women are by and large once again safely ensconced back in their famous 1950s homes:[6] this lessens the threat that arguably contributed to the 1940s insistence on the mother's evil possessive powers. (For the purposes of space and coherence, I will leave aside here the important 1950s "Rebellious (male) Youth" Films, typified by the James Dean movies, since these films deal only peripherally with mothers. While Jimmy's hen-pecking mother in *Rebel Without a Cause* suggests male anxiety about an overwhelming domestic sphere, these mothers have little direct impact on their children. The youth film is about father–son relations, and thus is tangential to this study.)

The maternal melodrama would continue to crop up in later decades: there is, as noted, a 1966 *and* a 1988 version of *Madame X*, and in 1990 a new version of *Stella Dallas* appeared (discussed in Chapter 9). But it no longer appeared routinely. Indeed, in the 1950s, select films manifest two main variations on earlier mother, and mother–daughter, paradigms. The first is that of the mother's claiming subjectivity and demanding access to the public sphere, albeit with her culture's disapproval. An example of this is Sirk's remake of Stahl's *Imitation of Life* (1959); the second is that of the daughter actively refusing the traditional mother position, as may be seen in *Picnic* (1955) and *Peyton Place* (1957). This contrasts with the earlier power-struggle with a negative phallic mother, as in *Now Voyager*. Sirk's *All that Heaven Allows,* meanwhile, manifests a complex meditation on the maternal melodrama and on traditional images of the mother–daughter relation, while Martin Ritt's powerful *No Down Payment* (1957) exposes the complex underlying tensions between men and women, as well as among classes; as men strive for success and to retain dominance, women appear confused and conflicted about appropriate roles.

Sirk (1959) [margin annotation]

While all of the films still assume that woman's place is in the home – that code remains intact as a governing ideology – all include some questioning of the code. In remaking *Imitation of Life* in 1959, Sirk allows us to gauge the distance travelled since 1934 in relation to the white mother, and to note the appalling lack of change in the situation of the black mother. Annie is simply a slightly younger and more elegant version of Delilah, but Lora (Lana Turner) articulates the desire for self-fulfillment through career in a way impossible for Bea Pullman in the earlier film.

It is Lora's intense desire for the public sphere that creates in this version a revealing parallelism with the mulatto (here called Sara Jane). Different as are the two heroines (they are separated by age, race and class), they both nevertheless represent intense, repressed desire, and the inability of social codes to accommodate this desire. Each in her own way strains against the codes that hem her in. This is not to deny the vast differences in their situations, nor to imply equivalent oppressions: Lora is privileged by being white and able to move up the social and career ladders, while Sara Jane, by virtue of her race and class, is forever doomed to marginality, exclusion and rejection. Indeed, the contrast precisely exposes these very imbalances. But the film usefully suggests through the parallelism certain links between otherwise polarized women whose desire exceeds the possibilities for its expression.

In both cases, as one might expect in high modernism, the film exposes the constraints that confine the heroine, the social codes which determine how her actions are read. In the case of Lora, it is her lover Steve and daughter Susie who judge Lora and position her deeds. Lora's determination to combine her career with mothering and having a lover, long after it becomes clear that she can give it all up and marry Steve, is seen by Steve and Susie as a stubborn, selfish desire. Their values (echoing those of the larger society) indicate that Lora is denying them both the life they deserve through her selfish ambition. They insist that she belongs in the home. The career the narrative chooses (i.e. film star) only supports the charges of narcissism, indulgence and promiscuity brought to bear on Lora. She is condemned for desiring to be desired in the public sphere, instead of confining this desire to the private marital sphere: she is painfully made to learn that life's "true" worth lies in the home – domesticity and the love of those close to her – where the film (ironically) repositions her.

Sara Jane's revolt is handled differently but with a similar end in view. Sara Jane's intense desire to be as free to be herself as are white people becomes the film's governing emotional core. The displacement of her frustration into sexuality is clearly a misconceived attempt to find freedom: she has not understood that patriarchy controls the sexual as well as the racial terrain – that there are limits and constraints for the black woman here as well (Flitterman-Lewis 1988). In this case it is her mother, Annie, who offers the socially acceptable codes: Annie (as had Delilah) counsels patience, humility, passive waiting. In the end, Sara Jane, like Peola, rescinds her demands to be white and to be sexual, succumbing to her mother's socially validated black maternal feminine.

Sirk's slightly earlier *All that Heaven Allows* (1957) is equally ironic and subtle in its critique of dominant 1950s codes. The film demonstrates the futility of the maternal sacrifice in an era when daughters are looking toward careers and sons no longer want to follow in Dad's footsteps. Having given up the possibility for love in order not to jeopardize her children's lives, Jane Wyman discovers that her children do not need her: they patly plan to replace themselves with the television set on which Jane Wyman will be able vicariously to enjoy life's (melo)dramas. The film also demonstrates the destructiveness of an apparently innocent conservative New England community who find the widow's open expression of sexual desire for her

F's nt. in Sirk indicates his int. in questioning the dominate codes

Figure 15a   Sirk's *Imitation of Life* (1959)
Annie nurtures Lora's daughter, while her own daughter looks bitterly on. Lora's
narcissism, which the film critiques, is indicated in the mirror shot.

gardener more than they can tolerate. The film's ironic ending – Jane Wyman
finally goes back to her now wounded lover, back, that is, to marriage and
domesticity – mimics the irony in *Imitation of Life*: Sirk is able in this way
in both films to condemn the narrow codes that confine female desire and
female subjectivity.

But it is the very possibility for such irony in the 1950s that indicates the
historical inadequacy of the codes being subtly critiqued – an inadequacy
that marks the high modernist moment. Another indication is evident in
the second alteration in codes, namely that pertaining to mother–daughter
relations specifically. Both the original *Peyton Place* (1957) and *Picnic* (1955)
have daughters rebelling now not as in the 1940s against an obviously cruel,
over-possessive mother, but against decent mothers expecting only what
Hollywood mothers have always expected, namely that their daughters would
want to follow in their footsteps. These daughters love their mothers but want

Figure 15b   Sirk's *Imitation of Life* (1959)
Sara Jane tries to "pass" in her stage job in a club. Sexual objectification at
least allows her entry into a white world otherwise closed to her.

to be different: they want to use their minds, to express themselves, and,
above all, they insist on indicating and satisfying sexual desire. Kim Novak,
the beautiful daughter so adored by her mother, who anxiously awaits her
marriage to the suitable local wealthy bachelor, is tired of being valued only
for her looks – of being "sold" (as it were) for those looks. She chooses instead
to risk running off with a drifter (William Holden). Meanwhile, Novak's
brainy little sister is on her way to college and career.

In *Peyton Place*, the daughter, after battling with her prudish and sexually
repressed mother for her subjectivity and sexuality, loses the man she loves
in war: she suffers a long trauma, but, by the film's end, has won her right
to go off to the city to try her hand at a writing career.

Martin Ritt's *No Down Payment* explores a complex series of tensions of various kinds in its study of several young married couples, some with children,

in a lower-middle-class California suburb. The film's main focus is the post Second World War male identity crisis, as returning veterans resist settling into ordinary, low-paying jobs, aspire far beyond their actual means, and are intent on proving their manhood to their wives through material success. Underneath it all, the men desperately need the women's love and support.

The wives, meanwhile, remain at home, even if they have no children, but seem lost as to how to fill time, and confused as to what is really demanded of them. The mothers among the group have more sense of identity, but marital tensions are high, and children necessary symbols rather than presented as giving pleasure. The one wife who gave a baby up for adoption because she was uncertain of who fathered it, yearns in vain for that baby or another one. Her husband wants his revenge for her infidelity, and envies, and finally rapes, the newest wife on the block, who is well educated and middle class.

All of these films, then, indicate that the institutional codes of post-war North America were becoming outmoded in the mid- and late 1950s. Gender codes, which modernism did not (per se) question or problematize, are strained – about to crack open – and it is perhaps for this reason that the age-old mother dichotomy (the angel versus the witch) is muted in the 1950s. Women are back in the home: on the surface, domestic bliss prevails. But the relatively ordered narrative surface of 1950s films is haunted by a sense of tension and artificiality that typifies high modernism. Sirk and Ritt are two of the few directors able to capture this conflict and express it: Sirk does it through his devastating irony, which reveals the reinscriptions of his heroines in the required social forms to be devastating failures. Ritt does it more directly through daring to expose the tensions that usually only underlie filmic surfaces. Ritt breaks this open to lay bare the dire situation of the modern North American family.

Select 1950s films may be seen as anticipating all the disruptions and disturbances of the late 1960s and 1970s. In Chapter 9 I will look briefly at the implications of these disturbances for representations of the mother. If the relatively very realistic and non-paranoid mother images I have focused on were produced by a period when women were making few explicit or public demands, we will see how quickly paranoid representations return once women begin to articulate their oppressions.

9

SEX, WORK AND MOTHER/FATHERHOOD

Consumerism, science and reproductive technologies in the postmodern era

In this final chapter, I will argue that we are witnessing a dramatic shift in the mother-paradigm analogous to that which took place in 1830 and which made that period a convenient starting place for this study. In a sense, the 1980s might well provide the starting-point for another book, although it might be difficult to write that book before the passage of enough decades to permit dominant tendencies to be traced. Partly, then, because I am too close to the period I want to write about to see it clearly, but also because of space limits (adequate treatment of the period from the 1960s to the 1990s really would require a book to itself), this chapter will consist in supplementary comments rather than a sustained argument. I will rely on data accumulated from representations in popular materials – in films and novels, but also in television programs, news articles, advertisements and women's magazines. In earlier periods, dominant paradigms were most clearly articulated in the theatre, commercial novel and film, which were the main popular media. After 1960, however, television increased, as did also coverage of relevant cultural events in newspapers and magazines, warranting some attention to these areas. The overwhelming mass of materials available necessitates even more selectivity than in previous chapters, however. I focus on different kinds of materials in different parts of the chapter, depending on which avenues seem to have offered the most significant data. The suggestions made in this chapter will provide the basis for later researchers to argue from.

The mother-paradigm shift that I am postulating may usefully be seen in relation to postmodernism – the term that has been used to talk about a general cultural paradigm shift. Postmodernism has been linked by theorists like Baudrillard (1983), Lyotard (1985), Jameson (1983) and Kroker and Cook (1985) to a new stage of multinational corporate capitalism and to all the new electronic and computer technologies circularly producing and proliferating in this stage. I am not arguing that technology determines culture, but rather that there is a complex circular interaction such that changes in one area have ramifications in the other. It is in this way that the separate terrains develop in relation to one another.

I began this book with the premiss that the modern motherhood paradigms that I trace emerged at about the same time as the first industrial revolution: the shift there was from a pre-industrial to an industrial (machine) economy and culture. I will argue that the west is experiencing an analogous paradigm shift emerging in relation to a second-stage industrial revolution marked by the move from the machine age to the electronic age.

As developed by Baudrillard, Jameson and others, postmodernism involves the blurring of hitherto sacrosanct boundaries and polarities, the elimination of any position from which to speak or judge, the reduction of all to one level, often termed that of the simulacra. The excitement of the various 1960s liberation movements arose from the challenges they offered to dominant establishment discourses and institutions. A clear polarity between dominant and counter-culture positions remained, as the terms themselves acknowledge. But North American capitalism, in its desperate search for ever new markets and its uncanny method of co-opting subversive discourses, has incorporated many of the 1960s oppositional discourses into dominant ones, blurring distinctions and boundaries and eliminating the sense of an "outside" distinct from the dominant culture. While this may have some beneficial aspects, these are hard to locate. Even more difficult to assess is the degree to which basic structures of North American society have *in fact* changed. Given my concerns here, I must leave that empirical issue aside and focus rather on the new *rhetorical* mother positions that can be read from representations.

I want then briefly to speculate about changes in the conception of mother/family/gender roles that are emerging culturally in tandem with changes on technological/economic/industrial levels. A summary glance at popular materials from 1970 to 1990 reveals a plethora of heterogeneous and contradictory motherhood discourses. Representations appear to gather up all of the past images as well as introducing new ones. As will be clear in the examples that follow, popular magazines show earnest reporters desperately trying to figure out what is going on. Their articles are interrogative and explanatory. Each is constructed on the basis of anecdotal interviews, only to be challenged by that of next week's reporting team.

Something that all the discourses have in common is anxiety – which is precisely what one would expect in a period of intense transition. In searching for a paradigm shift more specific than the global postmodern one – a shift that might encompass all the different forms of anxiety – I became aware that the overall change has to do with childbirth and child care no longer being viewed as an automatic, natural part of woman's life-cycle. In previous centuries, women's biological and reproductive roles were unquestioned: how each society or historical period *constructed* those functions, and the codes constraining or controlling them obviously varied enormously. I have

181

tried to show the emergence (in representations) of the angel/witch mother dichotomy, and how it finally came into its own as Freudian ideas entered the popular terrain. We saw how representations in different decades played with unconscious fears of the mother – fears which became increasingly evident as the nuclear family solidified as an institution. But the fact that women should only bear and nurture children was simply a *given* prior to our own period. As Luce Irigaray puts it, so well:

> As both natural value and use value, mothers cannot circulate in the form of commodities without threatening the very existence of the social order. Mothers are essential to its (re)production (particularly inasmuch as they are [re]productive of children and of the labor force: through maternity, child-rearing and domestic maintenance in general). Their responsibility is to maintain the social order without intervening so as to change it.
>
> (Irigaray 1985a: 78)

It is this "given" that recent developments have irrevocably called into question. One of the characteristics of the postmodern moment is the proliferation of subject positions that historical individuals occupy. Whereas in earlier periods, looking now from the semiotic perspective, the sound-image "woman" was congruent with "mother" (the only other possibilities were the "virgin" (nun-figure) or the unacceptable "whore"), things are now more complex. If we accept the visions of Arthur Kroker and David Cook (1985), gender will no longer per se be the problem: in their projection of an era in which the human body of either sort is no longer adequate to technological speed and sophistication, both men and women become victims.

Anxiety emerges just because there is now the "question" of whether or not to mother, and of what sort of context for mothering one wants or deems essential. The plethora of new reproductive technologies now available, including surrogacy and "open" adoption (L. Kaplan 1990), adds further complexities. That child-bearing is no longer automatic has spawned a whole series of discourses and representations that figure forth contradictory ideologies and unconscious fantasies. The feminist movement has itself contributed to the destabilizing of the mother, in turn creating a renewed *desire* to occupy the mother position. As one of my students recently noted, the choice now seems to be between an unacceptable "career woman" image ("unacceptable" because it seems to mean trying to be like a man), and the "bombshell" Madonna image (seemingly unacceptable to intellectual women). She regretted that it was no longer possible to choose the domestic mother-position, for this meant there was nowhere a woman could be "safe" any more.

My focus in what follows is on representations in fictional cultural productions, viewing these as indicative of generalized fantasies – fantasies that have ideological implications, or that serve specific cultural interests. My student's conceptualization of her choices may also be considered "representations," but I will focus for reasons stated in the book's introduction on representations geared for large audiences. I reserve the word "historical" for the level of lived experience – or, as Johnson (1987) put it, "lived culture" – which stands in complex relationship always to images, as also discussed in the book's introduction. "Mother" and "Father" as social roles are in transition in lived culture, but images deal with such changes in ideologically bound ways. It is the ideological force of images that concerns me in this chapter.

Representations partly support my student's sense that current female alternatives exclude the domestic, although we will see that many images promulgate a sentimentalizing return to the family and parenthood. Certainly, the old angel/witch mother dichotomy is imaged only occasionally after the 1970s: there are the early 1980s films, like *Frances* (1982), *Mommie Dearest* (1981) and *Ordinary People* (1981), where the "witch" mother reappears; or a recent new version of *Madame X*, repeating the *East Lynne* saintly-mother paradigm; or a postmodern pastiche form of the "witch" mother in *Throw Momma from the Train*. But some representations respond to the gap mentioned by the student, and begin to image mothering positively. What representations still cannot produce is images of sexual women, who are also mothers, and who, in addition, have fulfilling careers. "Sex, Work and Motherhood" is evidently too threatening a combination on a series of levels.

On the whole, then, we find a series of different representations all of which address issues (both conscious and unconscious) resulting from this new self-consciousness about mothering. A brief survey of subtle alterations in Mother's Day ads from 1986 to 1988 underlines that, each year, codes about the mother were changing: in 1986, a lot of fuss was still made about Mother's Day, but there were significant alterations in mother-images in the ads for presents. Instead of household goods (the norm in prior years), ads suggested sexy nightgowns and dresses, or glamorous perfume as presents. Women had won the right to be a "mother" and to be "sexy." In 1987, however, Mother's Day was a muted affair, with few ads at all, suggesting two possibilities: either, at a moment when women's numbers in the work-force were the focus of attention, women had managed not to be limited to the sign "Mother;" or, threatened by the gains via various women's movements, society now chose to ignore the mother.

In 1988, in keeping with the renewed interest in the self-fulfilled mother (see pp. 193–200), Mother's Day was again given attention: new in many ads was the inclusion of the baby in the Mother's Day image: mothers were unfailingly glamorous still, indicating that if by 1986, the mother/sexual-woman split was healed, in 1988 the mother can be sexy *and* have her child *with* her. New also in 1988 ads was the linking of the mother to machines – cameras, VCRs and CDs were now seen as suitable presents for Mom.[1]

Let me list the most obvious dominant motherhood discourses as I found them in select popular media, roughly in the order in which they surfaced as the 1980s got underway. Not accidentally, most of these discourses either address the white middle class or assume that speaking position when representing other classes and races. As before, I assume that detailing these white middle-class discourses is important as registering dominant social codes that in turn implicate (indeed themselves construct) other classes and ethnic groups.

The "Absent Mother" and the "Nurturing Father"

The 1980s began with new images of the nurturing father at first forced into the role by the mother's decision to leave the family. Perhaps indicating a cultural reaction to the prior decade when women's liberation had been a main theme, films and TV programs became obsessed with fantasies of the mother abdicating her role as wife and mother to pursue her own ends, leaving to the father the domestic terrain that he found increasingly rewarding. *Kramer versus Kramer* (1981) was the archetype for this imaginary paradigm, especially in the negativity accorded the departing mother, who later appears to regret her decisions, and its obvious invitation to the spectator to identify with the father. The fantasy was repeated in many other films. The 1980s became increasingly the decade for fantasies of the Father as nurturer – the Father as desiring to participate in child-rearing, the Father as necessary in child-rearing (David Sacks, "A New York Dad," *New York Times*, Saturday, 14 June 1986: 27). In one article, acceptance of the changing role of the father in the care of children is considered "the irreplaceable experience of paternal love and care" (Edward Zigler, "Parental Leave for Men, Too," *New York Times*, Saturday, 14 June 1986: 27). Frequent accounts of custody cases in which the father won bolstered the father's new imaginary role, as did psychological studies of the new roles fathers were supposedly adopting (*Psychology Today* April 1987).

Father's Day ads in 1988 exemplify the new focus of the Father in the Imaginary: in 1986, an article explicitly noted the new attention being paid to Father's Day and to the image of the nurturing father. This was seen as linked to the image of men as more "sensitive," itself given metaphorical import in the sixty new lines of male skin-care products introduced that year ("Selling of Father's Day: New Image Emphasized," *New York Times*, 14 June 1986: 1). But by 1988, Father's Day ads were as pervasive as Mother's Day ones, and featured more images of the Father holding a baby, sometimes with a daughter by his side, than had even been seen before.[2]

At the end of the decade, discourses about Fathers' rights in abortion cases emerge. An unparalleled series of film comedies about men raising children alone or closely involved with child-rearing has appeared. Examples include *Raising Arizona* (1987), *Parents* (1990), but the most popular is *Three Men and a Baby* (1988), whose sequel *Three Men and a Little Lady* (1990) has

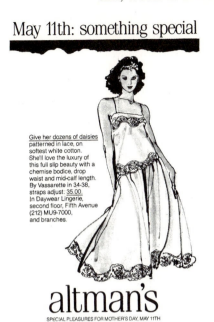

Figure 16a   Mother's Day advertisements

This 1986 Mother's Day ad depicts the mother as demurely sexual.

A 1990 ad shows the mother as more explicitly seductive and sexual.

This 1990 ad seeks to render the woman's newly gained power in terms of the kitchen.

185

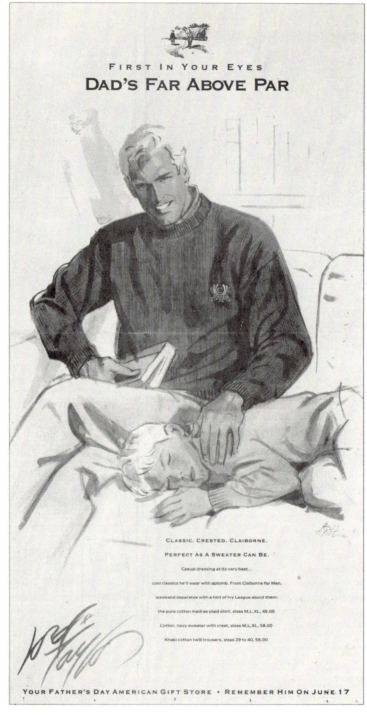

Figure 16b   This ad for a male cologne trades on the "New Father" focus. A
smiling businessman looks rested, attractive and sexy.

(*Left*)Father's Day ads from 1986 to the present show the new focus on the Father
in the Imaginary. Here in 1990 the father is masculine, but putting his son to sleep
by reading to him: 'First in Your Eyes: Dad's Far Above Par,' suggests the son's
hero-worship of the father and the high-class position of the father as well.

now appeared. A remake of the French film *Three Men* shows how single
men grow to love the baby (fathered by one of the men) that has been
dumped on them by the girlfriend who wants to pursue her career rather
than motherhood. The film ends, interestingly enough, with the creation of
a sort of communal family to care for the baby (see pp. 196–8 for longer
discussion of this film). Meanwhile at least two 1988 TV shows, *Full House*
and *My Two Dads*, feature males as sole parent, carrying on alone after the
mother has died.

It is perhaps significant that comedy is the preferred form for the image of changing family roles, particularly fathering. The shows are considered insulting, appealing to the image of the broken or complex family only in order to trivialize it (*New York Times* 13 March 1988). One might also wonder about the construction of this new father-image: what is culture's investment in this fantasy? How far are such images in the service of men co-opting a role being revalidated at the very moment that more women choose not to occupy it? Is there any empirical evidence that large numbers of historical fathers are in fact fulfilled in making child-care the center of their lives? There *is* empirical evidence to show that mothers are still blamed far more than are fathers for what goes wrong with children (P. Caplan 1989).

Discourses about the Working Mother

These discourses proliferated in the mid-1980s as the statistics about working mothers appeared: in 1987, 5.6 million single American women were said to be working while rearing children, while only 900,000 single men were doing the same. The figures cited in the late 1980s and early 1990s show 24 per cent of US children living with one parent, with the number expecting to rise to 50 per cent by the time those children reach adulthood (*New York Times* 9 May 1987; 16 June 1988; *Newsweek* 4 June, 1990: 64–7). Some articles debate the positive or negative effects of professional mothers on their children, especially daughters (*New York Times* 3 December 1987; 20 January 1988). Others (e.g. *New York Times* 9 September 1984) show concern for the "devaluation of (traditional) motherhood" (lamented by Phyllis Shlafly) in the new context of the working mother, and fear that domestic mothers are now burdened with feelings of inadequacy. It is noted that women should not feel guilty about staying home, and that "housewiving" is in fact compatible with contemporary attitudes toward women. As one woman in an article puts it, "Feminism is doing what you believe is right. And having a choice" ("Self-Image of Mothers a Concern," *New York Times*, 17 September, 1984).

Some of the articles critique the new representations of the "Executive Mom" (partly responsible for the Shlafly discourse) who calmly and easily manages to combine a high-level corporate position with mothering (significantly, there is no allusion to her sex life) (*Wall Street Journal* 5 October 1984). The worry here is that women are being encouraged to undertake more than they can, in fact, handle. In the early 1980s ads showed sleek, attractive mothers (but not sexy/powerful in the way that executive males in ads usually are), in business clothes, pushing elegant perambulators with cute, happy babies in them. (I recently found an ad with handsome executive *father* going to work with baby on his back in a carrier (see figure 16b). The caption links success with attending to baby, and its general tone was of high energy and smiling hurry.) Later on, we find the "Super-Mom," who usually has a job but whose energies are largely directed to furthering the progress of the baby from the moment it is born. The Super-Mom worries about getting the child into the best schools before the baby is born, takes the baby to swimming classes at 3 months, plies the baby with all the latest learning devices in hopes of increasing intelligence, strives for the healthiest diet for the baby, to ensure a trim body later on, and so on.

By the end of the 1980s both images are ripe for satire, marking both their excess and mediation by developmental psychology discourse. The best mockery of the "Super-Mom" may be found in *Baby Boom* (1988), which also expresses the impossibility of combining career, sex-life and motherhood (see pp. 196–8 for fuller discussion of this film).

In 1987 images emerge of the stressed "two-career" marriage (which is pursued for financial benefit) but in which most of the pressure lands on the woman. The question – does "Superwoman" thrive on her over-extension or is she overcome by it? – is left unresolved (*New York Times* 3 December 1987). A development of this sort of discourse is the concern about professional couples continuously off on business trips and out at nightly dinner engagements. The worry is that the rearing of children in these families is often left to naive babysitters, and that the real parents are rescinding their responsibility to raise their own children:

> What I see emerging is an entirely new category of professionals who spend little, if any, time with their children. There appears to be a new form of neglect on the part of the rich: absence. I am not talking about parents who must work but of families where a staff of one or two is taking the place of Mom and Dad.
>
> (Leigh Cowan 1989)

In the contradictory fashion we have come to expect in this period, we also find in 1987 articles that argue for motherhood and career as being quite compatible. Such articles typically ignore women's sex lives, as though sex is not appropriately discussed in connection with motherhood/career issues. Significantly, such discussion did not appear in the mainstream *New York Times*. A short piece in *Psychology Today* (June 1987: 14) shows that pursuing science does not detract from a woman's capacities to mother. By the end of the 1980s, even the *New York Times* is running articles which accept the fact of woman's career ambitions but which decry the difficulties mothers still face in the public sphere. A *New York Times* front-page article (8 August 1988) had the headline "Women in the Law Say Path is Limited by 'Mommy Track'" and went on to describe female lawyers' impossible choice between deciding not to have children, or being relegated to a lower status (and much lower salaries) in the law firms because they are working mothers. Cultural codes continue to promote belief that "good" mothers cannot be good workers:

> The highest barriers, female lawyers agree . . . are the traditional attitudes that say a man must give everything to his career or be

considered weak, and that a woman cannot give everything to her career and still be a good wife and mother.

(*New York Times* 8 August 1988: 1)

Another article (this time in the *Chronicle of Higher Education* 3 February 1988) notes that, in the face of no consistent and formal policy regarding maternity leave, the issue for non-tenured female faculty seems to be whether to grant priority to the "tenure clock" or to the "biological clock." The article states that women are afraid of asking for time off to have a child, fearing that if they do, they will fall behind in the competition for tenure, and argues for a coherent university maternity leave policy. Meanwhile, a *New York Times* article (23 September 1988) notes that "with legions of superwomen worn out and discontented, a new model has been suggested for married professional women; the 'sequencer.'" The piece goes on to show that a frequent outcome for women who take time out to have children is "a loss of professional ground."

Finally, a *New York Times* article (16 June 1988) asserts that "Working Mother is Now Norm, Study Shows." Quoting a Census Bureau report that within a year of giving birth "for the first time, more than half of new mothers are remaining in the job market" (in 1978 only 31 per cent did), the article concludes that "businesses must begin to cope (practically) with the needs of working mothers."

Discourses about Child Care

The above representations in turn spurred discourses about the effects of day care on the psychic health of the child, and prompted all kinds of research on the part of academic psychologists on children in day care programs. Articles described varied results, or argued either for the ill or the good effects of child care. The questions that such discourses raise include: are the growing number of working women threatening traditional family values, or even the institution of the family itself? Evidence of less secure attachments in children whose mothers worked in their first year of life are challenged by other psychologists who believe that child care is not threatening to child development (*New York Times* 25 November 1987).

By 1988, articles show acceptance of day care, given that mothers have careers; they begin to address practical issues, now including reference to the poor.[3] As noted earlier, most articles elide issues of class and race in dominant motherhood discourses in favor of the psychological dilemmas of middle-class women. An excellent example of this is a *New York Times* article (26 December 1988) about the child-care dilemma of a career woman. While the piece did note the incredibly low average wages for caregivers, the main focus was caregivers' undependability. The reader is told that many caregivers leave abruptly, and that they tyrannize over mothers who

THE NEW TRADITIONALIST.

SHE'S A WOMAN WHO LOVES HER JOB — EVEN WHEN ICICLES FORM ON HER HARDHAT.

When winter storms hit the Blue Ridge Mountains, Emily McCoy straps on her tools, and works through the night on high voltage lines.

Nobody said it was easy. Emily trained for the job when she was divorced and a single mother.

But today she's "real happy" about her job, her paycheck and her life with her 8-year-old daughter and her new husband.

Her energy, her attitudes, and her values embody the New Traditionalist movement that now affects almost every aspect of American life.

No magazine can speak to the New Traditionalist with the authority and trust of Good Housekeeping.

That's why there has never been a better time for Good Housekeeping – the Magazine, the Institute, and the Seal.

AMERICA BELIEVES IN GOOD HOUSEKEEPING

Figure 17 'The New Traditionalist'
This image seeks to reappropriate the woman's new role as worker back into the traditional nuclear family. It oppresses women's actual struggles with sexism on the construction site.

represses?

191

totally rely on them. The trials and tribulations of the job for women who are often illegal aliens, with children of their own to care for, are not explicitly mentioned. The class and race differences between the women involved are simply elided.

Discourses about the Abusive and/or Neglectful Mother

Linked to concerns about the psychological effect of day care on children at the start of the 1980s were increasing alarms about child abuse at day care centers as the decade ended. These concerns developed into a full blown discourse about abusive and neglectful mothers (*New York Times* 8 January 1989). More and more images of mothers harming children themselves were mingled with those leaving their child vulnerable to sexual or other abuse on the part of day care workers. An article, "When Courts Take Charge of the Unborn: Drug Abuse in Pregnancy" (*New York Times* 9 January 1989), summarizes many of the debates about abuse issues, as they have emerged in the past few years. The case of Brenda Vaughan provides the context for reviewing debates "about the increasing use of both child-abuse and drug laws to prosecute women who take illegal drugs while pregnant, and to take their newborn babies away from them." The judge in this case clearly took the side of the drug addicted newborns over the rights of the mothers. His statement that "It's appalling to see little babies shaking and quivering because they were born addicted" shows the emotional tone of the discourse, and the implied excoriation of mothers who put their foetuses at risk. One lawyer correctly notes that "Mother and Child are really one unit and should be treated together. When you create an adversary relationship between women and their foetuses, neither one wins." A judge remarks: "I see no authority for the state to regulate women's bodies merely because they are pregnant. . . . By becoming pregnant, women do not waive the constitutional protection afforded to other citizens." As Kathe Pollit recently noted (*The Nation* July 1990), few in authority explore the contexts of lives of abusive *mothers*, or the lack of social agencies to help them in the first place. Mothers are once again blamed, as individuals, rather than blame being placed on social structures and governmental priorities that steer funds in other directions.

In the late 1980s, the abusive mother takes the form of the cocaine-addict producing already damaged children, mistreating her child, or using it to finance her habit. Imaged in popular materials is the addictive (assumed to be promiscuous) mother with AIDS, bestowing on her child certain death in a period of time. In 1989, for instance, a frequent ad in the New York subway imaged a womb, unattached to any female body, with a foetus inside; just outside the cervical entry to the womb hung a drug addict's needle. These are the predominant representations about, and addressed to, the poor that usually speak from an implicit, judgemental, middle-class position. The discourses inevitably lean toward the mother-blaming that took a very different but analogous form in relation to middle-class mothers in the 1940s.

Much less popular attention has been given to abusive fathers, although the 1988 Joel Steinberg case, and other occasional articles, put the figure in the social imaginary. As always, it is precisely *because* of prevailing mother-constructs that we expect, or indeed demand, that mothers be gentle and self-sacrificing. Their deviation is then all the more reprehensible. Men, meanwhile, are not expected to be "gentle," and hence their abuse (when not discovered to be really severe, like Steinberg's) is more socially acceptable. According to Paula Caplan (1989) mothers are blamed for more than seventy kinds of problems; fathers almost none.[4]

Discourses About the Lesbian Mother

Articles on research into the Lesbian Mother also appeared in the late 1970s, as the Women's Liberation Movement legitimized lesbianism, and as that discourse entered the popular terrain. Results were again mixed: reports of custody cases in particular revealed anti-lesbian discourses and archaic assumptions about the effects of a lesbian household on children,[5] even when articles themselves were supportive (Philip S. Gutis "Homosexual Parents Winning Some Custody Cases," *New York Times*, 21 January 1987). Most recently issues regarding children born through new reproductive technologies (artificial insemination and in-vitro fertilization especially) to lesbian couples (now separating) have been discussed. Articles imply difficulties for the child involved (*New York Times* July 1990).

The few innovative movies that deal with lesbian sexuality, like John Sayles's *Lianna* (1984) or Donna Deitch's *Desert Hearts* (1985), avoid the issue of the lesbian mother. However, the issue is now being addressed by female scholars, who argue that the lesbian as mother challenges and explodes the mythic underpinnings of the patriarchal mother-construct that this book has analyzed.

The "Woman-Who-Refuses-To-Mother," or "The Selfish Non-Mother"

This woman is imaged as caring more for her own comforts than for nurturing. (One inevitably recalls Lois Weber's 1914 *Where Are My Children?* – see Chapter 7.) Articles discuss women calculating the financial and psychological costs of a child, and weighing this up against spending the time and money on themselves. Articles projecting this representation attempt on the surface not to judge such women negatively: however, anxiety about what will happen if women choose not to bear children inevitably underlies each text (*New York Times Week in Review* 15 March 1987; *New York Times* 8 April 1987).

The "Self-Fulfilled Mother"

These 1970s and early 1980s discourses lead, in the mid-1980s, to contrary images of women fulfilling themselves through bearing children. It is important that in the decades studied in the main part of this book, there was no talk about self-fulfillment for women in child-bearing and rearing. On the contrary, feminist scholars researching women's own records (letters, diaries, fiction) have found that the main nineteenth-century motherhood discourse is that of suffering and self-sacrifice in the service of a *duty* to mother that goes unquestioned. The late-twentieth-century reification of mothering, now not as a *duty* (women no longer *have* to mother), but as in itself *fulfilling*, is something new. Discourses are extremely complex and contradictory in themselves.

Films begin to image satisfaction in mothering, and the choice of mothering over career, as in *The Good Mother* and *Baby Boom*. (See below for more discussion.) *Heartburn* also shows pleasure in mothering, and the choice of children over an unsatisfactory marriage. A comedy like *Raising Arizona* shows the extreme lengths (in this case, kidnapping) that parents will go to in order to have a baby. On TV, meanwhile, we have sentimental images of "yuppies" in *Thirtysomething*, *Baby Boom* (started after the film's success) and *Almost Grown* satisfied in rearing children. In general, the end of the decade is marked first by a surprising number of films focusing on babies; second, by a series of films about mothers – many of them comedies; third, by films, yet once again, about *fathers*; and finally, by films about *parenting* in general.

The general points made so far about the major motherhood discourses prevailing from the 1970s through to the 1990s will be illuminated by brief focus on a few carefully selected films. I will first look at *The Good Mother* (1988), which addresses important contemporary issues having to do with divorce, custody and female sexuality within a still *high modernist* frame; I will turn second to explore contrasting *postmodern* images of mothering and fathering in *Baby Boom* (1989) and *Three Men and a Baby* (1988); and finally I will explore differently *postmodern* nostalgic family discourses in *Fatal Attraction* (1989).

The Good Mother, made from Sue Miller's (1981) novel of the same name, exposes the degree to which traditional mother images and myths remain deeply embedded within the United States' laws, legal institutions and their representatives. How these codes in turn constrain what the heroine is able to become – how they force her into traditional maternal positions that she has, in some ways, moved beyond – is made clear. Both texts take up the important problem of motherhood and sexuality as exposed via the situation of single-motherhood. In this case, Anna's (the mother's) sexuality is highlighted in a way that, within the traditional family, it need not be. Certainly, within the legal nuclear family (aside from the specificity of sexual abuse or of homosexual parents, so much a part of recent discourses), sexuality is considered a private matter. But the novel shows that this is not the case with the single-mother: her right to be fully sexual comes under criticism from the state (in this case, the divorced father, Brian, brings the state into the matter) when the child is involved.

Liberatory discourses about single-motherhood, female sexuality, child custody and the state are evident here. But they exist in complex relation to what I am here calling a renewed sentimentalizing motherhood discourse. Even the novel assumes that mothering is woman's only satisfying activity. Anna is destroyed when she loses primary custody for the child, Molly; she leaves her lover, Leo (who has stayed by her through the excruciating court case), and she does not take up any new professional interest.

The film exacerbates the subdued tendencies in the novel, placing even more emphasis on the idyllic mother–child relationship. The visual representation of the New England grandparents' home (not unlike that in *Baby Boom*) is almost embarrassingly nostalgic and stereotypical, as are also the grandparents themselves. This pre-modern, Thoreauvian world still haunts the American imagination, despite its being an archaic representation.

The film also slants things in favor of the husband in the construction of the ambivalent image of the lover and his relationship to the child. It supplies a scene, not in the novel, in which Anna flares up at Leo when he complains that her life is too narrow in being totally absorbed in the little girl. Anna, interestingly, points out that men previously wanted a home-body, and got it; they now want a woman with broader interests. She demands to know why nurturing is not enough, what is wrong with this focus? The scene prepares for the ending of the film, when Anna, having lost primary custody of the child, acts almost as if the child had died: her life is now seen to be empty, pointless; she is left to yearn for the girl, with nothing important at the center of her life any more.

Meanwhile, like the novel, the film lets us see how legal institutions construct mothers according to old codes. The lawyer suggests that the only hope of victory is to blame Leo, and when Anna argues for saying the "truth", she is persuaded that the jury is not yet ready for a "truth" that involves openness about sexuality, particularly outside of marriage. But the heroine's over-reaction to the outcome of the case, and her passive renunciation, do not provide helpful models. There is no analysis in the film as to why the heroine is caught in her dilemma on the level of the dominant ideologies that govern institutions like the law-courts. Further, why was the heroine not a fully-fledged career woman, who cared about her work as well as about her role as mother? Why have we still not seen Hollywood address the conflict between work and parenting from the mother's point of view in a serious drama such as was done for fathers in *Kramer versus Kramer*?

This film, then, betrays contradictory discourses: Anna at once stands for impassioned, extra-marital female desire (a desire released only outside of marriage); and for a sentimental self-fulfillment in mothering alone. If the terms have changed since the nineteenth century, the maternal sacrifice paradigm may be glimpsed returning beneath the narrative of a film like *The Good Mother*. The underlying definition of woman as "mother" and nothing else slyly returns. The film supports both this and the discourse of liberated female desire in a high-modernist manner, critiquing the old-fashioned nuclear family discourse and the legal institutions still embedded in it. It is a modernist film because it assumes that Anna's "truth" is achievable theoretically, if only legal institutions were rational. The film lacks the sort of "resisting" elements one finds in other work, like Atwood's *The Handmaid's Tale* (to be discussed shortly).

Meanwhile, a brief comparison of *Three Men and a Baby* (1988) and *Baby Boom* (1988) is instructive in relation to how contemporary culture *thinks* fathering versus mothering. Both *Baby Boom* and *Three Men* begin with comic satire on New York "yuppie" life. *Baby Boom* satirizes the new "Working Girl", later on dealt with rather differently in the film of that title, in showing Diane Keaton as a hustling, nervous, high-powered executive woman. She lives in a smart, well-equipped apartment, where she eats take-out food. Her lawyer boyfriend, equally wired, equally pressured, has equally little time for relaxation (Keaton and he take their work to bed with them, and *time* their sexual intercourse to seconds, it seems). Nothing could be further from family and the domestic. By some fluke, Diane Keaton inherits a baby, who is brought to her and then left with her. Keaton tries unsuccessfully to get rid of the baby, but, meanwhile, she increasingly grows to enjoy it. The baby has awakened, it seems, Keaton's assumed-to-be-dormant maternal self. Before we know it, she has quit her job, and bought a rambling old house in the country.

Three Men sets up a similar situation: the men have hectic, active lives, only here the focus is more on their promiscuity and their libidinal pleasures than on their work drives. That is, the contrast suggests woman's over-investment in her work (she's serious, devoted), and the three men's delight in bodily pleasures (they are playful, carefree, sensual). Once again, a baby arrives unannounced on their doorstep and they have to deal with it. This time, however, since men are not supposed to know about babies or to have parental yearnings, there is far more comedy around dealing with the baby's eating, defecating and cleaning than in *Baby Boom*. In fact, taking care of the baby becomes the film's main content, although there is a significant side-step into the detective genre through a sub-plot about smuggled drugs, as if to allude to the more serious matters (and genres) that men are normally associated with. A certain sexualizing of the baby reflects perhaps distaste for "mature womanhood" (Modleski 1988b: 71), but also the need to keep the aging men in the romantic mode. Unconscious anxiety about men in the domestic may be glimpsed here – an anxiety that surely has to do with historical women's new demands that men share child care. But the anxiety is defused through

Figure 18   Shyler's *Baby Boom* (1988)
The baby has awakened the marketing executive, J.C. Wiatt's (Keaton) assumed
(if dormant) maternal self. Baby soon takes precedence over career.

the comedy, and through making sure that nothing is actually at stake for
these men in relation to the baby. Fathering is not seen as part of any identity
they *need* to assume: the film shows how understandable it is that the men
would want to rid themselves of the baby, but also understandable that
some attachment to it might be there; fatherhood is chosen, not demanded,
as motherhood is.

The case is very different for Diane Keaton: since women are still *assumed* to
be linked to child-bearing and rearing, the film shows Keaton quickly altering
her personality and life-style; indeed, the focus of her life changes completely
to absorption in the baby and neglect of her work, until she is fired. This is
what we expect of women, as against men.

The second part of the film almost accidentally does offer a critique of
single motherhood. Keaton's idea of an idyllic country retreat turns into a
nightmare, when she and the baby are marooned in a ramshackle house in
the severe winter up in New York State. Soon, Keaton is nearly climbing the
walls with loneliness and boredom.

197

But this does not last long: the depressed mother, of course, needs only sex and romance to bring her to life again. Keaton soon finds this in the figure of the local animal doctor called in, for want of better, to treat her depression. Under his love, Keaton is soon re-energized, and an old American pastoral fantasy begins (one recalls Sirk's similar images in both *All that Heaven Allows* and *Written on the Wind*). Keaton hits upon the idea of producing healthy home-made baby apple-sauce, and soon has a highly successful business. So much so, that her old corporation plead for her to come back and bring them her business. Again, in tune with an old American fantasy for small free enterprise (a fantasy that here conveniently fits in with the desire for heterosexual coupling), Keaton refuses, choosing her country life, motherhood and her horse-doctor to hectic city strife. Of course, her city entrepreneurial skills come in handy, but the family is reconstituted safely in the film's end.

The contrast with *Three Men* is dramatic: it is not that the men don't also grow fond of the baby (they do); or that they are not sorry to see it leave (they rush to the airport to try to prevent the girlfriend from taking the baby away). But it is the film's cavalier, comic, distanced treatment of these emotions that makes the difference. Men cannot be truly invested in a baby, and their yuppie city jobs are never in jeopardy: this would deny their masculinity, their virility still, it seems (hence the anxiety beneath the comedy). Indeed, it is the (expected) *woman's* investment that seems about to break up their life with baby, since she found that *she* couldn't leave the baby. In the end, this film allows everyone's fantasy to come true: the woman returns, and they all decide to set up a sort of "communal" family around the baby.

Interesting in both films is foregrounding, newly, the desire for the baby on the part of the yuppie generation. North American culture seems ready to critique its drive for more money, more markets, for aggressive, ambitious pursuit (see, for example, a film like *Wall Street*). But it seems unable to find a way in which to do this without returning (especially in *Baby Boom*) to earlier American myths about nature as better than the city, the family as better than the single life. These films play out unconscious fantasies of abandonment (the bad mothers in these films who drop off their babies), of unrestrained libidinal desire (parenting is a responsibility for another, and is good for you), and end with the old values, in that the *mother* has to be re-inserted at the end, even if we are left with a slightly unconventional "family".

Fatal Attraction is perhaps the clearest example of the new ideological construction of the family as in opposition to the "liberated" career woman. "Liberation" in most Hollywood films still means "sexually promiscuous." Glen Close is shown at the start of the film as an independent career woman, who objects to being made a sex object, but who, in turn, has intense sexual desire and drive. The female spectator is invited to identify with the figure at the start of the film, only to have this identification sickeningly wrenched away as we watch Glen Close turn into a monster of horror film proportions before our eyes. We are now forced to identify with both the besieged husband and abused wife, and, finally, with the wretchedly tortured child. Glen Close, the repressed underside of the nuclear family, becomes intolerable. Like the ghastly mutations of science fiction and horror genres, she must be eliminated, at all costs, as the representative of everything that threatens the biological nuclear family. Like those mutations, she keeps returning in ever more vile forms, with ever more monstrous purposes, until finally, together, husband and wife manage to eradicate her. The sanctity of the nuclear family returns, albeit badly scarred: the wife has had to resort to an undesirable violence, contaminated by Glen Close; the child is damaged. Nevertheless, the trio reconstitute their little community once evil (the liberated woman) is exorcised.

The phenomenon of complex, contradictory discourses at work evidenced in these films has several possible meanings: it may mean that anxiety underlying the paradigm shift already noted is being defused through a combination of comedy images of the conflicted family sphere, together with horror images of the embattled family sphere. It may be that anxiety about AIDS is influencing the return to the family; finally, it is possible that the virulent anti-abortion crusade is having its impact, leaning on and thereby increasing the late 1980s pro-family sentiments.

However that may be, the 1980s images are contradictory. They include a validation of the domestic sphere for women having already been successful in careers, while also promoting the woman who finds fulfillment only in mothering. No longer is combining career and motherhood imaged as desirable; nor is choosing career over mothering seen positively (indeed, this possibility has rarely been shown, nor have there ever been regular images of the mother-woman's satisfaction in work or her needs for self-fulfillment through work). It is clear that in the late 1980s choosing the child over career (as happens in *Baby Boom*, 1988), or going to college or taking up some kind of business only *after* the daughter is grown up (the situation of most mothers in the "Mother–Daughter Pageant" discussed on pp. 200–20) represents the new ideal. As in the 1950s, this marks a return to idealizing the domestic after a period when women invaded the work-force in large numbers. The difference now is that the *single* working woman still has a hold on the social imaginary, as is evident from the success of Mike Nichols's *Working Girl* (also 1988) and an interesting corollary to *Baby Boom*. The film represses everything to do with children, mothering, the nuclear family and the domestic.

A film like *Parenthood* (1989) marks a return to focus on the father with which the decade began. Different now (significantly) is that the woman has not abandoned her mother-role for career; the wife/mother is very present in *Parenthood*, but clearly the father (played for laughs by Steve Martin) is the film's center. The problem of Fatherhood is the problem of the film, and the women are secondary. The film explores, quite interestingly, different kinds of fathers, raising questions about which kind is best. One wonders, once again, why there has not been an analogous exploratory film about *mothering*. One can only assume either that the cultural assumption of there being only one, universal way in which to mother remains, or that motherhood is simply still too deep and problematic a topic to be given similar treatment.

It seems that the end of the 1980s marks, in relation to women, a return to rigid polarization of sex, work and motherhood in the social imaginary. However, there are important variations in the images from those explored earlier in the book. Single women are now represented in high-level career positions, although they are usually depicted as masculinized or unpleasant. Mothers are represented as sexual, although not also as career women. Meanwhile, Fathers begin to steal the show in regard to parenting (they are the new heroes in this role), and the baby steals the show from both mothers and fathers.

The sentimentality of much of the pro-family discourse was typified in a rather extraordinary TV event early in 1989, which was repeated in 1990 in equally bizarre manner. This was the first "Mother–Daughter American Pageant." A significant (if not particularly progressive) aspect of the event was the mother–daughter coupling: hitherto in popular images mothers and daughters are either in hostile oppositional relationships, or are sentimentally separated from each other. In the late 1980s, on the contrary, we find mothers and daughters now proudly united, and publicly declaring their enduring love for one another. The event evoked complex responses because of this unusual aspect. In other ways, the show verged on the grotesque: mothers and daughters paraded in a series of elaborate, look-alike gowns, and indeed were themselves made up to look the same. Make-up covered any wrinkles the mothers might have had, and the pairs glowed with health, color and vitality. It seemed that we were confronting yet another attempt at eliminating the mother, since both women were smoothed and sleeked like young girls, not only sisters but also twins. The smooth, harmonious lines of the couple were unreal, uncanny, as if both had just been born, or rather, arisen all bright and new from clean waters. The eyes shone with love for one another. The projected family image was of harmony, contentment, comfort – a seamless, smooth, paradisal terrain, with nothing to ruffle it. It is as if mother–daughter symbiosis is now publicly declared an allowable fantasy, provided the values of the "new" couple are thoroughly white, Anglo-Saxon and middle class; and provided the women are carefully inscribed within the control both of the handsome male host and also of the commercial sponsors whose products dominated the evening.

The show exemplified many current American obsessions, such as the denial of aging (mothers become daughters, in a reversal of time), the denial of difference (all couples were thoroughly white, Anglo-Saxon and middle class), and the two beings, in addition, *looked* like one. The denial of pain, conflict, contradiction and disturbance was remarkable. In eliding the specificity of mothers different from, and differently positioned than, daughters, the show denied the need for separation, individuation or entry into the Symbolic. It was as if a pre-Oedipal utopian fantasy had managed to be realized, with the mother now absorbed into the daughter, eradicating any occasions for disjunction, hostility or separation (i.e. reverting to how it had been when the daughter was in the mother's womb). We were invited, then, to a kind of Baudrillardean experience of simulacra – two women, simulating each other, simulating mother/daughter as one. The show grotesquely pastiched some feminists' utopian dream of close mother–daughter (or even adult woman–woman) bonding: everything was self-conscious, studied and false; the stakes were entirely financial and self-enhancing.

A different kind of Baudrillardean postmodern simulation, again product of new electronic technologies, is the phenomenon of a commercial video-tape, called "Video Baby." The tape is one in a video series that includes "Video Cat" and "Video Dog," and that is linked to the host of videos enabling one to "experience" popular beauty spots without travelling there. Video, that is, is now being used, as theorists like Baudrillard and Kroker and Cook feared it would, to take the place of all kinds of experiences. In line with this, "Video-Baby" unabashedly privileges the simulacrum over the biological baby. According to a *Wall Street Journal* article ("Watch the Baby, See it Smile," August 1988) the marketers of "Video Baby" extol its virtues in precisely that manner: if one's break-neck career gives one no time to create a real family, well, one can have the next best thing, namely "The full, rich experience of parenthood without the mess and inconvenience of the real thing." Admittedly, marketers say, the tape "is tailor made for yuppies," who, it is implied, do not have the time, patience or commitment for the constitution of their own family, and who like to follow orders. "Video Baby" comes complete with soothing voice-over instructing these "adoptive parents" how to talk to their baby on the screen. Are we here one remove from the Baudrillardean fantasy of a world in which there are only simulacra, in which the television screen has indeed become the only "reality" that people know? The family, note, is still sentimentalized in such phenomena as "Video Baby," only now the family consists of images rather than biological entities.

Reproductive Discourses

The renewed interest in a nostalgic, sentimental stance to motherhood and the family is exacerbated by some aspects of new reproductive technologies. The newly contested practice of mother-surrogacy has brought attention to the specifically biological nature of dominant mother–child relations.[6] The celebrated Mary Beth Whitehead versus the Sterns' case (immortalized in 1989 by Whitehead's published account) unleashed unprecedented, contradictory, popular discussion centering on the special mother–baby closeness produced through the biological processes of gestation and birth. Readers will recall that Mary Beth Whitehead made a contractual agreement with the Sterns to bear Mr Stern's child, since his wife represented herself as sterile. (In fact, her mild form of a debilitating muscular disease might have been exacerbated by pregnancy.) On giving birth to the baby, Mary Beth Whitehead found herself unable to give up the child. A court-case ensued to determine which woman was legally the mother.

The heavy media interest in this case and its issues in itself suggests a society extremely anxious about bearing and nurturing children. Viewers and readers were exposed to intense emotionality in connection with who should retain the child. Other previous surrogate mothers joined in propagandizing the pathetic situation of surrogates who bear, and then feel too attached to, the babies to let them go. In 1988 Elizabeth Kane's *Birth Mother* appeared. Spoken in the first person (Kane narrating events chronologically), the book was a sensationalized plea against surrogate motherhood on the grounds of an inevitable biological bonding with the baby that a surrogate mother carries. Much the same can be said about Martha Field's *The Surrogate Motherhood* (1988).

Mary Beth Whitehead's book carries the same tone. All these books seek to reify the writer as a woman devoted to being a mother, and, in the case of Mary Beth, of wanting nothing else in life than bearing and nurturing children. "Being a mother was how I had always defined myself" (Whitehead 1989: 89). Surrogacy, for Mary Beth, was "a way for me to help someone less fortunate, by doing what I was born to do" (1989: 89). While the surrogacy contract necessitated that Mary Beth give up this particular child, she claimed that she was fulfilled in helping other women become the mother that was their proper position in life.

Mary Beth unwittingly participates in an anti-career woman discourse that was common in North America between 1930 and 1960:

> Betsy valued her career [says Mary Beth] with the same intensity that I valued motherhood. She was a twenty-nine-year-old Ph.D. the year she married Bill Stern. At the time of their marriage, I was only eighteen, but I was already the mother of two children.
>
> (Whitehead 1989: 92)

Noting that Betsy chose to wait another seven years before considering pregnancy, Mary Beth says: "I had felt so strong a desire to experience pregnancy that it would have been hard for me to comprehend that Betsy or any other woman might not want to" (Whitehead 1989: 92). Throughout, Betsy Stern is constructed in terms common to popular depiction of the career woman, namely as cold, unfeeling and selfish.

The ways in which feminists disagree about the Mary Beth Whitehead case were made clear in a 1987 article detailing positions from fierce support of

Mary Beth to concern for the Sterns and criticism of Mary Beth (*The Village Voice* 14 April 1987). Martha Rossler's provocative video, *Baby M* (1988), is excellent in terms of class analysis of the case. The video makes clear how class-based was much of the media and law-court bias against Mary Beth – how she was smeared with anti-working-class discourse. Correlatively, the Sterns gained media and legal support because of their middle-class life-style that was closer to the North American family mythology than that of Mary Beth. But in doing this, the video is forced to support sentimental motherhood values that feminists have fought hard to combat in recent years. It has to support the woman who claims that biological mothering is all there need be to woman's life.

Other feminists supported Mary Beth in principle: their fears were that society's acceptance of surrogacy would inaugurate and make acceptable hiring out women's uteruses. The fantasy of "baby farms" (see Murphy 1984) where Third World women would bear babies for wealthy North American couples led some feminists to stand behind Mary Beth's legal position.

The splits revealed over surrogacy can also be found in relation to other reproductive technologies, especially in-vitro fertilization. The increasing use of this latter technology is linked to a new centrality being given to the foetus in film comedies, and to the general prevalence of foetal imagery in literature, television and recent journalism. Since this has important ramifications for how the mother is being repositioned, I will explore select foetal representations.

To begin with, it is important to note the interaction between a new foetal interpellation, and developing medical and photographic technologies. From the 1960s on, photography and medicine together have brought new awareness of, and knowledge about, life in the mother's womb. The famous Swedish photographer, Lennart Nilsson, fascinated with the "mystery of life," has devoted himself to capturing the processes of life in the womb on film. His first series of color photos about conception and gestation were produced in his 1965 book, *A Child is Born*, and reproduced in *Life* magazine on 30 April of the same year. They created a sensation in relaying images of the sperm penetrating the egg, and of the almost daily growth of the foetus in the uterus. Significantly, his second series of color photos, this time mainly about the very moment of conception, appeared in the August 1990 *Life* magazine issue. This time, the focus, in *Life*'s words, is on "the earliest and least understood moment of creation." The introduction praises Nilsson's use of high-tech tools, and his devotion to seeing inside woman that entails rushing off to hospitals on the chance of getting a good picture. Both series of photos, but particularly the later ones, are made to suggest the abstract, cosmological import of the creation of life. Through incredible magnification, pictures look like those of the moon or of outer space.

Displacement of the mother and the world of her actual, material and complex body, is evident in the way photographic discourse renders inception

203

cm?

and gestation in cosmic terms. The inside of the woman's body is magnified tremendously until it looks like outerspace, an Other World. The brightly colored images of swirls and folds look like the images of earth's creation – conception on the grand scale: the foetus-as-miracle, as the wonder of "Man" (*sic*), far beyond the mundane scale of a simple, ordinary female body. That body is nowhere in sight, but is rather the repressed vessel for all this wonder.

Meanwhile, the incipient *humanity* of the foetus itself from the earliest days, is emphasized. Nilsson stresses the little shapes that will become eyes, or ears, or other organs. The foetus is presented as already a full-blown subject, a baby, rather than an entity *in process*. The emphasis is all on the baby-to-be read back into the zygote. Further, the fact that this is all taking place in the mother's body is, in *Life* magazine's reproduction, ignored. The photos have no boundary to them that might represent the limit of the mother's womb or fallopian tubes. The mother is simply not a part of anything. Significantly, Nilsson's *A Child is Born* itself ran on two tracks, one of which was that of the mother-in-the-world. But even there, the tracks were hardly united, as in reality they ought to be.

The photos, together with increasing medical access to and knowledge about, the foetus and its development, fed the militant anti-abortionists' campaign. Anti-abortionists disseminated numerous new images of the foetus, principally through their film *A Silent Scream*. It was sensational pictures of what happens to the foetus during an abortion that drew renewed interest in, and sympathy for, the foetus. These images, together with the ones featured in *Life* magazine, made the spectator identify with the foetus as *subject*, initiating what has now become commonplace, privileging of the foetus over, indeed to the exclusion of, the mother.

This new foetal subjectivity has entered popular discourse: a recent *New York Times* article on the new obsession with foetal operations, for instance, had enlarged images of how the surgeon obtains access to the foetus, but the mother's body was not otherwise in evidence. The image showed the surgeon's hand and implements entering the womb as if the womb were located in space, floating unattached to anything (*New York Times* May 1990). Another recent *New York Times* article about foetal heart surgery again imaged the foetus as if it had nothing to do with the mother's body. Discussion of the surgery mentioned nothing about discomfort to the mother in whose body this was taking place. But, significantly, the mother is *assumed* to be at her foetus's behest, and safely located in a nuclear family (*New York Times*, 30 January 1990). Yet another article, this one on foetal survival (*New York Times*, Gina Kolata, 18 April 1989) shows an enlarged image of the foetus, the umbilical cord moving out of frame. The cord is hanging in space, and the mother's body not imaged (nor even the womb). An article about conception images the sperm binding to an egg in the woman's body, but again the blown-up image floats in space, and the title says nothing about the woman (*New York Times* 28 July 1988).

Significantly, like the Nilsson text, the images of the foetus in the above articles, usually sketches and drawings, depict it as a small human with all the outward signs that mark it as such: eyes, nose, hands, fingers, legs, feet, toes; often, the foetus has a little smile on its lips, and a peaceful baby-like look. We all know that zygotes of six to eight weeks do not really have such features. Pictures always image the "baby" as white and sexless. Depicting the zygote this way, in pictures far larger than actual size, instigates the same feelings in the viewer as would a picture of an actual baby. The representational qualities of largeness, whiteness and humanness become moral determiners, misleading readers/viewers about the *actual* status of the zygote, and negating race/gender specificities.

The new interest in the foetus has entered into film, where it threatens to displace the mother as subject. Amy Heckerling's 1990 comedy, *Look Who's Talking*, shows us the actual moment of conception (presumably using Nilsson film and photo footage). Spectators are shown the inside of what we later realize is the heroine's body; an egg matures and drops into the fallopian tube (these images accompany the film titles). The camera then pans right to focus on a male hand feeling the heroine's leg. The adulterous couple are at work, but about to have sex. At this point, the camera pans left again, now imaging sperm racing through the fallopian tubes. The sperm are given male voices, which sound like men chasing, and competing for, women in a dance hall. The "winner" is seen diving into the egg, while tones of satisfaction fill the sound track.

The camera continues to take us, periodically, into the heroine's womb, where the *male* foetus talks to us about what it feels like there. The world-as-seen by the foetus returns as the heroine struggles with her baby's father over whether or not to marry. Things the heroine does are registered by the foetus in the womb. At one point, thirsty, the foetus suggests "we get some orange juice down here;" a moment later, the heroine is seen finishing a gallon of juice.

The birth is presented from the foetus's perspective, and, after birth, the baby continues to talk to the viewer, as if a fully cognizant being from the start. He has opinions about the heroine's boyfriends, and helps her choose the right one. While this makes for good comedy, the underlying significance of displacing the mother-as-subject and of assigning to foetus and baby thoughts and perceptions of adulthood should not be taken lightly. Indeed, the choice of a boy baby sets up an automatic Oedipal rivalry between baby and the heroine's boyfriends, and means that once again woman/mother is object of exchange between, if not "men" then "males." In the end, the baby and lover become the *real* couple, until the heroine gives in and agrees to marry the lover now bonded to the baby. The mother's authority and centrality are at stake, again, in such new images. Heckerling's film carries to a ludicrous

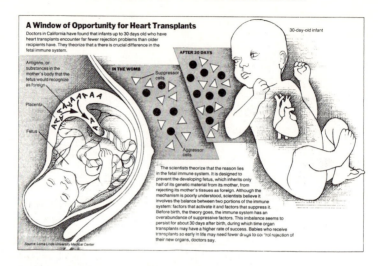

Figure 19a   *New York Times*, 30 January 1990. Note how the drawings misrepresent the foetus as already a baby, complete with facial features and an expression.

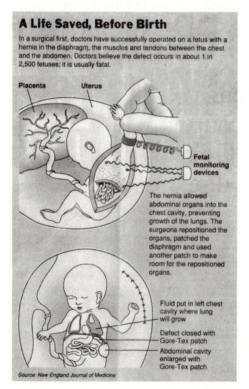

Figure 19b   *New York Times*, 31 May 1990. Again the foetus has facial features and an expression that suggests it is far more 'human' than it really is. In addition, the images show no evidence of the mother's body. The surgeon's hand interacts directly with the baby.

206

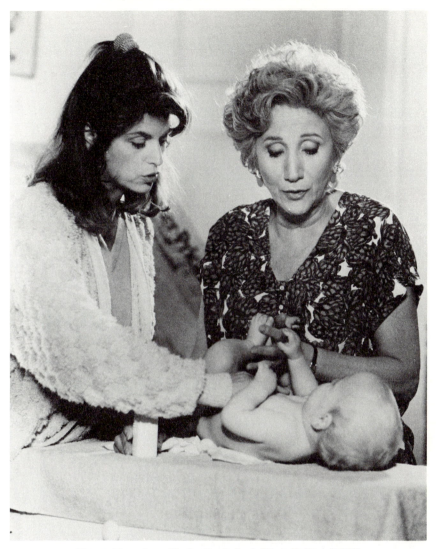

Figure 20a   Amy Heckerling's *Look Who's Talking* (1990)
Mikey, now born, being diapered by Mollie and her disapproving mother in a
rare moment of relative harmony.

extreme – it externalizes and literalizes – what is implicit in other foetal
imagery noted above.

   Look Who's Talking, Too (1990) has recently appeared. Evidently, the success
of the first film, as with *Three Men and a Baby*, spurred Hollywood to a follow-up
movie. *Look Who's Talking, Too* begins in a similar manner to the earlier film,
only now the heroine is making love to John Travolta, her husband, instead
of to a lover in the office. As before, as the film titles appear, the screen is

Figure 20b   Amy Heckerling's *Look Who's Talking* (1990)
Once again, the woman/mother is object of exchange between males. The baby
and the lover, James, constitute the *real* couple.

filled with the enlarged image of a woman's ovum floating in what looks like
cosmic, or under water, space. The camera moves right to find the heroine and
Travolta love-making, only now they are interrupted by Mikey's nightmare.
Back in bed, Travolta wakes his wife, they continue love-making, and once
again the screen is filled with an image of sperm racing toward a magnified
diaphragm. Once again, male locker-room dialogue ensues, the sperm, like
males, eager for a lay. The language of capture and penetration dominates,
and the sperm that manages to find a way around the diaphragm to the egg

moans "hot mama, hot mama" as it plunges down through the egg's resisting surface.

This time the foetus is female, but as before, it fills the screen and is given cute features, Roseanne Barr's deep voice, and in general made a full subject, with thoughts and language, long before the birth. After the birth, both the baby and her brother are given perceptions, thoughts and language, and the full voices of adults. The world of the film is seen from their points of view. While this could theoretically involve a certain empowerment of children, the way in which the scenes are done is closer to exploitation of the child-actors. We do not have something resembling young children's innerworlds (if one could ever approach such a thing), but only adult play with adult concepts of child-views. But, as with the first film, *Look Who's Talking, Too* reinforces the 1990s fashion of decentering adults and making children the heroes. Particularly troubling, still, is the representation of the foetus as *person*, and the disjunction between the image of the womb and the mother's body.

How do we account for this? Is the form of foetal interpellation such as to make it fulfill man's need for a hero? Is the foetus the new savior of mankind, delivering us from all the actual messes we have made? Is the focus on it part of man's dream to make the perfect being? Is the focus on the foetus the latest form of the age-long male utopian urge to control reproduction, to control the body, perhaps to the extent of eliminating it altogether?

Focus on the foetus may, indeed, indicate a renewed desire to write the mother out of the story (except as once more an unquestioned patriarchal function), or to marginalize and negate her subjectivity. This new discourse, apparently contradictory to that of a nostalgic return to a sentimentalized mother–child relationship, in fact colludes neatly with it. Instead of an intense mother–child relationship being idealized and hypostatized, we have obsession with conception and gestation – with foetal life within the mother. But the discourses are linked in both indicating, at least in dominant forms, a return to obsession with the biological child.

The differences are important, however. The sentimental mother-discourse speaks from the position of the mother's being absorbed in nurturing: however oppressively, it situates the mother as a subject, as in *The Good Mother*. The reproductive mother-discourse, on the contrary, marginalizes the mother again, in that it is only interested in the mother as the being that initiated the foetal discourse – by desiring to create a foetus. It also redefines *subjectivity*, and raises anew issues about what constitutes subjectivity in the first place.

Foetal interpellation manifests a new form of the old desire to absent (or deny) the mother: foetal imagery represents the foetus as an entity in its own right, unattached to the mother, or at least rendering her irrelevant to what is going on in the womb. Male fears of woman's ability to reproduce, on some primal level, have partly produced the mother-images I have studied in this book. The development of science has now made possible not only understanding but also *controlling* reproductive processes which have long caused envy in males.

All the discourses noted above collude in privileging the biological, nuclear family. Apparently, North American culture feels threatened by the legacies of the Women's, Gay and other 1970s liberation movements. It needs images of couples happily united around the biological baby.

To review briefly: the orientation toward the child which began with Rousseau (marking the start of the modern motherhood discourse) was further developed in psychoanalytic theory. This orientation largely entailed on the one hand, marginalizing the mother, and, on the other, over-valuing her for her sacrifices or denigrating her for her failures. As Evelyn Fox Keller has pointed out, the new push that science is making in relation to the foetus represents man's age-long desire to understand the mystery of woman's ability to give birth (Keller 1986). These strategies have now been carried to a wild extreme in taking the *idea* of the child back to the foetus. The mother is now asked to be responsible for (and subject to) her own foetus: the foetus now takes on a life of its own, with its own needs, demands and satisfactions.

The proliferation of foetal imagery in contemporary fiction is currently being studied by feminists as a phenomenon that requires situating in the context of both reproductive and nuclear technologies (Soufoulis 1984; Petchesky 1987; Squier 1989). Suddenly, the foetus is the center of the narrative, the main protagonist, taking the place of the mother. Science's new interest in the foetus coincides with renewed images of distaste for women's bodies and biological processes. Patriarchy's age-long distaste has been well-documented, but the renewed representations, in such films as *Aliens* (1986) for example, are significant as they dovetail with medical reproductive technologies (Creed 1986). The monster-mother's endlessly proliferating, ghastly body, consisting of sticky, sucking tubes which smother all in its path, emblematizes a whole host of male fears. Medical science's control of women's reproductive processes, in an ironical rewriting of Shulamith Firestone's *The Dialectic of Sex* (1970), rests on the fantasy of the "clean machine" which will in future produce babies. Whereas Firestone fantasized the possibility of an artificial womb with a view to relieving women of the necessity of going through childbirth, male scientists now engage in this fantasy with a view to *replacing* women as the creators of life.

Foetal interpellation coincides with representations of the cyborg – the artificially created human being – that is prevalent both in the male-oriented 1980s science-fiction film, such as *Blade Runner, The Man Who Fell To Earth, Brother From Another Planet, Brazil* and also in science fiction. Hollywood is fascinated by inter-species body-boundary loss in these cyborg films; but often the body-boundary destruction is viewed with horror or suspicion, as in *The Fly* or *Videodrome*. Occasionally, as in *Robocop*, there is a positive image of human/machine blends, but these often take the form of a human brain within a totally mechanical body.

This sort of cyborg-fantasy suggests another way in which males desire to control reproduction: women are not needed at all, since human look-alikes can be created totally independently of ovum or sperm. The male urge to create such fantasies has to do first, with a desire to reinvent morality in a version not fully human, as if "human" is a discredited concept within which any longer to develop moral views. But male science fiction, and the scientists doing cutting-edge artificial intelligence work, also yearn to be rid of the body altogether. David Rorvik (1977) quotes scientists enthusiastic about the fantasy of the human brain alone being retained of what was "man," and the new being is imaged as pure points of radiation communicating in outer space.

Since female sci-fi fantasies are strikingly different, I will briefly review such work from the late 1960s to the present. I will also point to significant changes within women's imaginary relation to reproductive technologies that parallels, and questions, male scientific developments as well as representations such as those noted above in popular media.

The struggle for control of women's bodies originally meant freeing women of a culturally imposed and not necessarily desired reproductive role – the main role open to women up until the 1970s. Firestone's book represents feminist fantasy about reproduction in this period, but such utopian ideas involving artificial wombs and so on also appeared in sci-fi women's novels. Naomi Mitchison's *Memoirs of a Spacewoman* (1962/1985), for example, imagines a diverse array of reproductive possibilities, only one of which is the standard human male and female mating to make a baby. In Mitchison's utopian future world, women are able to decide, based on any number of criteria, with whom they want to have children. They usually decide among human males, but Mary, the spacewoman, has two interesting reproductive experiences with "Others." She participates in an experiment that involves a graft that grows on to a living body – sort of exterior womb without a womb. The grafts produce in Mary a great deal of motherly love, and the whole experience is presented positively. There is no need to reject the "other" form.

The second reproductive experience is when a Martian accidentally activates Mary's reproductive cycle; she gives birth to a haploid child, who is composed of two parts mother, and no part Martian. The construction of "otherness" is thereby confused, since the child has double all the mother's characteristics rather than being a *distortion* of the mother, or something else entirely.

Another utopian sci-fi imaginary world can be found in Marge Piercy's *Woman on the Edge of Time* (1976), which envisions reproduction entirely outside the woman's body. All children are born from artificial wombs, thereby freeing the mother and simultaneously discarding the nuclear family as the ideal. Women and men are equally involved in raising children, and each child has three parents, consisting of at least one woman, one man and

211

a third person of either gender. Piercy sees placing reproduction outside of women's bodies as a way of making possible her utopian, egalitarian world, and replacing the sort of male abuse of women with which the novel begins.

Meanwhile, Joanna Russ's *The Female Man* (1975) constructs a planet where women are the only inhabitants, and they successfully rear children themselves, in groups. This novel looks back to Charlotte Perkins Gilman's *Herland* (1915) (discussed in Chapter 7) where the ideal of the "Virgin Birth" in a land without men was first developed.

In the 1960s, then, before abortion was legalized, women wanted to remove themselves from being inscribed within female bodies that were not within their control. In the 1980s, however, two developments changed these unconflicted female fantasies about the liberating possibilities of reproductive technologies. On the one hand, male scientists began indeed to develop reproductive technologies not that far removed from the fantasy of the artificial womb. At least, artificial insemination and in-vitro fertilization became possible, as did also technologies for surrogate motherhood, for foetal gender detection, gene-splicing and finally for foetal operations. On the other hand, women themselves began to have a series of options available to them, as outlined above in the discourses I've traced. At this point, then, insistence on the "clean machine" and on male scientists' research appears like male meddling in women's reproductive freedom and male control of our bodies.

In addition, the AIDS crisis has drastically altered feminists' 1960s conception of a liberated sexuality; while feminists continue to debate pornography and its effects, the centrality of the debate is being replaced by that on the effects on women of new reproductive technologies. This marks an important shift in priorities from sexual difference, and male abuse of the female body, to male meddling in women's reproductive processes and women's reproductive choices (Reissman 1983). Already underway in the 1960s, these technologies only captured feminist attention when their psychological and physical impacts on women became clear. Patriarchal investment in women's reproductive bodies is now equated with that already explored in pornography.

As Robyn Rowland has pointed out (1987; 1990), it is the remaining maternal (pro-natalism) discourse that has supported the new reproductive technologies in an era when more and more women are apparently finding that they are infertile. Figures may be misleading (Terry, 1989), but according to Rowland, infertile women describe an intense feeling of being outside their community because they cannot get pregnant. The discourse of pregnancy, then, is individualized and leads to women giving it precedence over all else. In this way, women unknowingly collude with male scientists' new interest in proliferating, and experimenting with, the reproductive technologies that represent the cutting edge of medicine.

Significantly, women's science-fiction depicts the contradictory positions women hold in relation to new technologies. Dystopias sometimes replace 1960s utopias, as in Margaret Atwood's *The Handmaid's Tale* (1986). The enunciative position in this novel could be described as a "resisting postmodernism" (or a postmodernism like the one which governs my own text, representing a modernist look within a postmodern universe); sometimes, as in Octavia Butler's *Dawn* (1987) and *Imago* (1988), fiction radically shifts the issues at stake, writing from another position altogether, one that I would call "postmodernist" in the sense of an acceptance of new cultural tendencies, an attempt to work with new technological possibilities. A brief look at each of these novels will make the differences clear.

The Handmaid's Tale (1986; made into a film in 1990) is a dystopic fantasy of a totalitarian North America, now called The Republic of Gilead, in which a group of right-wing religious fundamentalists are in control. Most women are infertile due to the excessive chemicals in the air and radiation released from an earthquake on the San Andreas fault. Many of the babies who are born are "unbabies," that is deformed, and there are also "unwomen," that is infertile women. Since the military take-over, women have been denied access to their money and property, which was given over to their husbands. Reduced once again to mere bodies (more thoroughly than in earlier periods), women are refused literacy and education, being used simply for reproduction. Surrogacy is the main reproductive mode (only now by intercourse itself rather than insemination, the right-wing group eschewing other technologies for religious reasons), and the distress of this practice made only too evident.

Octavia Butler's *Dawn* provides an example of fiction speaking from an altogether other position *vis-à-vis* new technologies – a position first articulated by Donna Haraway (1985) in her ground-breaking essay arguing "for *pleasure* in the confusion of boundaries and for *responsibility* in their construction." With similar aims in mind, Butler is concerned in *Dawn* with the problem of xenogenesis between an Earth woman, Lilith, and a species from another planet, the Oankali. A post-apocalyptic tale, *Dawn* traces the events after a great nuclear destruction of the Earth. The Oankali land on Earth and take several Earth beings up to their planet, where they mate with them, so as to produce a new species, neither human nor Oankali, which will be returned to reproduce on Earth. Lilith, the heroine, experiences a new, organic, plant-like world, which is organized predominantly through touch. She also experiences the magnanimity and peacefulness of highly refined, sensitive aliens, and the pathetic selfishness and evil of captured humans who refuse to adopt the modes of the aliens. The novel ends with Lilith pregnant, but she does not yet know what the result of her non-genital mating with an Oankali will be.

Imago, a sequel to *Dawn*, is the story of Lilith's child, Jodhas. Striking in *Imago* is how Lilith's offspring has a completely new genetic make-up and new possibilities. While the Oankali have all along shown incredible healing powers, Jodhas has even greater bodily possibilities. It is this depiction of

213

a world in which the body, as against the mind, is highly refined that sets Butler's fantasies apart from popular male ones. While male writers fantasize the abolition of the body in favor of pure mind, Butler imagines worlds where the body is vastly improved. The new body is able to detect sickness in another body, and immediately effects cures through touch. The new body is especially sensitive to gene mutations produced in the humans remaining on Earth through the nuclear holocaust that has taken place. Jodhas can detect and cure cancerous growths through linking her body to the sick one for periods of time.

Communication in *Imago* is largely through the body. The body becomes the supreme entity, able to sense everything about other bodies. Touch is highly sexualized, and intercourse is no longer genital in the old senses. Indeed, Jodhas has no genital organs per se at all. In this sense, Butler opens up the creative possibilities of new reproductive technologies, linked as they are to genetic scientific discoveries. Her novels challenge our species-hierarchical, nineteenth-century concept of the human body as the only valorized one, as Donna Haraway (1989) has noted. Corporeal borders are confounded when something which is not the same enters. The distinction between kinds of bodies disintegrates when separations between species begin to be eroded by inter-species reproduction. Donna Haraway (reading Butler and building on her prior work) opens up the possibility of liberatory aspects to destroying body boundaries as hitherto defined, whether these be animal human or machine human. Butler demonstrates how reproductive technologies will, when carried to a science-fiction extreme, not only save humankind from destruction but also free men and women from the stifling notions of difference recent feminisms have exposed.

While most Hollywood science-fiction fantasies stress man's construction of human–computer interface entities, a film like *Demon Seed* is particularly interesting because of its preoccupation with inter-species reproduction specifically. In this film, Julie Christie plays a restless, angry wife of a government researcher, involved in top-secret developments in artificial computer intelligence. The husband's computer-creation gains intelligent autonomy from its creator, and begins to seduce the wife with the aim of reproducing itself through links with human flesh. The grotesqueness of the intercourse – its possible entirely evil/negative representation – is mitigated by the computer's benevolent aim in reproducing itself. Like the Oankali in Butler's *Dawn*, it wants to create a more humane world for humankind. The film ends with the husband's attempt to kill the inter-species foetus, while the wife seeks to save it. The new being finally emerges from its external "womb," with an ambivalently coded appearance, leaving to spectators the decision regarding its results for the world.

In this movement from *Memoirs of a Spacewoman* at the end of the 1960s, to *Demon Seed* (in the late 1970s) and *The Handmaid's Tale*, *Dawn* and *Imago* at the end of the 1980s, we see how a feminist utopia, in which women control and

214

use reproductive technologies to free themselves of an oppressive patriarchy, gives way to narratives preoccupied (either negatively or positively) with post-holocaust worlds. Writing in the context of extreme proliferation of nuclear weapons and of projected life-threatening environmental effects of radiation and chemicals, women writers imagine postmodern worlds where the issue of the nuclear family is no longer central. Indeed, this very shift away from contesting dominant sexuality, marriage and the family arguably signals the end of the feminisms that the 1960s gave rise to.

The negative position argues that the 1970s positions failed to recognize what might happen if women were no longer needed for their reproductive organs. If male babies can be created artificially outside the womb, and if homosexuality can, as in the Greek period, easily become generally satisfactory for men, then what need does a society have for women? Men could simply abolish women, or artificially produce them as a "slave" class.

It is the prospect of this new potential scenario that has resulted in the 1980s paradox, in which struggle for control of woman's body involves putting the womb *back* in the woman's body. Women now rediscover pleasure in giving birth and in nurturing: maternal pleasures can be returned to us because mothering is no longer an irrevocable male mandate. Women have won the right to choose or not to choose motherhood. When this is the case, women can accept the pleasures of maternity. In the 1980s, then, the female body is a site of contestation between women seeking to retain a hard-won control, and male scientists newly fascinated with gaining control over women's bodies through new reproductive technologies.[7]

The complex and contradictory motherhood discourses outlined in this chapter show that extremely complicated adjustments are evidently being made on the Symbolic level in response to new technologies, to postmodern multinational capitalisms, and revolutions in female sexuality and social roles. Women's finally declared move from the domestic to the public sphere, which has been steadily in progress in Euro-centric nations since the turn of the twentieth century and that I have tried to trace in this book, has produced, and been produced by, unprecedented cultural upheaval. While the consumerist perspective largely welcomes this move (women wage-earners at the new high levels are clearly a rich source of markets), and while dominant advertising representations indicate no trouble with the new female positions, things are obviously more complex on the deeper cultural levels. For instance, alongside discursive acceptance of women's new career roles, there exist, as indicated, representations returning (1950s fashion) to the idealization of woman in the home, which embodies patriarchal need to control and restrict woman.

The complexities of the new situation, indeed, suggest the need for a new theoretical paradigm. Culture arguably confronts a post-feminist historical moment, that is a moment in which prior feminist interventions, having had their effects, can no longer be undertaken in the old ways. The various feminist interventions, as they occurred from 1960 to 1980, are partly responsible for the current changes in women's actual institutional situations. But modern capitalism has found ways to co-opt, integrate and thereby subtly reverse the very interventions that have benefited women, thus putting them into question.

If post-structuralist feminism has demonstrated the need to analyze the language order through which we learn to be what our culture calls "women" as against "men," as we seek to bring about change, now we need to re-evaluate the usefulness of "feminist" as a concept, since it has been appropriated by dominant consumerist culture. "Feminism" may now be seen as an essentializing term that looks back to the individualist frameworks of early feminist positions, which may no longer serve in the postmodern era. The concept of an oppositional cultural stance like feminism becomes more and more difficult once society's *rhetoric* has integrated what were earlier feminist demands.

However, it is precisely in such moments that we have to struggle to keep oppositional positions alive. But the question remains as to the best strategies for doing this. In relation to the mother, we find a diversity of theories, strategies and actions. While some feminists, like Judith Kegan Gardiner (1989) and Marianne Hirsch (1990), argue that the mother should begin to represent "herself," others, such as Nancy Wood (1983) or Parveen Adams (1983), fear that any "mother-self" is inevitably already a patriarchal construct, part of a patriarchal ideology that depends for its coherence on the binary opposition, "Father/Mother," and on an unconscious repression of the mother's *jouissance*, of her possibility to become something "other" than a mother. Yet others, like Donna Haraway (1989), from within some postmodern theoretical frameworks, would argue that the mind is already turned inside out, its mechanisms therefore open to view; indeed, in the new age of what Baudrillard (1983) has called "communication, contact, ecstasy," that replaces the old "Faustian, perhaps Promethean" Oedipal world, the unconscious is no longer possible.

A final group (Birns 1988; Rothman 1989) would want to look at motherhood as an institution. On this sociological level, researchers address the inadequacy of our institutions to new social developments regarding the mother. The argument might roughly be as follows: North America retains the nineteenth-century concept of the nuclear family as its predominant *concept* for child-rearing, despite the fact that the social roles, and the division of labour required in such a family, no longer routinely apply, as most of this chapter has tried to show. Technology, combined with the new liberation movements, has made possible forms of relating that move far beyond the traditional nuclear family. But it is largely women who bear the brunt of the gaps and imbalances on the level of daily, lived experiences. More men are now rearing their children from birth, and certainly men are sharing in child-rearing tasks in North America in an unprecedented fashion. Yet, the

216

argument continues, women who combine mothering and career continue to feel that they do neither job adequately, and remain confused as to how they ought to be arranging their lives. As middle-class women have increasingly entered the professions in the wake of 1960s movements, and as women intellectuals and artists have increasingly made scholarship and artistic creation their main goals in life, so for the historical female subject, it has become more and more difficult (and perhaps undesirable) to develop and retain an identity as "mother" (M. Kaplan 1991).

On this level, it might be argued that if Rousseau can be seen as initiating the modern motherhood discourse in the eighteenth century, the twenty-first century will witness its demise. Motherhood, as an institution, is perhaps victim of capitalism's postmodern attempt to simultaneously blame women for not nurturing while seeking to control motherhood through reproductive technologies that eradicate the biological mother–child relation. In this way, mother-women can remain in the work-force, useful to the economy as workers and consumers, while society decides their fate.

Let me in concluding address briefly the contradictions among these varied discourses, themselves exemplifying the theoretical difficulties that we face today. The two theoretical extremes are exemplified by the gap between women's dystopic, postmodern fantasies, in which the very possibility for any inner, psychic mental life seems erased, and psychoanalytic feminists, who, despite the many differing theories and perspectives, keep alive the sense of an intricate, unconscious realm. Psychoanalytic theorists like Julia Kristeva (1980; 1985), Juliet Mitchell (1974) or Jessica Benjamin (1988), to mention three women developing different kinds of theories, continue in the 1980s, more perhaps than before, to work on difficult psychoanalytic problems, such as depression, love, the female Oedipal trajectory, mother–infant interaction, or the relationships among Freudian drives, the Lacanian Symbolic and the realm of the Imaginary. In between are the feminists working on the level of social institutions, changing social roles, on relations among different ethnic and class groups, or on the impact of technological developments on social interactions or social forms.

All three kinds of research are essential for understanding fully what is going on today. But each level, for the time being, is perhaps best studied in isolation from the others. The ultimate goal ought to be the integration of these three broad perspectives, but scholars are far from being sufficiently theoretically sophisticated to achieve such integration. It is easier to take one of the perspectives and apparently account for everything in its terms; but it is precisely because of this ease that we should beware of the temptation to reduce one of the levels to any other. In terms of motherhood, in any case, we simply do not know enough to be able to account for any particular phenomenon in terms of only one theory. For instance, one could use psychoanalytic theory to explain foetal imagery and the postmodern fascination with reproductive technologies

217

in cultural products. In this view, such representations would manifest increasing unconscious fear of the mother – indeed a pathological fixation on her displaced into an obsessive need to control and/or erase her very being, to take charge of the very functions that define her and that have created individuals' unbearable dependence on her. From the perspective of postmodern theory, such representations prefigure the universe of the twenty-first century, in which, indeed, there is no "interaffective sharing" (Stern 1985) and in which prior so-called "natural" reproductive processes have been disrupted or eliminated. Or we could explain such representations as a result of actual scientific and political developments (a mimetic reflection of the real, nuclear-age, world), and look at the impact on social relations, on the structure of the nuclear family, and on political or economic factors, of such developments.

Each of these explorations would contribute something to the understanding of the contemporary cultural dilemmas *vis-à-vis* the mother. As I noted in Chapter 1, I started this project with the ambitious aim of exploring the relations between the psychic/cultural levels in regard to the mother, and those of the social institutions and ideologies we encounter in daily experience. This perspective naturally leads at this point to the following question: if the modern unconscious that I have been trying to illuminate by exploring literature and film – if this unconscious was an integral part of the modern nuclear family and was produced through specific culturally coded relations to the mother – does it change as new technologies alter our social relations? And if that unconscious changes, then does the mother's hitherto negatively central place in the old unconscious begin to shift? Does her displacement to the margins change?

Research has not yet reached a level in which this question is answerable. The mother-in-the-unconscious, the Imaginary mother, continues to be powerful, despite the ideological and social changes that the various feminisms have brought about. Psychically, the mother still fails to satisfy, the phallus is still longed for, despite an increasingly postmodern society that (for good or ill) is finally challenging the nineteenth-century concept of the nuclear family.

But all the work that feminist scholars have done on the mother in the unconscious, on mother–child relations, and on the mother in representation, has itself had an impact, and influences how the Imaginary mother is now constituted. The very understanding of a difference between an historical and an unconscious imaginary mother permits better *conscious* attitudes towards the mother, even if the unconscious desire for her (with its attendant problems) remains.

Arguably, all the feminist theorizing about women in social structures, about women and psychoanalysis, and about women in representation over the past twenty-five years (theorizing that obviously made this book possible) is playing its part – that of a meta-language – in displacing the old negative mother-position in the patriarchal unconscious that has hitherto encompassed us all. But the 1990s represent a painful transitional period, as indicated by the plethora of contradictory mother-discourses outlined earlier – discourses which in some circular fashion impossible to analyze arise from our complex, post-industrial, postmodern society. If we can begin to glimpse the possibilities of new female subjectivities, of female as well as male desire, and of a mutual recognition of the Other – whether that other be a male, one's mother or father, a female, or whether that other be ethnically, nationally or socially "Other" – we will have achieved a lot. In other words, as subjectivities, including female ones, are in general conceived of as dispersed, multiple, unstable, in process, so the concept "mother" may, in turn, no longer signify such supreme importance. The de-essentializing of subjectivity and, in a related move, of *identity*, should free women and minorities of their simultaneous subordination and fetishization. For women, one of the most subordinated *and* fetishized positions has been that of "mother." Once this position is opened up as only a part of any specific woman's subjectivity, not the all-consuming entirety of it; once any specific woman is seen to be constituted "mother" only when interacting with her child; once "mother" is no longer a fixed, essentialized quality, then women may be freed from the kind of discursive constraints and burdens studied in this book.

NOTES

1 Introduction

1 Let me note that Vidor does redeem himself to a degree in both films by allowing the mother a voice – particularly in *Stella Dallas* – as will be clear in Chapter 8. It is possible that here and in the scene in *The Crowd* Vidor is being ironical.

2 See for evidence of the effect of maternal ideas on empirical mothers, interviews of Ann Oakley in her *Housewife* (1974), and Meryl Kaplan's study on *Images of the Mother* (1991).

3 See bibliography for list of authors and titles.

4 Also relevant to theorizing a "master" discourse are first, Juri Tynjanov, and second, Louis Althusser. Juri Tynjanov's concept of the dominant was developed by Roman Jakobson (see Tynjanov 1971). Althusser's concept of Ideological State Apparatuses (ISAs), linked to the notion of the dominant, may be found in the essay on ISAs (Althusser 1971: 127–86); for Jameson's reworkings, see Jameson (1982).

2 The Historical Sphere

1 For evidence of the discourses and technological developments that prepared for the changes at the Industrial Revolution, see Cott (1977); for evidence for the period, see Welter (1966); for summary of scholarship on these issues, see Degler (1980); for summary of and bibliography for changing Motherhood discourses, see Ehrenreich and English (1978).

2 Each of the books contains numerous references to further important sources; see also bibliography to this book for more reading on these areas.

3 Historians claim that Badinter overstates the case of both the Mother's indifference and the absence of value for the child prior to Rousseau. Her work has been criticized by Louise Tilly and Miriam Cohen (1982) for "shaky documentation", and the empirical studies by George D. Sussman call into question some of Badinter's facts and figures. See in particular Sussman (1977).

4 See Cora Kaplan (1983: 15–30) for discussion of Wollstonecraft's responses to Rousseau.

5 See also Chapter 7, where I discuss several child-care experts' discourses; see bibliography for citations of texts.

6 See for example statements in *The German Ideology* (1845–46), Chapter 3, Section D ("Hierarchy"), reprinted in Padover (1975: 61–2). Marx and Engels here argue that "Historically the bourgeoisie gives the family the character of the bourgeois family, wherein boredom and money are the binding links, and to which also belong the bourgeois dissolution of the family, which does not prevent it from

220

constantly continuing its existence. Its dirty existence corresponds to the holy concept of it in official phraseology and universal hypocrisy." And "the real body of the family: property relation, the excluding relation toward other families, forced living together . . . remained . . . because the existence of the family is made necessary by its connection with the mode of production that is independent of the will of bourgeois society." Again, in *Manifesto of the Communist Party* (1848), Part II, Marx says: "On what foundation is the present family, the bourgeois family, based? On Capital, on private gain. In its completely developed form, this family exists only among the bourgeoisie. But this state of things finds its complement in the practical absence of the family among the proletarians, and in public prostitution" (Padover 1975: 67).

7 It is poignant but instructive to read narratives of the personal lives of Darwin, Marx and Freud, all of whose families suffered loss and pain on the level of daily, lived existence. Testimony and letters by Jenny Marx, collected by David McLellan, detail the suffering of bearing and losing many children, of poverty, shame, illness, while Marx continued to write his important but enormously abstract theories, which, for all their attention to the *human being*, still only see that human in his political/social/economic dimension, and not as a subject, produced through psychic interchange; or Darwin, who lost his mother at an early age, and who over-venerated his father, and depended utterly on his intelligent, responsible wife to provide the conditions for his abstract research. Freud does deal with the intimate sphere, finally, in contrast to the two other main modernist theorists; but, poignantly, blinds himself to the suffering going on within his own home. It is this level of the domestic, the personal, the psychic, then, the world that women have long inhabited, that feminist research has tried to address, and that this book hopes to contribute to.

3 The Psychoanalytic Sphere and Motherhood Discourse

1 See Appendix B (pp. 54–5) for discussion of Freud's "A Case of Successful Treatment by Hypnotism," which involves a mother (Freud 1951).

2 See Appendix A (pp. 52–4) for details of such feminist responses to psycho-analysis.

3 See for example French authors, such as Kristeva, Luce Irigaray and Hélène Cixous (to be discussed shortly); but many feminist theorists in other countries have used and developed Lacanian theories.

4 For good discussions of differences between these two groups of theorists, see introductions by Jacqueline Rose and Juliet Mitchell to their edited volume (Mitchell and Rose 1982).

5 I am grateful to Jessica Benjamin in particular for these points, and to members of the New York Institute for the Humanities Seminar on "Sexual Difference and Psychoanalysis" (led jointly by Jessica Benjamin, Muriel Dimen, Adrienne Harris and Virginia Gouldner) for a lively discussion of these issues.

4 Woman's Writing, Melodrama and Film

1 This spate of books was published all about the same time.

2 Mary Ann Doane has recently re-evaluated feminist film theory in an impor-tant essay, "Remembering Women: Psychical and Historical Constructions of Women," in E.A. Kaplan (1990).

3 For more discussion of mass culture and the feminine, see Huyssen (1986). Huyssen is correct in seeing this designation as a representation valid primarily

for the late nineteenth century. But he agrees that it is only recently that the underlying dichotomy has begun to lose its power as women become *visible* in *high* art, and also emerge as new kinds of performers and producers in mass culture (Huyssen 1986: 205).

5 The Maternal Melodrama: The Sacrifice Paradigm

1 I am using "pre-Symbolic" to refer explicitly to the Lacanian psychoanalytic paradigm (see Chapter 3 for a full discussion). Much of what I discuss in this chapter has to do with the persistence of desire in the adult psyche left over from the Imaginary phase. While both Mother and Father have Symbolic functions (that of the Mother subservient to the Father), there is no pre-Symbolic Father. The significant Mother relation is the pre-Symbolic one: the Mother in the Symbolic has very specific, patriarchally defined roles.

2 Narratives in some texts themselves expose links between the mother-types: see, for example, the mother in Basil Deardon's 1947 film, *Frieda*, whose good-natured efforts in fact betray a desire to control her son's life; Harriet Beecher Stowe's *Uncle Tom's Cabin* actually explodes the patriarchal mother paradigms in the figure of Cassy, the much-abused mulatto. The text shows how it is the brutality of patriarchy toward mother–child relations that drives Cassy to murderous excess.

3 A forthcoming book by Judith Walkowitz deals with the relationship between melodrama and professional Samaritans like Joseph Butler or self-stylized muck-raking journalists, like Stead, who exposed the brothel and under-world London life of the nineteenth century.

4 Judith Walkowitz's "Melodrama, Sexual Scandals, and Victorian Political Culture," read at a New York Institute for the Humanities Seminar in May 1986, is a draft version of parts of the forthcoming book.

5 I am here using "ideology" in the senses first developed by Louis Althusser and also by Deleuze and Guattari in their *Anti-Oedipus* (1983). For Althusser, "Ideology is a representation of the imaginary relationship of individuals to their real conditions of existence" ("Ideological State Apparatuses," in Althusser (1971) *Lenin and Philosophy*, p. 1,620). It is the way in which the subject is constituted through the Lacanian mirror phase that renders him/her vulnerable to being "hailed" (as Althusser puts it) by ideology, and made into an *ideological* subject (necessarily – there is no being outside of ideology). But the specific *kinds* of ideal images (of, that is, fantasy political relations) will vary from one cultural context and historical period to another. And they will change, as on a level at which the individual is not aware, his/her "real" conditions of existence change. For a full discussion of many of these matters see Jameson (1982).

6 Research on the play done in the Lincoln Center Library, New York.

7 Cf. Kilgariff (1966: 276). Kilgariff notes the large number of what he calls "mutilators of this lachrymose work," including Gus West, Charles Embley, Ned Albert, J. Itt Hardacre, Lilla Wilde, Herbert Shelley and T.A. Palmer.

8 See Brian J. Burton's (1965) version of *East Lynne*, Birmingham, UK: Combridge Ltd. The author here situates his play as a deliberate and nostalgic attempt to keep alive a melodrama tradition now obviously defunct. He specifically notes that he returns to the original novel.

9 Obviously the *femme fatale* figure has a long tradition in western culture, but she was rather rare in American representations from 1830 to the turn of the century. My thesis about the "Master Mother Discourse" in these years in part accounts for the paucity of *femme fatale* images.

6 The Maternal Melodrama: The "Phallic" Mother Paradigm

1 Freud implies that female analysts were given material that he was denied because of his gender, whereas I would assume that female analysts were interested in mothering issues for their own sake and by virtue of their own mothering experiences. For a discussion on Freud's allusions to female analysts, see Sarah Kofman (1985: 11–19). Kofman exposes Freud's reluctant genuflection to the discoveries of the female analysts, while at the same time he attempts to control the material by assuming that they will further develop *his* belated ideas on the subject.

2 For details regarding psychiatrists in the Hollywood film, see Gabbard and Gabbard (1987). While psychiatry entered the German film early on – *The Cabinet of Dr Caligari* (1919) and *The Secrets of a Soul* (1926) – the first American film to figure the godlike psychiatrist was *Blind Alley* (1939), according to the Gabbards. Earlier American treatments were largely comic.

3 Philip Wylie (1942) *A Generation of Vipers*, New York: Farrar. Wylie's brand of "momism" lingered on in North American culture, as evidenced in a song that was commonly sung in 1950 by returning war veterans, aged 26–30, training to be psychiatric clinicians. It parodies a well-known song that idealized the Mother, and some of its lines were as follows:

M is for the many Maladjustments
O is for the Oedipus of Old;
T is for the Things she did to torment me,
H is for her Heart as Black as coal . . .
    Put them altogether, they spell MOTHER
    The one who made a wreck of me.

I should note that a new interest in "Momism" appeared in 1976, hot on the heels of the Women's Movement in Hans Sebald's *Momism: The Silent Disease of America.*

4 Indeed one could argue that it is precisely in genre's other than the maternal melodrama or maternal woman's film that the deepest fears regarding the mother lie. cf. pp. 209–15 for more discussion on this.

5 Both films perhaps look back to the nineteenth-century novel that often combined melodrama and thriller. For discussion of one such text, see Chapter 5, and E.A. Kaplan (1987b).

6 For a text that, by contrast, deals sensitively precisely with such "difficulties," see Mannoni (1970).

7 Critics like Raymond Durgnat have hypothesized a great deal about the mother's feelings and position from her scenes in the film – see Durgnat (1974: 357–8) but this material is read into the characters rather than being articulated in cinematic devices.

7 The "Resisting" Text Within the Patriarchal "Feminine"

1 In a ground-breaking book that shaped future research, Helen Papashvily (1956) argued that there was a bitter, hostile tone beneath most sentimental novels that betrayed women's resentment at their powerlessness in the heyday of repressive Victorian patriarchy.

2 See Harriet Beecher Stowe (1966) *Uncle Tom's Cabin*, New York: Signet, pp. 43–6. All page citations are from this edition. For fuller discussion of these scenes, see E.A. Kaplan (1988).

3 For example, Marie St Clare is unequivocally disapproved of for being self-absorbed, while Miss Ophelia gains stature as she undertakes the mothering role. Cassy's bonding with Emmeline – i.e. her re-entry into the mothering position – ultimately "cures" her of her violence.

4 Her own book, for all its historical progressivity on the slave issue, unfortunately introduced derogatory black stereotypes in American culture, that were to be oft repeated up until recent black liberation movements.

5 For a recent survey of the development of these ideas about eugenics, see a series of articles in the *New Yorker*, especially 27 October 1984 and 29 October 1984.

6 For fuller treatment of this and other Weber films see my forthcoming essay "Lois Weber and her Films: Discourses of Early Cinema, Realism and the Feminine."

8 The "Resisting" Maternal Woman's Film 1930–60

1 Mulvey/Wollen's short film, *Amy!*, made from an explicitly feminist position, enables us to read Arzner's film "against the grain." Their analysis of Amy Johnson, the British flier upon whom Arzner's film is modelled, allows us to see the radical implications of Darrington's deeds that Arzner's text does not foreground. For full discussion of the Mulvey/Wollen film, see E.A. Kaplan (1983b: 163–70).

2 I am referring here to Darwinian ideas adapted to the level of the social, so that Man was thought of as having a series of evolutionary stages, culminating in white European civilization. Such stages were in turn related to innate genetic capabilities. These ideas were popularized in writings by Joseph-Arthur, Comte de Gobineau, Houston Stuart Chamberlain, Alfred Rosenberg, and others.

3 See, for example, Raymond W. Smock (1988) and Joseph P. de Marco (1983).

4 See Marjorie Baumgarten's review in *Cinema Texas Program Notes* 17(1) (20 September 1979). Baumgarten notes that the film would probably have contained even more racial slurs than it does had not Louise Beavers "gotten the NAACP to help her get the word 'nigger' stricken from the script" (47). There was critical debate about the film in the press, and Fannie Hurst evidently defended lines like "once a pancake, always a pancake" by saying that blacks should be more grateful for all the opportunities the script did give them (47).

5 For more details regarding this scene, and for a fuller reading of the film, see my "The Case of the Missing Mother: Maternal Issues in Vidor's *Stella Dallas*," in *Heresies* 16, (1983): 81–5. See also Linda Williams, "'Something Else Besides a Mother;' *Stella Dallas* and the Maternal Melodrama," first published in *Cinema Journal* 24, (1) (Fall 1984): 2–27.

6 For discussion of such homes, see the well-known, now "classic" texts by Betty Friedan (*The Feminine Mystique*, 1965), Phyllis Chesler (*Women and Madness*, 19?), Adrienne Rich (*Of Woman Born*, 1976), Marilyn French (*The Woman's Room*, 19?), among many others.

9 Sex, Work and Mother/Fatherhood

1 Mother's Day ads in the *New York Times* between 1 May and 7 May 1988 included the following examples.

First, a Saks Fifth Avenue ad: two full pages of children, a girl and a boy, thinking about possible gifts for Mom: the girl thinks about pearls, hat, ruffly dress (quite traditional), and the boy thinks about chocolates (also traditional, but the child has a sly look – that is, he knows it's *bad* for Mom's figure for her to eat chocolates). What is new in both is the message that they want to go to Saks with Dad to buy Mom gifts "because Mom says that's her favorite place."

Second, more divergent from previous norms were the many ads for high-tech gifts for Mom: Grand Central Camera featured an ad for sale of VCRs, cameras, camcorders and TVs for a high-tech mom. A Bloomingdale ad echoed the new idea of children in search of gifts for Mom, now featured carefully as a young teacher-cum-mother figure, in long skirt, sweater and blouse, with textbook in one hand, shopping bag in the other. The figure is carefully neither too domestic, nor too professional, neither sexy nor "housewifey" nor urban-Mother: she is civil servant and sovereign, all in one, the ad managing to code itself for all the new contradictions and possibilities.

Third, ads for lingerie from Bloomingdales now had models posed in languid, erotic, slightly vulnerable ways, making mother's sexuality overt, but innocent and non-aggressive. An Altman ad, on the other hand, permitted less shame about maternal sexuality. Several lingerie ads included babies or young children in with the "sexy" mother – this is a new development, I believe.

2 Conventional Father's Day ads in 1988 included, first, Sak's Fifth Avenue: "Sak's Fifth Avenue puts Dad at ease," *New York Times* (15 June 1988), with full page spread of bathrobes. Second, J and R Music World: "Dads and Grads of '88 Sale," *New York Times* (19 June 1988), with stereo, typewriters and watches. Third, NBO's Sportswear Sale: "For the Big Sport in Your Family," *New York Times* (15 June 1988). Fourth, Lord and Taylor, ad for ties: "American Dads tie things together . . . ," *New York Times* (15 June 1988). We then get a list of eminent American Dads who were famous for ability to tie things together, such as Rodgers and Hammerstein, John F. Stevens (Panama Canal) and Alexander Graham Bell.

Unconventional Father's Day ads in 1988 included, first, Bonsai Designs: "Bonsai – the Father's Day Gift for the Gardener in us all," *New York Times* (15 June 1988) (Bonsai, the pathetic symbol of confinement, discipline and objectification). Second, Manufacturers Hanover, *New York Times* (24 May 1988), photograph of father holding baby daughter at his side; family values – ad for low-rate credit line designed especially for families.

3 See "A Crisis in Child-Care," *Newsweek* (15 February 1988): the article notes that "While middle and upper income employees have been moving toward more tax-subsidized help, the poor have been getting less." See also "Broader Day Care is Aim of Harvard Union Drive," *New York Times* (28 February 1988). The article notes that clerical workers claim they cannot afford child care offered on campus, and that in any case the services are too limited for the demand that exists for them.

4 Joel Steinberg, a New York lawyer, and his companion, Hedda Nussbaum, adopted a little girl, Lisa, who was found beaten to death in 1988. Steinberg's abusive behaviour to both wife and child emerged in the shocking court case that followed.

For examples of articles about acceptability of male abuse, see "Mothers on the Run," *US News and World Report* (13 June 1988), which deals with an organization that helps women escape abusive husbands. The article, however, casts doubt on the competencies of the mothers involved in helping, and the old sentimental mother-sacrifice theme predominates. In Fall and Winter 1988–9, almost daily coverage was given in the popular press and television to the Steinberg case, in which increasing attempts were made to implicate Hedda Nussbaum.

5 Michael D. Newcomb (1985) "The role of perceived relative parent personality in the development of heterosexuals, homosexuals, and transvestites," *Archives of Sexual Behavior* 14 (April): 147–64; Terri A. Lyons (1983) "Lesbian Mothers' Custody Fears", *Women and Therapy* 2 (Fall): 231–40; Audrey Steinhorn (1982) "Lesbian mothers – the invisible minority: role of the mental health worker,"

Women and Therapy 1 (Winter): 35–48; Teya Scheiffer (1984) "Mother in the lesbian community," *Off Our Backs* 14 (July): 4–5; Susan Wolfe (1982) "Jewish Lesbian Mother," in Evelyn Beck (ed.) *Nice Jewish Girls*, Watertown, Mass: Persephone Press; S. Golombok, A. Spencer and M. Rutter (eds) (1983) "Children in Lesbian and Single-Parent Households: Psychosexual and Psychiatric Appraisal," *Journal of Child-Psychology and Psychiatry* 24 (October): 551–72; G.A. Javaid (1983) "The Sexual Development of the Adolescent Daughter of a Homosexual Mother," *Journal of the American Academy of Child Psychiatry* 22 (March): 196–201; Evelyn Torton Beck (1983) "The Motherhood that does not Speak its Name," *Women's Studies Quarterly* 11 (Winter): 8–11.

6 See "Sex and Politics: Tough Decisions Along a New Ethical Frontier," *New York Times Week in Review* (15 March 1987): and "New Anxiety over the Sexual and Medical Revolutions," *New York Times* (8 April 1987).

7 This is not to deny medical scientists' and clinicians' concern to help distressed and infertile women who want to conceive. Any fantasies of "control" of female reproduction are surely unconscious. Financial rewards of the research and practices of reproductive technologies are another matter.

BIBLIOGRAPHY

Abbott, J.S.C. (1834) *The Mother at Home or The Principles of Maternal Duty*, London: John Mason.

Abraham, R. (1979) *Freud and "Mater": The Influence of Sigmund Freud's Mother on his Life and Work*, Davis, Calif: University of California Press.

Adams, P. (1983) "Mothering," *m/f: A Feminist Journal* 8: 40–52.

Ainsworth, M.D., Bieher, M.D., Waters, E. and Wall, S. (1978) *Patterns of Attachment: A Psychological Study of the Strange Situation*, Hillsdale, NJ: Erlbaum.

Alcott, W. A. (1838) *The Young Houskeeper; or, Thoughts on Food and Cookery*, Boston, Mass: George W. Light.

Allen, J. (ed.) (1986) *Now Voyager*, Madison, Wis: University of Wisconsin Press.

Alpert, N. (1941) *East Lynne*, New York: Samuel French.

Althusser, L. (1971) *Lenin and Philosophy and Other Essays*, trans. Ben Brewster, New York and London: Monthly Review Press.

American Matron, An (1972) *The Maternal Physician: A Treatise on the Management of Infants, From Their Birth until Two Years Old*, 1911, New York: Arno.

Arcana, J. (1979) *Our Mother's Daughters*, Berkeley, Calif: Shameless Hussey Press

Aries, P. (1962) *Centuries of Childhood*, London: Cape.

Arney, W. R. (1980) "Maternal Infant Bonding: The Politics of Falling in Love with your Child," *Feminist Studies* 6(3): 547–82.

Atwood, M. (1986) *The Handmaid's Tale*, New York: Fawcett.

Auerbach, N. (1978) *Communities of Women*, Cambridge, Mass: Harvard University Press.

——(1982) *Woman as Demon*, Cambridge, Mass: Harvard University Press.

Bachofen, J.J. (1967) *Myth, Religion and Mother-Right*, trans. R. Mannheim, Princeton NJ: Princeton University Press.

Badinter, E. (1980) *The Myth of Motherhood: An Historical View of the Maternal Instinct* trans. R. DeGaris, London: Souvenir Press.

Balderston, L.M. (1919) *Housewifery*, Philadelphia, Pa: J.B. Lippincott.

Balint, A. (1954) *The Early Years of Life: A Psychoanalytic Study*, New York: Basic Books.

——(1965) "Love for the Mother and Mother-Love," 1939, in M. Balint (ed.) *Primary Love and Psycho-Analytic Technique*, New York: Liveright Press.

Bannan, H. M. (1979) "Warrior Women: Immigrant Mothers in the Work of their Daughters," *Women's Studies* 6(2): 165–77.

Barthes, R. (1984) "Upon Leaving the Movie Theater," in Theresa Hak Kyung Cha (ed.) *Apparatus*, New York: Tanam Press, pp. 1–4.

Baudrillard, J. (1983) "The Ecstasy of Communication," in H. Foster (ed.) *The Anti-Aesthetic: Essays in Postmodern Culture*, Port Townsend, Washington: Bay Press.

Baym, N. (1978) *Women's Fiction: A Guide to Novels by and About Women in America 1820–1870*, Ithaca, NY: Cornell University Press

——(1984) "The Mad Woman and her Language: Why I Don't Do Feminist Literary Theory," *Tulsa Studies in Women's Literature* 3(1/2): 45–59.

Beard, M. R. (1946) *Woman as Force in History: A Study in Traditions and Realities*, New York: Macmillan.

Beecher, C. E. and Stowe, H.B. (1869) *The American Woman's Home; or Principles of Domestic Silence*, New York: J.B. Ford.

Benjamin, J. (1980) "The Bonds of Love: Rational Violence and Erotic Domination," *Feminist Studies* 6(1): 144–73.

——(1988) *The Bonds of Love: Psychoanalysis, Feminism and the Problem of Domination*, New York: Pantheon.

Bennett, T. (1980) "Popular Culture: A Teaching Object," *Screen Education* 34: 17–29.

——(1986) "Texts in History: The Determinations of Readings and their Texts," in D. Attridge, G. Bennington and R. Young (eds) *Post-Structuralism and the Question of History*, Cambridge: Cambridge University Press.

Bentley, E. (1967) *The Life of the Drama*, New York: Atheneum.

Berger, P. L. and Luckmann, T. (1966) *The Social Construction of Reality*, Garden City NY: Doubleday.

Berke, J. (1979) "'Mother, I Can Do It Myself': The Self-Sufficient Heroines in Popular Girls' Fiction," *Women's Studies* 6(2): 187–203.

Bernard, J. (1974) *The Future of Motherhood*, New York: Dial Press.

——(1975) *Women, Wives, Mothers*, Chicago: Aldine Press.

Binstock, J. (1972) "Motherhood: An Occupation Facing Decline," *The Futurist* 6: 99–102.

Birns, B. (1988) "The Mother–Infant Tie: Fifty Years of Theory, Science and Science Fiction," in B. Birns and D.F. Hay (eds) *The Different Faces of Motherhood*, New York: Plenum.

Blair, K. J. (1980) *The Clubwoman as Feminist: True Womanhood Redefined 1868–1914*, New York and London: Holmes & Meier.

Bloch, R. H. (1978) "American Feminine Ideals in Transition: The Rise of the Moral Mother, 1785–1815," *Feminist Studies* 4: 101–26.

Booth, M.R. (1965) *English Melodrama*, London: Herbert Jenkins.

Bowlby, J. (1966) *Maternal Care and Mental Health*, 1951, New York: Schocken.

——(1979–80) *Attachment and Loss*, Vol. 1: "Attachment," 1973; Vol. II: "Separation," 1980; Vol. III: "Loss," New York: Basic.

Brehan, W. (1804) *Advice to Mothers*.

Breitbard, V. (1974) *The Day Care Book*, New York: Knopf.

Brody, S. (1956) *Patterns of Mothering: Maternal Influence During Pregnancy*, New York: International University Press.

Broner, E.M. and Davidson, C.N. (eds) (1980) *The Lost Tradition: Mothers and Daughters in Literature*, New York: Frederick Ungar.

Bronstein, P. and Pape Cowan, C. (eds) (1988) *Fatherhood Today: Men's Changing Role in the Family*, New York: John Wiley.

Brooks, P. (1976) *The Melodramatic Imagination: Balzac, Henry James, Melodrama and the Mode of Excess*, New Haven: Yale University Press.

Brunsdon, C. (1983) "*Crossroads*: Notes on Soap Opera," in E.A. Kaplan (ed.) *Regarding Television: An Anthology – Critical Approaches*, Los Angeles: American Film Institute.

Buchan, W. (1972) *Advice to Mothers*, 1890, reprinted in *The Physician and Childrearing: Two Guides 1809–1894*, New York: Arno.

Burgin, V. (1982) *Thinking Photography*, London: Macmillan.

Burman, S. (ed.) (1979) *Fit Work for Women*, New York: St Martin's Press.

Burton, B. J. (1965) *East Lynne*, Birmingham: Cambridge University Press.

Butler, O. (1987) *Dawn: Xenogenesis*, New York: Warner Books.

——(1988) *Imago*, New York: Warner Books.

Callahan, S.C. (1972) *The Working Mother*, New York: Warner.

Canfield, D.F. (1914) *Mothers and Children*, New York: Henry Holt.

Caplan, P. (1989) *Don't Blame Mother: Mending Mother–Daughter Relations*, New York: Harper & Row.

Case, S.E. (1989) "Toward a Butch-Femme Aesthetic," in L. Hart (ed.) *Making a Spectacle: Feminist Essays on Contemporary Women's Theatre*, Ann Arbor, Mich: University of Michigan Press.

——(ed.) (1990) *Performing Feminisms: Feminist Critical Theory and Theatre*, Baltimore, Md, and London: Johns Hopkins University Press.

Chafe, W. H. (1972) *The American Woman: Her Changing Social, Economic and Political Roles, 1920–1970*, New York: Oxford University Press.

——(1977) *Women and Equality: Changing Patterns in American Culture*, New York: Oxford University Press.

Chasseguet-Smirgel, J. (1970a) *Female Sexuality*, Ann Arbor, Mich: University of Michigan Press.

——(1970b) *Sexuality and Mind*, Ann Arbor, Mich: University of Michigan Press.

Chodorow, N. (1978) *The Reproduction of Mothering: Psychoanalysis and the Sociology of Gender*, Berkeley: University of California Press.

Cixous, H. and Clément, C. (1986) *The Newly Born Woman*, trans. B. Wing, Minneapolis, Minn: University of Minnesota Press.

Cominos, P.T. (1963) "Late-Victorian Sexual Respectability and the Social System," *International Review of Social History* 8: 216–50.

Comolli, J.-L. and Narboni, J. (1976) "Cinema/Ideology/Criticism," in B. Nichols (ed.) *Movies and Methods*, vol. 1, Berkeley: University of California Press.

Cook, A. H. (1978) *The Working Mother: A Survey of Problems and Programs in Nine Counties*, Ithaca, NY: Cornell University Press.

Cott, N. F. (1977) *The Bonds of Womanhood: Woman's Sphere in New England 1780–1835*, New Haven, Conn., and London: Yale University Press.

Creed, B. (1986) "Horror and the Monstrous-Feminine – an Imaginary Abjection," *Screen* 27(1) (Jan./Feb.): 44–71.

Dally, A. (1982) *Inventing Motherhood: The Consequences of an Ideal*, London: Burnett.

Davis, A. (1981) *Women, Race and Class*, New York: Random House.

de Beauvoir, S. (1972) *The Second Sex*, Harmondsworth: Penguin.

Degler, C. N. (1980) *At Odds: Women and the Family in America from the Revolution to the Present*, Oxford and New York: Oxford University Press.

de Lauretis, T. (1984) *Alice Doesn't: Feminism, Semiotics, Cinema*, Bloomington: Indiana University Press.

——(1987) "Stategies of Coherence: Narrative, Cinema, Feminist Poetics, Yvonne Rainer," *Technologies of Gender: Essays on Theory, Films and Fiction*, in T. de Lauretis (ed.) Bloomington and Indianapolis: Indiana University Press.

Deleuze, G. and Guattari, F. (1983) *Anti-Oedipus: Capitalism and Schizophrenia*, trans. R. Hurley, Minnesota: University of Minnesota Press.

de Marco, J.P.(1983) *The Social Thought of W.E.B. Du Bois*, Lanham, London: University Press of America.

Deutsch, H. (1926) "The Psychology of Women in Relation to the Functions of Reproduction," *International Journal of Psychoanalysis* 6: 405–18.

——(1944) *The Psychology of Women*, New York: Grove & Stratton; (1946) London: Research Books.

Diner, H. (1973) *Mothers and Amazons*, 1930, ed. and trans J. P. Lundin, intro. B. Berger, Garden City, NY: Anchor.

Dinnerstein, D. (1976) *The Mermaid and the Minotaur: Sexual Arrangements and Human Malaise*, New York: Harper & Row.

Disher, M. (1954) *Melodrama: Plots that Thrilled*, New York: Macmillan.

Doane, J. and Leight Hodges, D. (1982) "Looking for Mrs Goodmother: D.W. Winnicott's 'Mirror Role of Mother and Family in Child Development'," *Enclitic* 6(2): 51–6.

Doane, M.A. (1982) "Film and the Masquerade: Theorizing the Female Spectator," *Screen* 23 (3–4): 80.

——(1984) "The Woman's Film: Possession and Address," in M.A. Doane, P. Mellencamp and L. Williams (eds) *Re-Vision: Essays in Feminist Criticism*, Los Angeles: American Film Institute.

——(1987) *The Desire to Desire: The Woman's Film of the 1940s*, Bloomington, Ind: University of Indiana Press.

——(1990) "Remembering Women: Psychical and Historical Constructions of Women," in E.A. Kaplan (ed.) *Psychoanalysis and Cinema*, London and New York: Routledge.

Donzelot, J. (1979) *The Policing of Families*, New York: Pantheon.

Douglas, A. (1977) *The Feminization of American Culture*, New York: Knopf.

Dudden, F. (1983) *Serving Women: Household Service in Nineteenth-Century America*, Middletown, Conn: Wesleyan University Press.

Durgnat, R. (1974) *The Strange Case of Alfred Hitchcock*, Cambridge, Mass: MIT Press.

Dyer, R. (1981) "Entertainment and Utopia," in R. Altman (ed.) *Genre: The Musical – A Reader*, London: Routledge.

Ehrenreich, B. and English, D. (1978) *For Her Own Good: 150 Years of the Experts' Advice to Women*, Garden City, NY: Anchor.

Elsaesser, T. (1972) "Tales of Sound and Fury: Observations on the Family Melodrama," *Monogram* 4: 2–15, reprinted in C. Gledhill (ed.) (1987) *Home is Where the Heart is: Studies in Melodrama and the Woman's Film*, London: British Film Institute.

Engels, F. (1972) *The Origin of the Family, Private Property and the State*, ed. E. Burke Leacock, New York: International University Press.

Epstein, B. (1983) *The Politics of Domesticity*, Middletown, Conn: Wesleyan University Press.

Ewen, S. (1976) *Captains of Consciousness: Advertising and the Social Roots of Consumer Culture*, New York: McGraw Hill.

Fairbairn, W.R.D. (1952) *An Object-Relations Theory of Personality*, New York: Basic Books.

Fiedler, L. (1966) *Love and Death in the American Novel*, New York: Stein & Day.

Field, M. A, (1988) *Surrogate Motherhood*, Cambridge, Mass. and London: Harvard University Press.

Fildes, V.A. (1986) *Breasts, Bottles and Babies*, Edinburgh: Edinburgh University Press.

Filene, P. (1986) *Him/Her Self: Sex Roles in Modern America*, Baltimore, Md, and London: Johns Hopkins University Press.

Firestone, S. (1970) *The Dialectic of Sex*, New York: William Morrow: 1972, London: Paladin.

Fischer, L. (forthcoming) *Imitation of Life: Douglas Sirk Director*, Rutgers Films in Print, New Brunswick, NJ: Rutgers University Press.

Flax, J. (1978) "The Conflict between Nurturance and Autonomy in Mother/ Daughter Relationships and within Feminism," *Feminist Studies* 4(1): 171–89.

——(1980) "Mother–Daughter Relationships: Psychodynamics, Politics and Philosophy," in H. Eisenstein and A. Jardine (eds) *The Future of Difference*, Boston, Mass: G.K. Hall.

Flitterman-Lewis, S. (1988) "*Imitations(s) of Life*: The Black Woman's Double Determination as Troubling Other," *Literature and Psychology* 34 (4): 44–57.

Foucault, M. (1970) *The Order of Things: An Archaeology of the Human Sciences*, New York: Random House.

——(1978) *An Introduction to the History of Sexuality*, trans. R. Hurley, New York: Pantheon.

——(1984) "Nietzsche, Genealogy, History," 1971, in P. Rabinow (ed.) *Foucault Reader*, New York: Pantheon.

Fraiberg, S. (1977) *Every Child's Birthright: In Defense of Mothering*, New York: Basic Books.

Freud, S. (1951a) "A Case of Successful Treatment by Hypnotism," 1893, *Standard Edition*, vol. 1, London: Hogarth Press.

——(1951b) "Family Romances" 1909, *Standard Edition*, vol. 9, London: Hogarth Press.

——(1953a) "Three Essays on the Theory of Sexuality," 1905, *Standard Edition*, vol. 7, London: Hogarth Press, especially pp. 135–243.

——(1953b) "Female Sexuality," 1931, *Standard Edition*, vol. 21, London: Hogarth Press.

——(1974) "Femininity," 1933, *New Introductory Lectures on Psychoanalysis*, reprinted in *Women and Analysis*, ed. Jean Strouse, New York: Grossman.

Friday, N. (1981) *My Mother, My Self: The Daughter's Search for Identity*, New York: Dell.

Friedan, B. (1965) *The Feminine Mystique*, Harmondsworth: Penguin.

Friedman, S.S. (1987) "Creativity and the Childbirth Metaphor: Gender Difference in Literary Discourse," *Feminist Studies* 13 (1): 49–82.

Fuller, M. (1845/1971) *Woman in the Nineteenth Century*, New York: Norton.

Gabbard, K. and Gabbard, G.O. (1987) *Psychiatry and the Cinema*, Chicago and London: University of Chicago Press.

Gardiner, A.K. (1974) *Conjugal Sins Against the Laws of Life and Health and their Effects Upon the Father, Mother and Child*, 1870, New York: Arno.

Gardiner, J.K. (1978) "The New Motherhood," *North American Review* 263 (2): 72–6.

——(1986) "Maternal Metaphors, Women Readers, and Female Identity," Paper read at a Rutgers Seminar Series on Representations of Motherhood, organized by E. Ann Kaplan and sponsored by the Institute for Research on Women. Revised version included in Gardiner (1989).

——(1989) *Rhys, Stead, Lessing and the Politics of Empathy*, Bloomington, Ind: Indiana University Press.

George, V. and Wilding, P. (1972) *Motherless Families*, London: Routledge & Kegan Paul.

Gerard, J. (1988) "TV Mirrors a New Generation," *New York Times* 30 October.

Gillis, J.R. (1985) *For Better, For Worse: British Marriages, 1600 to the Present*, New York and Oxford: Oxford University Press.

Gilman, C.P. (1898) *Women and Economics*, Boston, Mass: Small, Maynard.

——(1910) *The Home: Its Work and Influence*, New York: Charlton.

——(1915) *Herland*, with an introduction by A.J. Lane, 1979, New York: Pantheon.

Gledhill, C. (in dialogue with E. Ann Kaplan) (1986) "Comments on Melodrama and *Stella Dallas*," *Cinema Journal* 25(4): 44–53.

——(ed.) (1987) *Home is Where the Heart is: Studies in Melodrama and the Woman's Film*, London: British Film Institute.

Goldstein, R.D. (1988) *Mother-Love and Abortion: A Legal Interpretation*, Berkeley, Calif: University of California Press.

Goode, W. (1963) *World Revolution and Family Patterns*, New York: Free Press.

Gordon, L. (1977) *Woman's Body, Woman's Right: Birth Control in America*, New York: Penguin.

Gould, J. (1980) "Law, Custom and Myth: Aspects of the Social Position of Women in Classical Athens," *JHS* 100: 38–59.

Green, M. (1976) *Fathering*, New York: McGraw Hill.

Greenberg, M. and Morris, N. (1974) "Engrossment: The Newborn's Impact upon the Father," *American Journal of Orthopsychiatry* 44: 520–31.

Grimstead, D. (1986) *Melodrama Unveiled: American Theatre and Culture, 1800–1850*, Chicago: University of Chicago Press.

Gruenberg, S.M. and Krech, H.S. (1957) *The Modern Mother's Dilemma*, Public Affairs Pamphlet 247, New York.

Gunning, T. (1988) "The Opium Den and the Theatre of Morality: Moral Discourse and the Film Process in Early Cinema," *Art and Text* (Sydney) 30 (Sept./Nov.).

Habegger, A. (1982) *Gender, Fantasy and Realism in American Literature*, New York: Columbia University Press.

Hammer, S. (1976) *Daughters and Mothers: Mothers and Daughters*, New York: Signet.

Hamon, M.-C. (1983) "L'Ane Dossier," *m/f: A Feminist Journal* 32–3.

Hansen, M. (1983) "Early Cinema: Whose Public Sphere?" *New German Critique* 29: 147–84.

——(1991) *Babel and Babylon: Readings in American Silent Film*, Cambridge, Mass: Harvard University Press.

Haraway, D. (1985) "A Manifesto for Cyborgs: Science, Technology, and Socialist Feminism in the 1980s," *Socialist Review* 80: 65–108.

——(1989) "The Biopolitics of Postmodern Bodies: Determinations of Self Immune System Discourse," *Differences: A Journal of Feminist Cultural Studies* 1(1): 3–43.

Heath, S. (1982) *The Sexual Fix*, London: Macmillan.

Heffner, E. (1978) *Mothering: The Emotional Experience of Motherhood after Freud and Feminism*, New York: Doubleday.

Hegel, G.W.F. (1931/1967) *The Phenomenology of Mind*, trans. J.B. Baillie, New York: Harper Row.

Heilman, R.B. (1968) *Tragedy and Melodrama: Versions of Experience*, Seattle: University of Washington Press.

Hewitt, M. (1958) *Wives and Mothers in Victorian Industry*, London: Rockcliff.

Hirsch, M. (1981a) "A Mother's Discourse: Incorporation and Repetition in *La Princesse de Clèves*," *Yale French Studies* 62: 67–87.

——(1981b) "Mothers and Daughters: A Review Essay," *Signs* 7(1) 200–21.

Honey, M. (1976) "Images of Women in the *Saturday Evening Post*, 1931–1936," *Journal of Popular Culture* 10: 352–8.

Horney, K. (1967a) "The Dread of Woman," in H. Kelman (ed.) *Feminine Psychology*, New York: Norton.

——(1967b) "Maternal Conflicts," 1933, in H. Kelman (ed.) *Psychology*, New York: Norton.

Hurst, F. (1933) *Imitation of Life*, New York.

Huston, N. (1985) "The Matrix of War: Mothers and Heroes," in S.R. Suleiman (ed.) *The Female Body in Western Culture: Contemporary Perspectives*, Cambridge, Mass: Harvard University Press.

Huxley, J. and Kettlewell, H.D. (1965) *Darwin and his World*, London: Thames & Hudson.

Huyssen, A. (1986) "Mass Culture as Woman: Modernism's Other," in T. Modleski (ed.) *Studies in Entertainment: Critical Approaches to Mass Media*, Bloomington and Indianapolis: Indiana University Press.

Irigaray, L. (1981) "And the One Doesn't Stir Without the Other," trans. H. V. Wenzel, *Signs* 7 (1): 60–7.

——(1985a) "The Power of Discourse and the Subordination of the Feminine: An Interview," in *This Sex Which Is Not One*, trans. C. Porter and C. Burke, Ithaca, Cornell NY: University Press.

——(1985b) "When Our Lips Speak Together," in *This Sex Which Is Not One*, Ithaca, NY: Cornell University Press.

——(1985c) "This Sex Which Is Not One," in *This Sex Which Is Not One*, trans. C. Porter with C. Burke, Ithaca, NY: Cornell University Press.

Jakobson, R. (1971) *Fundamentals of Language*, The Hague: Mouton.

Jameson, F. (1979) "Reification and Mass Utopia," *Social Text* 1: 130–48.

——(1982) *The Political Unconscious: Narrative as a Socially Symbolic Act*, Ithaca, NY: Cornell University Press.

——(1983) "Postmodernism and Consumer Society," in H. Foster (ed.) *The Anti-Aesthetic: Essays in Postmodern Culture*, Port Townsend, Washington: Bay Press.

Johnson, R. (1987) "What is Cultural Studies Anyway?" *Social Text* (winter/spring): 38–80.

Johnston, C. and Cook, P. (1975) *Dorothy Arzner: Toward a Feminist Cinema*, London: British Film Institute.

Jolly, H. (1973) *Commonsense about Babies and Children*, New York: Times Ltd.

Jorden, E. (1603) *A Briefe Discourse of a Disease Called the Suffocation of the Möther*, London.

Jung, C.G. and Kerenyi, C. (1967) *Essays on a Science of Mythology: The Myths of the Divine Child and the Divine Maiden*, New York: Harper.

Kane, E. (1988) *Birth Mother*, New York: Harcourt, Brace, Jovanovich.

Kaplan, C. (1983) "Wild Nights: Pleasure/Sexuality/Feminism," in *Formations of Pleasure*, London: Routledge & Kegan Paul.

Kaplan, E.A. (1983a) "The Case of the Missing Mother: Patriarchy and the Maternal in Vidor's *Stella Dallas*," *Heresies* 4 (4): 81–5.

——(1983b) *Women and Film: Both Sides of the Camera*, London and New York: Methuen.

——(1983c) "Missing Mothers," *Social Policy* 14 (2): 56–62.

——(1983d) "Theories of Melodrama: A Feminist Perspective," *Women and Performance* 1 (1): 40–8.

——(1985a) "Dialogue: Ann Kaplan Replies to Linda Williams' 'Something Else Besides a Mother': *Stella Dallas* and the Maternal Melodrama," *Cinema Journal* 24 (2): 40–3.

——(1985b) "Dialogue: E. Ann Kaplan Replies to Petro and Flinn" (continuing *Stella Dallas* debate), *Cinema Journal* 25 (1): 51–4.

——(1986) "Dialogue: 'Thoughts on Melodrama.' Reply to Christine Gledhill" (continuing *Stella Dallas* debate), *Cinema Journal* 25 (4): 49–53.

——(1987a) "Mothering, Feminism and Representation: The Maternal in Melodrama and the Woman's Film from 1910 to 1940," C. Gledhill (ed.) *Home is Where the Heart is: Studies in Melodrama and the Woman's Film*, London: British Film Institute, pp. 113–37.

——(1987b) "The Political Unconscious in the Maternal Melodrama: Ellen Wood's *East Lynne* (1861)," in D. Longhurst (ed.) *Gender, Genre and Narrative Pleasure*, Manchester: Allen & Unwin.

——(1988) "Women and Morality: A Discourse Analysis," in N. Eisenberg, J. Reykowski and E. Staub (eds) *Social and Moral Values: Individual and Societal Perspectives*, New York: Erlbaum, pp. 347–61.

——(ed.) (1990) *Psychoanalysis and Cinema*, London and New York: Routledge.

Kaplan, L. (1990) "An Open Adoption," *New Yorker Magazine*, 21 May.

Kaplan, M. (1991) *Images of the Mother*, New York: Routledge.

Kardiner, A. (1954) *Sex and Morality*, Indianapolis, Ind: Bobbs-Merrill.

Keller, E.F. (1986) "Making Gender Visible in the Pursuit of Nature's Secrets," in T. de Lauretis (ed.) *Feminist Studies/Critical Studies*, Bloomington Ind: Indiana University Press, especially pp. 74–5.

——(1990) "From Secrets of Life to Secrets of Death," in M. Jacobs, E.F. Keller and S. Shuttleworth (eds) *Body/Politics: Women and the Discourses of Science*, London: Routledge.

Kelly, M. (1981) "Post-partum Document," *m/f: A Feminist Journal* 5 (6): 124–48.

Kerber, L. (1980) *Women of the Republic: Intellect and Ideology in Revolutionary America*, Chapel Hill, NC: University of North Carolina Press.

Kilgarriff, M. (ed.) (1974) *The Golden Age of Melodrama: Twelve Nineteenth-Century Melodramas*, London: Wolfe Publishing, Ltd.

Klein, M. (1930) "The Importance of Symbol Formation in the Development of the Ego," in *Love, Guilt and Reparation and Other Works, 1921–1945*, London: Hogarth Press,

Kofman, S. (1985) *The Enigma of Woman: Women in Freud's Writings*, trans. C. Porter, Ithaca, NY, and London: Cornell University Press.

Kohut, H. (1971) *The Analysis of the Self*, New York: International University Press.

Kolata, G. (1989) *New York Times* 18 April.

Komarovsky, M. (1953) *Women in the Modern World*, Boston, Mass: Little, Brown.

Kristeva, J. (1980) "Motherhood According to Bellini," trans. T. Gora, A. Jardine and L.S. Roudiez, *Desire in Language: A Semiotic Approach to Literature and Art*, ed. L.S. Roudiez, New York: Columbia University Press.

——(1982) *Powers of Horror: An Essay on Abjection*, trans. L.S. Roudiez, New York: Columbia University Press.

——(1985) "Stabat Mater," (trans. A. Goldhammer) in S.R. Suleiman (ed.) *The Female Body in Western Culture: Contemporary Perspectives*, Cambridge, Mass: Harvard University Press.

Kroker, A. and Cook, D. (1985) *The Postmodern Scene: Excremental Culture in the Age of the Hyperreal*, London: St Martin's Press.

Kroker, A. and Kroker, M. (1987) "Body Digest: Theses on the Disappearing Body in the Hyper-Modern Condition," *Canadian Journal of Political and Social Theory* XI (1–2): i–xvi and v.

Lacan, J. (1979) *Écrits: A Selection* trans. A. Sheridan, New York: Norton.

Laclau, E. (1980) "Populist Rupture and Discourse," *Screen Education* 34.

——(undated) "Politics and the Construction of the Unthinkable," unpublished paper.

Lane, A. J. (1979) "Introduction," Charlotte Perkins Gilman, *Herland*, ed. A.J. Lane, New York: Pantheon.

Leigh Cowan, A. (1989) "Women's Gains on the Job: Not Without a Heavy Toll", *New York Times*, 21 August.

Lerner, G. (1978) "The American Housewife: An Historical Perspective," *Feminist Perspectives on Housework and Child Care*, ed. A. Swerdlow, Bronxville, NY: Sarah Lawrence College.

Leverenz, D. (1980) *The Language of Puritan Feeling: An Exploration in Literature, Psychology and Social History*, New Brunswick, NJ: Rutgers University Press.

Levy, D. (1943) *Maternal Overprotection*, New York: Columbia University Press.

Lilienfeld, J. (1977) "'The Deceptiveness of Beauty': Mother-Love and Mother-Hate in *To the Lighthouse*," *Twentieth-Century Literature* 23: 345–76.

Liston, R. (1962) "Dateline: *East Lynne*: 1962," *Show* January: 14–15.

Llewelyn Davies, M. (ed.) (1978) *Maternity: Letters from Working Women*, London: Virago.

Lorber, X. Coser, R. Rossi, A. and Chodorow, N. (1983) "On *The Reproduction of Mothering*: A Methodological Debate," *Signs* 6(3): 482–514.

Lyotard, J.–F. (1985) *The Postmodern Condition*, Minneapolis: University of Minnesota Press.

MacCabe, C. (1974) "Realism and the Cinema: Notes on some Brechtian Theses," *Screen* 15(2): 7–27.

McGlory, R.J. *Racism in America: From Milk and Honey to Ham and Eggs*, Chicago, Ill.: Fides/Claretian.

McLellan, D. (1971) *The Thoughts of Karl Marx: An Introduction*, London: Macmillan.

——(1979) *Marxism After Marx: An Introduction*, London: Macmillan.

Mannoni, M. (1970) *The Child, his "Illness", and the Others*, London: Tavistock.

Margolis, M. (1984) *Mothers and Such*, Berkeley, Calif: University of California Press.

Mead, M. (1954) "Some Theoretical Considerations on the Problem of Mother–Child Separation," *American Journal of Orthopsychiatry* 24: 471–83.

Miller, J.B. (1977) *Toward a New Psychology of Women*, Boston, Mass: Beacon Press.

Miller, S. (1981) *The Good Mother*, New York: Harper Collins.

Minturn, L. and Lambert, W.W. (1964) *Mothers of Six Cultures*, New York: John Wiley.

Mitchell, G. and Brandt, E.M. (1972) "Paternal Behavior in Primates," in F. Poirier (ed.) *Primate Socialization*, New York: Random.

Mitchell, J. (1974) *Psychoanalysis and Feminism*, London: Pantheon.

——(1982) "Introduction I," in J. Mitchell and J. Rose (eds) *Feminine Sexuality: Jacques Lacan and the Ecole Freudienne*, London and New York: Norton.

Mitchell, J. and Rose, J. (eds) (1982) *Feminine Sexuality: Jacques Lacan and the Ecole Freudienne*, trans. J. Rose, London and New York: Norton.

Mitchell, S. (ed.) (1984) *East Lynne*, reprinted New Brunswick, NJ: Rutgers University Press.

Mitchison, N. (1962/1985) *Memoirs of a Space Woman*, London: Women's Press.

Modleski, T. (1983) "The Rhythms of Day-Time Soap Operas," in E.A. Kaplan (ed.) *Regarding Television: An Anthopolgy – Critical Approaches*, Los Angeles: American Film Institute.

——(1986) *Loving with a Vengeance*, London and New York: Routledge.

——(1988a) *The Women Who Knew Too Much: Hitchcock and Feminist Theory*, London and New York: Routledge.

——(1988b) "Three Men and Baby M," *Camera Obscura* 17 (May): 71.

Mulvey, L. (1977–8) "Notes on Sirk and Melodrama," *Movie* 25: 54.

Murphy, J. (1984) "Egg Farms," in R. Arditti, R. Duelli Klein and Shellen Minden (eds) *Test Tube Women: What Future for Motherhood*, London: Pandora Press.

Nietzsche, F. (1954) *The Genealogy of Morals in the Philosophy of Nietzsche*, New York: Random House.

Nilsson, L. (1977) *A Child is Born*, 1965, New York: Delacourte.

——Photos, *Life* magazine, April 1965 and August 1990.

Nowell-Smith, G. (1977) "Minnelli and Melodrama," *Screen* 18(2): 113–18.

Oakley, A. (1974) *Housewife*, London: Allen Lane.

——(1979) *From Here to Maternity*, Harmondsworth: Penguin.

——(1987) "From Walking Wombs to Test-Tube Babies," in M. Stanworth (ed.) *Reproductive Technologies: Gender, Motherhood and Medicine*, Minneapolis: University of Minnesota Press.

Padover, S.K. (ed. and trans.) (1975) *The Karl Marx Library*, New York: McGraw-Hill.

Papashvily, H. (1956) *All the Happy Endings: A Study of the Domestic Novel in America, the Women Who Wrote it, the Women Who Read it, in the 19th Century*, Port Washington, NY: Kennikat Press.

Peary, G. and Kay, K. (1975) "Interview with Dorothy Arzner," in C. Johnston (ed.) *Dorothy Arzner: Toward a Feminist Cinema*, London: British Film Institute.

Pêcheux, M. (1982) *Language, Semantics and Ideology*, London: Macmillan.

Petchesky, R.P. (1987) "Fetal Images: The Power of Visual Culture in the Politics of Reproduction," *Feminist Studies* 13(2): 263–92, 281 (cited V. Burgin 1982: 9).

Piercy, M. (1976) *Woman on the Edge of Time*, New York: Knopf.

Plaza, M. (1981) "The Mother/The Same: The Hatred of the Mother in Psycho-analysis," *Feminist Issues* 2(1): 75–99

Radl, S. (1973) *Mother's Day is Over*, New York: Charterhouse.

Radway, J.A. (1984) *Reading the Romance: Women, Patriarchy and Popular Literature*, Chapel Hill, NC: University of North Carolina Press.

Robert, M. (1980) *The Origins of the Novel*, trans. S. Rabinovitch, Brighton, Sussex: Harvester Press.

Rorvik, D. (1977) *Brave New Baby: Promise and Peril of the Biological Revolution*, London: New English Library.

Rose, J. (1982) "Introduction II," in J. Mitchell and J. Rose (eds) *Feminine Sexuality: Jacques Lacan and the Ecole Freudienne*, London and New York: Norton.

Rossi, A. (1978) "A Biosexual Perspective on Parenting," *Daedalus* 106(2): 16–21.

Rothman, B.K. (1989) *Recreating Motherhood: Ideology and Technology in a Patriarchal Society*, New York: Norton.

Rousseau, J.-J. (1974) *Emile*, 1911 trans. B. Foxley, London: Dent.

Rowland, R. (1990) *Living Laboratories: Women and Reproductive Technology*, Bloomington Indiana: Indiana University Press.

Ruddick, S. (1980) "Maternal Thinking," *Feminist Studies* 6(2): 342–423.

——(1989) *Maternal Thinking: Toward a Politics of Peace*, Boston, Mass: Beacon Press.

Rupp, L.J. (1978) *Mobilizing Women for War: German and American Propaganda, 1939–1945*, Princeton, NJ: Princeton University Press.

Russ, J. (1975) *The Female Man*, New York: Bantam.

Rutter, M. (1972) *Maternal Deprivation Reassessed*, Harmondsworth: Penguin.

——(1979) "Maternal Deprivation 1972–78: New Findings, New Concepts, New Approaches," *Annals, Academy of Medicine* 8(3): 312–23.

Schaffer, R. (1977) *Mothering*, London: Fontana.

Schofer, P. (1982) "Marcel Pagnol: Family and Friends: The Brick and the Flat," unpublished paper.

Schwab, G. (1987) "Cyborgs: Postmodern Phantasms of Body and Mind," *Discourse: Journal for Theoretical Studies in Media and Culture* (spring/summer): 64–84.

Schwartz-Cowan, R. (1976a) "The 'Industrial Revolution' in the Home: Household Technology and Social Change in the Twentieth Century," *Technology and Culture* 17: 1–23.

——(1976b) "Two Washes in the Morning and a Bridge Party, at Night: The American Housewife between the Wars," *Women's Studies* 3: 147–71.

——(1983) *More Work For Mother: The Ironies of Household Technology from the Open Hearth to the Microwave*, New York: Basic Books.

Sears, R.R., Maccoby, E.E. and Levin, H. (1957) *Patterns of Child Rearing*, Evanston, Ill: Row, Peterson.

Sebald, H. (1976) *Momism: The Silent Disease of America*, Chicago: Nelson Hall.

Shapiro, B.A. (1983) *The Romantic Mother: Narcissistic Patterns in Romantic Poetry*, Baltimore, Md. and London: Johns Hopkins University Press.

Shevrin, H. and Dickman, S. (1980) "The Psychological Unconscious," *American Psychologist* 35: 421–34.

Shorter, E. (1977) *The Making of the Modern Family*, London: Fontana.

Sigourney, L. (Mrs) (1839) *Letters to Mothers*, New York.

Silverman, A. and Silverman, A. (1971) *The Case Against Having Children*, New York: David McKay.

Silverman, K. (1988) *The Acoustic Mirror: The Female Voice, in Psychoanalysis and Cinema*, Bloomington, Ind: Indiana University Press.

——(1990) "Historical Trauma and Male Subjectivity," in E.A. Kaplan (ed.) *Psychoanalysis and Cinema*, New York: Routledge.

Silverstein, L.B. (1990) "Transforming the Debate about Child Care and Maternal Employment," *American Psychologist* (October): 1025–32.

Smith, J.L. (1973) *Melodrama: The Critical Idiom*, London: Methuen.

Smock, R.W. (1988) (ed.) *Booker T. Washington in Perspective: Essays of Louis R. Harlan*, Jackson: University Press of Mississippi.

Sofoulis, Z. (1984) "Exterminating Fetuses: Abortion, Disarmament and the Sexo-semiotics of Extraterrestrialism," *Diacritics* 47–59.

Spoto, D. (1983) *The Dark Side of Genius: The Life of Alfred Hitchcock*, New York: Ballantine.

Squier, S.M. (1991) "Fetal Voices: Speaking for the Margins Within," *Tulsa Studies* 10(1) (spring): 17–30.

Staiger, J. (1980) "Mass-Produced Photoplays: Economic and Signifying Practices in the First Years of Hollywood," *Wide Angle* 4(3): 12–27.

——(1985) "The Eyes are Really the Focus: Photoplays, Acting and Film Form and Style," *Wide Angle* 8(4): 15–17.

Stern, D. (1976) *The First Relationship: Infant and Mother*, Cambridge, Mass: Harvard University Press.

——(1985) *The Interpersonal World of the Infant*, New York: Basic Books.

Stewart, G.B. (1979) "Mother, Daughter, and the Birth of the Female Artist," *Women's Studies* 6(2): 127–45.

Stolz, L.M. (1960) "Effects of Maternal Employment on Children: Evidence from Research," *Child Development* 31: 749–82.

Stone, L. (1977) *The Family, Sex, and Marriage in England 1500–1800*, New York: Harper.

Stowe, H.B. (1966) *Uncle Tom's Cabin*, 1861, New York: Signet.

Suleiman, S. (1985) "Writing and Motherhood," in E. Showalter (ed.) *New Feminist Criticism*, New York: Pantheon.

——(1990) *Subversive Intent: Gender, Politics and the Avant-Garde*, Cambridge, Mass: Harvard University Press.

Sunley, R. (1963) "Early Nineteenth-Century American Literature on Child Rearing," *Childhood in Contemporary Cultures*, Chicago: University Chicago Press

Sussman, G.D. (1977) "Parisian Infants and Norman Wet Nurses in the Early Nineteenth Century: A Statistical Study," *Journal of Interdisciplinary History* 11(4): 637–53.

Suter, J. (1976) "Feminine Discourse in Christopher Strong," *Camera Obscura* 1(2): 135–50.

Terry, J. (1989) "The Body Invaded: Medical Surveillance of Women as Reproducers," *Socialist Review* 19 (Summer): 26–32.

Tilly, L. and Cohen, M. (1982) "Does the Family have a History? A Review of Theory and Practice in Family History," *Social Science History* 6(2) (spring): 131–79.

Todd, J. (1980) *Women's Friendship in Literature*, New York: Columbia University Press.

Tompkins, J. (1981) "Sentimental Power: Uncle Tom's Cabin and the Politics of Literary History," *Glyph* 8: 95–9.

——(1986) *Sensational Designs: The Cultural Works of American Fiction, 1790–1880*, New York: Oxford University Press

Toril Moi (1986) *Sexual/Textual Politics: Feminist Literary Criticism*, London and New York: Routledge

Tynjanov, J. (1971) "The Dominant," in L. Matejka and K. Pomorska (eds) *Readings in Russian Poetics: Formalist and Structuralist Views*, Cambridge, Mass. and London: MIT Press.

Ulrich, L.T. (1982) *Good Wives: Image and Reality in the Lives of Women in Northern New England 1650–1750*, New York: Knopf.

Vardac, N. (1977) *Stage to Screen: Theatrical Method from Garrick to Griffith*, New York: Benjamin Blom, especially "Introduction," and pp. 20–67.

Viviani, C. (1987) "Who is Without Sin?: The Maternal Melodrama in American Film, 1930–39," in C. Gledhill (ed.) *Home is Where the Heart is: Studies in Melodrama and the Woman's Film*, London: British Film Institute.

Walkowitz, J. (1986) "Melodrama, Sexual Scandals, and Victorian Political Culture," unpublished paper.

Weinberg, S.S. (1988) *The World of Our Mothers: The Lives of Jewish Immigrant Women*, Chapel Hill, NC: University of North Carolina Press.

Welter, B. (1966) "The Cult of True Womanhood: 1820–1860," *American Quarterly* 18: 151–74.

Wenzel, H.V. (1981) "Introduction to Luce Irigaray's 'And the One Doesn't Stir Without the Other'", *Signs* 7(1): 56–9.

Westcotte, M. (1978) "Mothers and Daughters in the World of the Father," *Frontiers* 3(2): 16–21.

White, A. (1983) "Why Did the Signifyers Come Out to Play?" unpublished paper.

Whitehead, M.B. (1989) *A Mother's Story*, New York: Bantam.

Willemen, P. (1972) "Distanciation and Douglas Sirk," in L. Mulvey and J. Halliday (eds) *Douglas Sirk*, London: Edinburgh Film Festival.

Williams, L. (1984) "'Something Else Besides a Mother': *Stella Dallas* and the Maternal Melodrama," *Cinema Journal* 24(1): 2–27.

——(1989) *Hard Core: Power, Pressures and the "Frenzy of the Visible,"* Berkeley, Cal.: University of California Press.

Winnicott, D.W. (1964) *The Child, the Family and the Outside World*, Harmondsworth: Penguin.

——(1971) *Playing and Reality*, New York: Basic Books.

Wolfenstein, M. (1955) "Fun Morality: An Analysis of Recent American Child Training Literature," in M. Mead and M. Wolfenstein (eds) *Childhood in Contemporary Cultures*.

Wollstonecraft, M. (1975) *A Vindication of the Rights of Women*, 1792, Harmondsworth: Penguin.

Women's Co-operative Guild (1915) *Maternity: Letters from Working Women*, London: G. Bell & Sons.

Wood, Mrs Henry (also Ellen) (1861/1984) *East Lynne*, ed. Sally Miller, New Brunswick, N.J.: Rutgers University Press.

Wood, N. (1983) "L'Ane Dossier: An Introduction," *m/f: A Feminist Journal* 8: 17–21.

Wylie, P. (1942) *A Generation of Vipers*, New York: Farrar.

Zaretsky, E. (1976) *Capitalism, the Family and Personal Life*, New York: Harper.

NAMES INDEX

SUBJECT INDEX

245